Resilient Marriages

Resilient Marriages

From Alcoholism and Adversity to Relationship Growth

Karen J. Shirley

ROWMAN & LITTLEFIELD PUBLISHERS, INC.
Lanham • Boulder • New York • Oxford

ROWMAN & LITTLEFIELD PUBLISHERS, INC.

Published in the United States of America
by Rowman & Littlefield Publishers, Inc.
4720 Boston Way, Lanham, Maryland 20706
http://www.rowmanlittlefield.com

12 Hid's Copse Road
Cumnor Hill, Oxford OX2 9JJ, England

British Cataloging in Publication Information Available

Library of Congress Cataloging-in-Publication Data

Shirley, Karen J., 1951–
Resilient marriages: from alcoholism and adversity to
relationship growth / Karen J. Shirley.
p. cm.
Includes bibliographical references and index.
ISBN 0-8476-9382-1 (cloth : alk. paper)—ISBN 0-8476-9383-X (pbk. : alk. paper)
1. Alcoholics—United States—Family relationships.
2. Alcoholics—Rehabilitation—United States—Case studies. I. Title.

HV5132.S56 1999
362.292'3'0973—dc21 99-044766

Printed in the United States of America

∞™ The paper used in this publication meets the minimum requirements of American National Standard for Information Sciences—Permanence of Paper for Printed Library Materials, ANSI Z.39.48–1992.

for Matthew and Zoa
and in memory of my mother, Jean B. Shirley

Contents

Acknowledgments

There are many people who helped bring this book to fruition, but before it was even an idea I received the encouragement to imagine doing it from my mentors, Nettie Bartel and Barbara Krasner.

In the initial stages I was encouraged by friends Susan LaDuca, Jane Buhl, and B. Hibbs. B. was especially helpful with the interviews—her contribution was invaluable. Several people helped me arrange interviews and encouraged me to move forward: Kathleen D., Tom G., Dick S., and Marvin G. Without their help this book simply would not be. I also want to acknowledge Frank Selgrath, past CEO of the Mustard Seed Foundation, for his endorsement of this project.

Throughout the entire process, Annette Lareau and Erin MacNamara Horvat read and edited drafts, guided the manuscript development, and offered moral support and friendship. In the most trying times of finishing the manuscript, they remained steadfast.

My family has been there in every way. My husband has offered various kinds of support from the initial idea to the final formatting. Our children have kept up on my progress and encouraged me at all times. I am grateful that other family members have taken an interest as well: Sydney and Xin-nan, the Yuns, Bob and Lynne, Bob Getzen, Jack, Dad, and Ilene. Beverly and Rufus Getzen volunteered to edit the final manuscript. Their eyes for both detail and meaning were right on target. I could not have asked for better assistance.

Several friends encouraged me throughout: Sue Bitner, Bea Blasdell, Patti Bourke, Peg Bryner, Hedy Cerwinka, the D'Ancona Family, Bob Downie, Linda Goncalves, Cara Herald, Lynn Moyer, Ginny Peckham, Joan Severino, Linda Stern, and Amy Steffan.

I am especially indebted to Dean Birkenkamp, executive editor at Rowman & Littlefield, and Susan Jones, for their careful readings and thoughtful suggestions.

I am particularly grateful to all of the people who agreed to be interviewed. Their willingness to speak openly is what made this book possible.

Preface

Resilient Marriages is an exploration of relational repair. It provides firsthand accounts of how couples have rebuilt their relationships following prolonged periods of trust-demolishing interactions. The portraits of the Gundersons, Royers, Bertolinos, and Abbotts are based on in-depth interviews with couples and individuals in long-term marriages who have weathered the crisis of alcoholism and sobriety. The narratives are supported by the work of researchers, clinicians, and writers who suggest that our commonalities and what is healthy within and between each of us is at least as significant as what is less healthy and tends to keep us at arm's distance.

The framework for this exploration is the identification of *residual resources* within the relationship, the acknowledgment of *moments of choice* that are often pivotal in moving spouses toward, rather than away from, one another, and the ongoing struggle to build or rebuild a firm relational foundation through *trust building*. There are two benefits of this approach: visualization of the possibilities for relational growth and demystification of the important process of relational resiliency.

The audience for this book includes anyone in a marriage, especially anyone whose marriage has experienced the turmoil and heartache of a crisis. It is also appropriate for clinicians and social service agency employees who work with couples and families. The introduction provides an overview of the entire book, including a description of resiliency and resiliency research; an explanation of a resource perspective for thinking about individuals, couples, and families; and a comment on the importance of trust in relationships. For those who would be helped by having more background on alcoholism, there are many public information sources and books available. The appendixes briefly define alcoholism and describe some of its effects and provide an overview of the benefits and critiques of the notion of codependency, as well as descriptions of Alcoholics Anonymous and Al-Anon, the two primary self-help support groups for alcoholics and their families.

What follows is perhaps best described as a book of hope. But it is hope that is born of hard work, determination, and the willingness of people to acknowledge their failings and to begin anew. It is hope born of the capacity to see one's partner from a new vantage point and to reassess what is expected and what one owes. *Resilient Marriages* adds to the growing literature on resiliency by expanding it beyond a primarily individual realm to the relational realm. It is my sincere hope that the book offers some piece of truth for all who read it and an impetus for relational hope and trust building.

Resiliency: An Introduction to the Process

During the first interview for this book, Cara Gunderson, married to an alcoholic who had been sober for the majority of their married life, spoke emphatically about couples in the aftermath of active alcoholism. "I think you can survive if you really want to. You have to have your mind made up. And, I think, there has to be *something between* two people—but you can survive." In fact, not only do many marriages survive after a crisis, but also the couples go on to have strong and vibrant relationships. What facilitates the growth of a relationship after a crisis? How does a couple make its way through such stressful and often destructive times? What exactly is that "something between" that Cara Gunderson spoke of?

We actually know very little about this process of marital survival. There are many excellent books and articles on divorce and marriage, and a few outstanding pieces of work on what makes marriages good, but there is little understanding of what enables a couple to navigate its relationship through the treacherous waters of a crisis to create a sound and satisfying marriage. Yet, most long-term relationships are bound to face crises over the years. The causes of these crises may vary—unemployment, the critical illness of a child, an affair. Over the years, and in the aftermath of life trauma, some relationships are destroyed and some remain intact but stagnant, while other couples find their way through these dark waters to build rewarding relationships. It is this story that is ultimately most compelling, complex, and potentially helpful. The questions are: What is it that enables marriages to survive crises and even grow? What is required of the spouses? And what eases their way?

To begin to answer these questions, I interviewed spouses who have been through at least one major life crisis: the trauma of alcoholism. A total of twenty-one couples and five individuals took part in in-depth interviews. Married between eleven and fifty-six years, with the average length of marriage being thirty-three years, most have adult or nearly adult children. All were married prior to the crisis of alcoholism and remain married today. It is their stories, particularly the detailed accounts of four couples, upon which this book is based. I also bring to this work my training in educational psychology and my own experience as the wife of an alcoholic. Married for more than twenty-five years and the father of two grown children, my husband, Mac, has been sober nineteen of those twenty-five years.[1] Thus, we have spent many more years with my husband in long-term sobriety than actively drinking. If my husband and I were to describe his years of drinking, it would surprise many to know that today we have a deeply satisfying marriage. Although this book took root from my own experiences, it took form from the interviews I conducted over several years.

When I first started the interviews, I wanted to understand what enabled marriages that share the common thread of alcoholism to persevere and heal. Like many travelers, we don't always end up exactly where we thought we would. Along the path of trying to understand how "alcoholic marriages" heal and grow, I realized that at the same time I was learning more about the strength of human commitment, the tenacity of determination, and the flexibility of the human heart and psyche. As I researched marital satisfaction, good marriages and bad, enduring marriages, and the resources that make relationships both liberating and comforting, I started to see that although the book's original focus was on alcoholism and long-term sobriety—a story rarely acknowledged and little studied—it had also become a book about the rebalancing of relationships so that people can move forward in trust and satisfaction. In short, I was learning what makes relationships resilient.

Much of the existing research on families and marriage focuses more on their pathology than on their health. Understanding what builds relationships is a largely unexplored territory. This is true for a variety of reasons. For one, pathology tends to be easier to identify and trace than health.[2] Compared with true pathology, health can be less dramatic and, to some people, less apparent and less interesting. Pathology, too, is usually more "fundable" and attractive to research agencies. This is for a good reason: Our society invests in attempts to cure people, to ease their suffering. Funds are directed toward the study of cancer, schizophrenia, diabetes, depression—any number of afflictions. Unfortunately, this has meant that illness and pathology have often been the thrust of research, while strength and health have largely been ignored. Instead of attempting to understand how people get through crises, we are often content to identify the pathology of the crisis and go no further. Simply identifying what causes depression is not enough; we have to know how to arrest it to make people healthy and whole again. Ideally, we need to learn how to prevent depression. For relationships, we need to learn what facilitates health and resiliency.

Psychological research has been dominated by attempts to identify and articulate pathological behaviors, and attempts to identify what brings about relational health and resiliency have been largely ignored. In recent years, that domination has abated as more significant efforts have been made to understand health and strength.

This emerging shift toward a greater focus on identifying strengths and resiliency is not restricted to psychology but has become a new focus in a variety of fields, including education, sociology, and family studies. Perhaps the shift marks a turning point in our collective thinking from that of a culture of victims and victimizers to a more balanced recognition that resources and pathology typically exist side by side. This shift has been identified as a "sea change," a true paradigm shift from what damages to what strengthens.[3] In *Resilient Marriages*, the existence of pain and pathology is not denied. Instead they are viewed alongside the individual and relational resources and strengths that these couples harbored, tended, and brought to bear.

What exactly are resources in a relationship? Mark Karpel suggests that they are "individual and systemic characteristics among family members that promote coping and survival, limit destructive patterns, and enrich daily life."[4] In other words, resources are anything that helps individuals, couples, and families function in a way that promotes health and fairness and limits exploitation. A number of researchers identified common resources, including respect; reciprocity, or fairness of give and take; reliability; trust; forgiveness; repair; flexibility; family pride; cooperation; humor; communication; a capacity for dialogue; realistic hopefulness;[5] loyalty; and appropriate investment and reinvestment of caring.[6] These are in addition to the traditionally recognized resources—financial security, a home, kinship ties, a job. Whatever the resources are, they limit pain and destructiveness and promote an easier, richer, and, thus, more rewarding life.

The couples interviewed for this book have surely known relational injustice and pain. Yet they managed to harness the available resources, no matter how apparently inconsequential and limited, and to find ways to rebuild their relationships. They did it slowly, painstakingly, awkwardly. They stumbled and began again. As one alcoholic said, "The war is over, and we came out of hell." Yet having been in hell, they have not forgotten it, and they have not lost all of the scars. They acknowledge that even today, all is not perfect. "*It isn't*," in the words of one spouse, "*that grand bouquet*."

The couples introduced in the following chapters came into their marriages, like most people, with certain expectations born of their own childhood experiences, life goals, fantasies, hopes, and dreams. When life took a long and dangerous detour into alcoholism, they were severely tested. But, in the final analysis, they found ways to activate resources to move toward one another, to test the possibilities between them, and to build a stronger foundation or to construct one where none had previously been. These couples offer us an inside view into who they are and how they accomplished this.

THE COUPLES: WHO ARE THEY, WHAT DO THEY TEACH US?

This book is based on composite portraits of four couples—Cara and Ken Gunderson, Peg and Dave Royer, Ann and Mike Bertolino, and Jan and Luke Abbott.

In the following chapters, you will meet each of them and hear about each person's upbringing, how the couples met, the early years of their marriages, the times of alcoholic drinking, and what enabled them to remain in their respective marriages. Three of the couples—the Gundersons, the Bertolinos, and the Abbotts—describe the resources, choices, and actions that facilitated relational growth. The fourth couple, the Royers, describe a relationship still mired in anger and disappointment.

Why include the Royers? Nearly 25 percent of the couples interviewed for this book described relationships that had endured but had not undergone significant relational growth. The Royers's inclusion serves two purposes: The first is as a tool to identify the resources that may still exist for them in the midst of their distance and stagnation. The second purpose for including the Royers is because they serve as a kind of backdrop against which we can see the other couples more clearly. This contrast is helpful because it brings the Gundersons, Bertolinos, and Abbotts into sharper focus.

None of these marriages is ideal. Each couple and each individual still struggles with some area of their relationship. But neither are they pathological. Instead, we see that their relationships contain a mixture of what helps and what hinders.[7] One of the more important but often overlooked aspects of relational resources is that they exist in the most troubled relationships as well as in relationships that are doing well. Resources that exist in good times are also found in the midst of injustice and mistrust.[8]

Each couple describes a distinctly different journey and a distinctly different kind of marriage. Some of what we see is flattering, and some less so. In fact, all marriages have many moments that are difficult—even ugly. Bitterness and anger can become explosive. During the interview with the Bertolinos, Ann states with great emotion that Mike has a "*social disability*," and Dave Royer refers to Peg as his "*maid*." Although less flattering aspects of relationships are not limited to marriages affected by alcoholism, they are certainly a fairly common aspect of alcoholic marriages. As Ann Bertolino says, *"alcoholism throws a harsh light on the human condition."* She is correct. The challenge is to not allow the glare of this very harsh light to blind us from seeing who these people really are or who they might become.[9] In doing so, we gain insight into how relationships endure and become resilient.

WHY RESILIENCY?

Resilience is the active process of self-righting. Although I started this book to understand healing, the more I heard from the couples and individuals interviewed, the more I realized that they were describing a long and circuitous process of becoming resilient. The book is about couples picking themselves up by the bootstraps and going on, of trying again and again, even when the situation looked hopeless. Resilience seemed to be a fitting description because these couples described building something better. It is not simply about eliminating pain from relationships; it is also about creating something new and healthy within relationships. The more interviews I did, the more I came to see that the majority of the couples did not live in marriages that simply endured; they lived in satisfying relationships that exhibited resilience—the ability to bounce back and recover, to try again. They had managed not only to jettison much of the pain and distrust but also to build a new life for themselves as individuals and as partners.

Early studies of resiliency grew, in part, out of epidemiological research on heart disease, where it was noted that some people appeared to be "insulated" from developing heart problems.[10] Similarly, sociological and psychological researchers discovered that many children born and raised under some of the harshest circumstances, including chronic poverty and even alcoholic, abusive, or psychotic parents, were able not only to avoid leading lives characterized by failure but to transcend their circumstances and live healthy and productive lives. Over the past forty years, the field of psychology has identified people who excel under the worst of circumstances and defy the odds against them. Psychologists Emmy Werner and Ruth Smith studied children from impoverished backgrounds.[11] They found that many of these children, reared in poverty, instability, and lacking proper education and health care, fared well as adults. Werner states that, resilient adults "are planners and problem solvers and picker-uppers."[12] In her book about resilient adults, psychologist Gina O'Connell Higgins explores the common characteristics of resilient adults.[13] All of the adults she interviewed had endured extreme trauma and deprivation as children but today lead balanced and productive lives. As Higgins notes, they emerged "loving well."[14]

In recent years, more attention has been directed toward the study of resiliency.[15] A greater understanding has led to the realization that resiliency is, in fact, a paradox that captures the ability to rebound from a bad experience, yet maintain an awareness of the damage done and of scars to heal.[16] Given this, the fact that people can emerge from terribly difficult situations to find balance and contentment, to "love well," is reason for pause. It makes it more difficult to maintain the belief that we are given a script at birth, or during early childhood development, that limits individual or relational growth and possibility. Excessive focus on human determinism results in an underestimate of human resiliency and adaptiveness.[17] For example, our understanding of human trust has shifted from a sole focus on disruptions occurring at a critical stage of infant development to the realization that trust is continuously shaped and reshaped through reciprocal care or its lack. Although we once thought trust was developed in a finite amount, we now recognize that it is not a "one shot deal."[18] Likewise, what many couples do with their lives, with their relationships, is not a one shot deal. The couples described in this book are a testament to that.

THEMES OF RESILIENCE: RESIDUAL RESOURCES, MOMENTS OF CHOICE, BUILDING TRUST

One spouse said of the couple's journey together, *"The fabric is so interwoven that you really can't trace a thread very well."* Although each interview was unique and each couple different from the others, there were three common threads that emerged repeatedly: residual resources, moments of choice, and building trust. Each thread, or theme, was part of the complex tapestry of resiliency. The themes provide a useful template, or framework, for understanding how couples journey through the dark days of mistrust to emerge with their relationships more balanced and satisfactory.

Residual resources was the first theme to emerge. Residual resources enabled the couples to hold on to their marriages in the worst of times and to risk trusting their partners, even in the face of likely disappointment. Even when all visible or apparent evidence suggested that any good between them was long ago extinguished, residual resources functioned to hold the couples together and to give them the will to work toward an improved relationship. One spouse said, *"My husband and I are good friends . . . I do love him and he loves me—and that does make a difference."* Karpel contends that three of the most important relational resources are respect, reciprocity, and reliability.[18]

Respect is something that most people can identify when they see it. It refers to one person conveying to another (through words, deeds, or simply being present) that the other is valued for his contributions. Respect promotes self-respect, which helps to "feed" the relationship in positive ways. A person who is respected is likely to show respect to others.

Reliability in relationships refers to the expectation that another will be there for us on an ongoing, fairly consistent basis. This includes being present and helpful in day-to-day life and, in particular, during times of great stress or need. Karpel points out that reliability is concerned more with actions than with words. It is "measured" by what a spouse actually does, rather than what they say they will do.

Reciprocity in relationships refers to the balance of giving and receiving care and consideration. It has been referred to as relational justice.[19] Balanced reciprocity contributes to the development of healthy relationships among family members because they feel fairly treated and they find ways to offer care and consideration to others. When this is the case, no family member is left in a permanent state of either benefit or burden.[20] Rather there is relative balance between giving and receiving. This balance teaches people to learn to expect fair treatment and enables them to offer fair treatment to others. When respect, reliability, and reciprocity are compromised, the likely outcomes are distrust and despair.[21]

The residual resources that came into play for the couples interviewed included feelings of both loving and liking between partners; being friends; exhibiting commitment to the other, to family, and to the institution of marriage; trust in the other as a person; similar backgrounds; and a shared religion. Other residual resources included early acceptance by the nonalcoholic spouse of the alcoholic's drinking, the capacity for personal insight, hopefulness, determination, the ability to maintain a "double vision," which consisted of a vision of the problems as well as a vision of good things from their past, and the fact that even as their relationship was being destroyed it was also being built in some significant ways.[22] Residual resources held these relationships together, even as they were threatened with destruction.

The second recurrent theme to emerge was references to moments of choice. For the Gundersons, Bertolinos, and Abbotts, moments of choice were pivotal decisions that moved each spouse toward his or her partner and toward the possibility of relationship building.[23] The couples themselves often used terms such as "turning points" to refer to moments of choice that had had a profound effect on the repair and rebuilding of their marriages. Examples of moments of choice include an alcoholic's decision to get sober, to return to one's spouse after a divorce or separation, to offer exoneration and unconditional love, to seek help, and to give up anger and rage. Moments of choice for the Royers seemed to move them away from one another: Dave Royer's moment of choice was the decision that Peg was unable to be more than a "*maid*" in his life. The result of this moment of choice is ongoing relational distance and despair.

For most of the couples, these turning points, or moments of choice, contributed to the rebalancing of their relationships. Marriage, like most of life, involves an ongoing array of choices. Some choices are better than others; some help and some hinder. Moments of choice jump-started the relationships of the Gundersons, Bertolinos, and Abbotts. These were choices that turned the partners toward one another.

The third theme to emerge was building trust. When spouses are disrespectful to one another and perceived as unreliable by their mates, the relationship is largely defined by fundamental imbalance. When there is an ongoing imbalance of giving and receiving care and consideration, the resources of a relationship are squandered and trust is eroded and slowly replaced by mistrust. Mistrust is galvanized when the relational resources of reliability, reciprocity, and respect are diminished; trust is fortified when these resources flow easily between people. When this happens, a "climate of trust" is maintained.[24] This climate of trust tends to have a forward-moving, health-promoting effect. In fact, trust has been referred to as the rudimentary resource of relational growth.[25] As such, trust is always a relational property of at least two people. By definition, it cannot be simply psychological.[26] Although some peoples' individual personalities may be naturally more trusting than others', it is primarily through relating to other people that we develop our sense of trust or mistrust. Once a relationship is characterized by mistrust, the very foundation on which it rests is eroded. If a person mistrusts his or her partner, it might be impossible to invest further in the relationship. When this happens, the relationship is in danger of either ending or remaining stuck at the level of accusation and distance. Thus, trust is of primary concern in attempting to understand relational growth.

Alcoholism, like any other violation of the relationship's bond, chips away at trust resources. People who are "married" to the bottle often convey to their spouse that they are not important. Many such spouses said during the interviews that they felt they were "second fiddles." Alcoholics are notorious for not showing up, for not being involved, and for not being supportive. One spouse said, *"he was married to the booze—he wasn't married to me, and my feelings, and what I wanted, and everything was secondary."* A person who is drinking is less likely to reciprocate because he/she is consumed by a compulsion to drink. Of course, alcoholism is not the only event in a marriage that erodes trust. A marriage in which one partner is a workaholic and is never available to spend time with the family also creates an imbalance. Such an imbalance diminishes trust. The same is true when there is an imbalance resulting from other circumstances—psychological depression, an affair, the inability or failure of one partner to consider the needs of the other partner. Situations that create an imbalance have the potential to erode trust. In short, long-term imbalances of giving and receiving in relationships violate trust and breed distrust.

In contrast, when people feel that they are being treated fairly, they feel secure and cared for, and in turn are able to give to others. The existence of trust in relationships facilitates the ability to find a balance between self-interest and the interests of others. When both partners offer and receive care in appropriate ways and amounts, a sphere of "fundamental trust" emerges.[27] Among the couples I interviewed, this sphere of "fundamental trust" had nearly been extinguished many years earlier because of alcoholism. Through great effort, trust was nourished and took root once again for the majority of the couples.

What does trust building look like? As Karpel observes,

> Trust building relies on dialogue, that is, verbal discussion, but its heart is action. It depends on action taken to initiate dialogue and can generate actions that change long-term relational patterns. . . . Trust building has a positive snowball effect. One person's willingness to consider the other's claims makes the other more likely to try to consider that person's claims. One person's demonstrated investment in the relationship makes it easier for the other to express caring.[28]

Among the couples interviewed for this book, trust building took a variety of forms, including the nonalcoholic spouse accepting alcoholism as a disease, the couple learning to speak the same language (e.g., the language of Alcoholics Anonymous), and both spouses becoming more independent. Independence for a spouse included finding his or her own "voice;" expressing feelings; investing in his or her own career, job, or hobby; and learning to consider his or her own needs. In particular, these individuals learned to no longer please their partner at their own expense; to take deliberate actions to rebalance the relationship; and to acknowledge the pain of the past. They learned to listen and to consider who their spouses were by considering the spouses' opinions, positions, and emotions. For the alcoholic, making efforts to reenter the family constellation was also part of building trust. Mike Bertolino took a step toward trust building when he realized he had to stop reading the newspaper at the dinner table if he wanted to have conversations with Ann. *"It was clear,"* he recalls, *"that if I wanted the marriage to continue, I'd have to make sure I spent time with her."* Such deliberate actions were common. Spouses also took responsibility for harm done. For Luke Abbott, taking responsibility meant finally facing the fact that he had not been responsible for a mere "fender bender," but for a full-scale "smash-up." Spouses and couples sometimes entered therapy, and all had the capacity to assess their own need to change.

Residual resources, moments of choice, and building trust are intertwined. For the sake of clarity, these themes are presented as discrete entities, but in fact there is considerable overlap. For example, moments of choice and residual resources contribute to trust building. However, moments of choice usually arise from a single decision rather than long-term, ongoing efforts like those required to build trust. For the couples in this study, residual resources were the parts of the relationship that, for the most part, had existed throughout the relationship. At critical and varying times in the relationship, these residual resources served as the "glue" that held these couples together, but also enabled them to risk building trust. Cara Gunderson loved Ken even at the worst of times, and Mike Bertolino had a special ability to accept Ann's drinking as part of her fundamental being. Such small but significant resources helped to hold their marriages together.

The three common themes of residual resources, moments of choice, and building trust provide a logical structure and also serve as a useful correction to some of the ongoing preoccupation with pathology. For, in the end, it was the residual resources that held the couples together, the moments of choice that catapulted them toward one another, and their often incremental efforts that activated trust and facilitated relational repair. Together, these movements built resiliency for the Gundersons, the Bertolinos, and the Abbotts. I have attempted to use this thematic framework to show different ways the couples moved from destructive and stagnant marriages to marriages in which both spouses find genuine satisfaction.

THE RESEARCH

There are several important points to be raised about what this book is and isn't and about my role as interviewer and writer. For interested readers, I have included a detailed description of the research methodology in the appendixes. Several aspects of my approach to research should, however, be noted here.

My particular interest is in how growth and healing occur in marriages that have been damaged, not in an investigation of the ingredients of divorce. With a divorce rate of approximately 50 percent in the United States, the widely acknowledged costs of divorce—both economic and emotional—and increasing public concern for the state of marriage, it is useful to identify the factors that contribute to improved or restored relationships. In many cases, divorce is clearly the best option. As Ann Bertolino said of Mike during her interview, *"I truly believe that enlightenment for some means divorce."* The purpose of this manuscript is not to question people who choose divorce, but to identify causes of growth and resilience among those who choose to stay married and work to rebuild their relationships.

The very choice of a research question is interesting in and of itself. Past research on the family has been criticized as being overly concerned with power, control, organization, communication, and having an excessive focus on the visible structure. Some researchers suggest that different kinds of research questions would be more fruitful. For example, what is it that motivates parents to deal continuously with their screaming infant, obstinate toddler, rebellious teen, adult child who "returns to the nest," or middle-aged child who cannot keep a job?[29] Why do adult children continue a relationship with a parent for whom they feel no affection, with whom they share no apparent interests, and who insists on giving them unsolicited advice? Why do they provide care for their infirm parents when providing this care disrupts their lives and the lives of their own children and spouses?[30] James Orford wrote that, "[t]o ask why a wife does not leave her drinking husband, or why a parent is not tougher with a drug-taking youngster, and to assume that these 'coping failures' imply some kind of pathology is, in my view, to misunderstand the profound dilemmas that excessive behavior in others poses for those of us who witness it or are affected by it."[31] I would add that to focus exclusively on 'coping failures' would in fact be a failure of the research to recognize inherent strengths in relationships.

Marriage relationships, although they take different forms, are about peoples' needs to be wanted, comforted, cared for, respected, sought out, and treated fairly. In alcoholic marriages, the alcohol fuels both exaggerated behaviors and disruption of family interactions. The marriages studied in this research are "different" in that they have an extensive history of alcoholism. However, the ways the couples resurrect their relationships have more to do with the human condition than with alcoholism and addiction recovery as such. Indeed, alcoholism ought not be viewed as a "special case" of marital disruption because so many of the same symptoms and responses commonly appear in nonalcoholic relationships during times of great stress and adversity. The challenge is to identify what strengthens, rather than what destroys, any marriage that faces adversity.[32]

Contextual family therapy, a paradigm of family therapy explicitly concerned with family and individual resources, trust building, and fairness, has been important as a basis for this research.[33] The contextual paradigm, as elaborated by Ivan Boszormenyi-Nagy, Margaret Cotroneo, Barbara Krasner, and others, is one of the more positive and realistic ways of thinking about individuals and families. In the case of these interviews, it provides a useful framework for understanding the couples' experiences from a perspective of resources rather than one of pathology.

An example of the difference between a resource-based perspective and a pathology-based perspective arose during my doctoral dissertation research on spina bifida. Spina bifida is a severe neuromuscular disorder, which typically causes paralysis, brain malformation, incontinence, and a variety of continual medical crises. I interviewed parents and their severely disabled adult children to gain a better understanding of family interactions, specifically, reciprocity. I reported to one of my mentors that these families, with the exception of the disability, looked and sounded like caring, concerned, "high functioning" families who personified grace under pressure. My mentor smiled at me and said something I will never forget: "That's because the disability is one small part of their humanity. Their humanity is not a part of their disability." Thus, what emerged in those interviews was how the disability was shaped *by* their humanity, not how their humanity was distorted by or confined within their "disability." The bottom line is that writers and researchers must be cautious not to overlook the humanity while more easily magnifying the disability or crisis in whatever form it happens to be. In my dissertation, that was spina bifida. Here, it is alcoholism. In reality, alcoholism is one and *only one* part of who these couples are.

My work as interviewer, translator, summarizer, and presenter of the interviews also bears mention. The presentation of findings from research based on interview data comes with great freedom as well as tremendous responsibility. Interview-based research is particularly vulnerable to being influenced by the interviewer's vantage point. The interviewer chooses what direction to move the interview; the writer chooses the comments to ignore, the quotes to use, and which to eliminate. In other words, the "shape" and message of the work are largely determined by the interviewer and writer. The responsibility, then, is to present a realistic and honest overview firmly grounded in the actual discussions. To some extent, how one shapes the work depends on how one perceives the world and what one believes.

This may raise the question: Did I simply hear what I wanted to hear?[34] Certainly, I have the bias of someone who has chosen to remain in a long-term marriage to an alcoholic. This identity gave me entree into the homes of many of these couples. More importantly, it is this experience that initially moved me to do the research. Additionally, it is possible that deep down inside I wanted to see some "ideal" marriages.[35] Did I "see" only the good parts of these relationships and ignore the more problematic aspects of them? I would argue I did not. Although I was originally cautious about the couples' claims that they had surpassed their problems to create satisfying marriages, the detailed exposure during the research was revealing. Most of the couples reported struggles and problems. At the same time, I saw some very good marriages—even a few apparently outstanding marriages. Yet each had its own quirks, tensions, and regrets.

Just as the interviewer shapes the findings, he or she is shaped by the people interviewed, because they are the primary conveyors and interpreters of their life stories. What I have attempted to do is to use a simple, common sense litmus test:

What is *this* individual or couple saying about *their* relationship and the processes that have held *them* together. Still, some critics might think that such accounts cannot be trusted or taken at face value; that they need interpretation by experts. In particular, the fact that these couples are in "alcoholic marriages" might be enough to make some assume that these marriages are, by definition, unhealthy. In the end, there is only so much one can say about such concerns, except to suggest a thorough reading of the accounts on the following pages, so the reader can make his or her own assessment. It should be kept in mind that none of these couples is claiming to have ideal marriages or offer instantaneous cures. Mike Bertolino proudly informed me that he and Ann were *"getting closer by inches."* He did not say by leaps and bounds.

A word about the organization of the book might be helpful. It is divided into four narratives, one each for each couple. The order of the couples is as follows: the Gundersons, the Royers, the Bertolinos, and the Abbotts. By placing the Royers's account, whose relationship is stagnant, between those of two more resilient couples, I hope to make it easier to view them from a resource perspective just as the other couples are viewed. Although each narrative is primarily the story of that particular couple, I have included notes and comments on prior research, which helps to elucidate different aspects of that couple's experience. At the end of each section, there is a brief summary that highlights the main points raised by the couples. These summaries are primarily reviews of the common themes of residual resources, moments of choice, and building trust. The four narratives are followed by an overall conclusion that describes the main findings. The appendixes include a more thorough description of the research methodology; a brief description of alcoholism and its effects, Alcoholics Anonymous (A.A.), and Al-Anon; and a description of *codependency,* including a brief discussion of the criticisms of that term and the notion of alcoholism as a disease.

Finally, this is not a self-help book per se. It does not offer exercises to improve communication skills or emotional states. *Resilient Marriages* points toward the resources that enable some couples to move from disaster to success, from the pathology of alcoholism (which may set any of us apart from one another and from our very selves) to what connects us as human beings. The complexities of marriage make the notion of a programmatic self-help book unrealistic. Marriage involves many things, including bringing together two different people with unique constellations of life experiences, family backgrounds, genetic traits and tendencies, individual psychological makeups, and influences from the rest of the world. It is more prudent and more honest to present the stories of people who are in long-term marriages and long-term sobriety as a way of showing what contributes to relational growth after a crisis. These stories provide rich accounts of real situations and relationships. They document the subtle shifts as well as the dramatic leaps that moved these partnerships from emotional and relational poverty to warmth and relational wealth. It is likely that readers will be able to draw on these accounts to help them reflect on their own relationships.

This book is about the complex as well as the relatively simple aspects of what makes marriages resilient. It is an attempt to identify what seems to help couples survive adversity by creating a more fair and balanced foundation. These couples serve as examples of reconciliation with dignity. They eloquently and honestly capture the elusive, the complex, the heartwarming and the heartrending, and make it accessible to us all. In doing so, their stories bring us squarely to the crossroads where relational mistrust and the resources of the human condition meet head-on. It is here that we see the paradox of relationships: the ability to find trust and meaning where it is least expected, to find resiliency in the wake of destruction.

NOTES

1. "Mac," like all names in this book, is a pseudonym used to protect the identities of interview participants.

2. I am not certain that imbalance in relationships is actually easier to identify than balance. It may seem this way because our culture has focused so much on pathology and imbalance that we naturally think in those terms.

3. D. Blum, "Finding Strength: How to Overcome Anything," *Psychology Today* 31, no. 3 (1998): 32–38.

4. M. A. Karpel, ed., *Family Resources: The Hidden Partner in Family Therapy* (New York: Guilford Press, 1986). This book provides a thorough discussion of relational resources.

5. E. S. Strauss, "The Therapist's Personal Impact on Family Resources," in *Family Resources: The Hidden Partner in Family Therapy*, ed. M. A. Karpel (New York: Guilford Press, 1986), 305–324.

6. M. Cotroneo, "Families and Abuse: A Contextual Approach," in *Family Resources: The Hidden Partner in Family Therapy*, ed. M. A. Karpel (New York: Guilford Press, 1986), 413–437.

Some traits can act as positive resources or negative resources. For example, shame is positive when it encourages honest behavior, but it is negative when it becomes an overpowering emotion that leads to depression and self-loathing.

7. J. Kagan, *Three Seductive Ideas* (Cambridge, Mass.: Harvard University Press, 1998), 191. "Humans are selfish and generous, aloof and empathic, hateful and loving, dishonest and honest, disloyal and loyal, cruel and kind, arrogant and humble."

8. B. R. Krasner, *Towards a Trustworthy Context in Family and Community*. Paper presented at Villanova University, Villanova, Pennsylvania, July 1983.

9. The field of addiction study in particular has been criticized for being overly simplistic. As such, it has usually portrayed the alcoholic and the alcoholic's spouse as pathological. There has been some lessening of this in recent years with the recognition that most people are a combination of good and bad. By saying this I do not mean to suggest that alcoholism is not destructive, just as I would never suggest that epidemics, floods, and famines are not destructive. Rather, I am suggesting that just as people in the aftermath of floods, famines, and epidemics have a way of pulling together, of learning from misfortune and tragedy, and of tapping undreamed-of strengths so that they can move on with their lives, so too do people in the aftermath of relationship crises such as alcoholism.

Instead of being defined and delimited by misfortune and tragedy, it is often our response to such situations that is the true measure of our inner being, a measure of what we are capable of becoming.

10. E. J. Anthony and B. J. Cohler, *The Invulnerable Child* (New York: Guilford Press, 1987).

11. R. Smith and E. Werner, *Vulnerable but Invincible: A Longitudinal Study of Resilient Children and Youth* (New York: McGraw-Hill, 1982).

12. J. P. Shapiro, D. Friedman, M. Meyer, and M. Loftus, "Invincible Kids," *U.S. News & World Report* (November 11, 1996): 62–71.

13. G. O. Higgins, *Resilient Adults: Overcoming a Cruel Past* (San Francisco, Calif.: Jossey-Bass, 1994).

14. Higgins, *Resilient Adults,* 352–353.

Common characteristics of the resilient adults that Higgins interviewed included: (1) above average to superior IQ; (2) exceptional talents; (3) attained higher economic levels than their families of origin; (4) are able to sustain close ties with people and often form important relationships with adults outside their family; (5) frequently have highly psychologically compromised siblings; (6) are invested in social and political activism; (7) are committed to reflection, looking at things from new angles, and ongoing therapy; (8) believe that knowledge is power and that their futures will be better if they are active change agents; (9) are life-long learners; (10) make positive meaning out of their experiences; (11) have the capacity to form and nurture a vision of an interpersonal world that is more satisfying than the one in which they were raised; (12) tend to be authentic, buoyant, and friendly; (13) maintain a distant but comprehending view of their families of origin; (14) believe that the adversity they have experienced has made them stronger than they would have been otherwise.

15. D. R. Hawley and L. DeHaan, "Toward a Definition of Family Resilience: Integrating Life-Span and Family Perspectives," *Family Process* 35, no. 3 (1996): 283–298. Hawley and DeHaan also comment on the need to understand resilience over time. They suggest that short-term results or changes are not necessarily good in the long run. In the interviews for *Resilient Marriages* the focus was on the couples and not their children. Extrapolating from Hawley and DeHaan's suggestion of the need to understand resilience over time raises the question that what is indicative of resilience for the couples may or may not translate into resilience for their children. As noted in the appendix, it was not within the scope of this project to attempt to understand the effects of the parents decisions on the lives of their children.

F. Walsh, "The Concept of Family Resilience: Crisis and Challenge." *Family Process* 35, no. 3 (1996): 261–281.

16. D. Blum, "Finding Strength."

17. J. Kagan, *Three Seductive Ideas.*

Cotroneo, "Families and Abuse," 413–437.

B. J. Hibbs, "The Context of Growth: Relational Ethics between Parents and Children," in *Children in Family Contexts: Perspectives on Treatment*, ed. L. Combrinick-Graham (New York: Guilford Press, 1989), 26–45.

18. According to Karpel (1994), there are four primary relational resources: respect, reliability, reciprocity, and repair. Repair involves efforts to make up for damage done to the relationship. These efforts can take different forms, including verbal apology and acknowledgment of wrongdoing.

19. L. C. Krone, "Justice as a Relational and Theological Cornerstone," *Journal of Psychology & Christianity* 2 (1983): 36–46.

20. Cotroneo, "Families and Abuse," 413–437.

21. It should be noted that giving and receiving in close relationships must be evaluated over time. In any close relationship, such as marriage, there are bound to be times when one person gives more than the other. For example, a husband might take over care of home and children while working full time, so that his wife can attend graduate school out of state. Although this is a temporary imbalance of responsibility, it must be understood over time and in the full context of their relationship. Perhaps the wife has repeatedly put her needs second to support her husband's career aspirations. This may be an opportunity for them to balance the ledger between what each one owes in the relationship and what each one deserves. Although it appears the husband is giving more than the wife during this time, she in fact may be offering her husband the opportunity to repay her for past support. Thus, the distinction between who is giving more and who is giving less is not always as obvious as it may seem.

22. The presence of a double vision was previously noted by Wallerstein and Blakeslee in their research on good marriages. They found a double vision, the ability to keep positive memories of the relationship's past when going through a crisis in the present, to be a primary task for maintaining a good marriage. J. S. Wallerstein and S. Blakeslee, *The Good Marriage: How and Why Love Lasts* (New York: Houghton Mifflin, 1995), 322.

23. Moments of choice are akin to *points of choice,* a term used by Peter Steinglass et al. (1987). The authors suggest that alcoholic families follow a trajectory that is variable, but they commonly experience "points of choice." These points of choice refer to critical decisions made by alcoholics during the course of their condition. In this text, "moments of choice" refers to critical insights and actions by both the alcoholics and their spouses. P. Steinglass, L. A. Bennett, S. J. Wolin, and D. Reiss, *The Alcoholic Family* (New York: Basic Books, 1987), 9.

24. L. C. Krone, "Justice as a Relational and Theological Cornerstone."

25. B. R. Krasner, "Trustworthiness: The Primal Family Resource," in *Family Resources: The Hidden Partner in Family Therapy*, ed. M. A. Karpel (New York: Guilford Press, 1986), 116–147.

26. B. R. Krasner, "Trustworthiness."

I. Boszormenyi-Nagy and G. M. Spark, *Invisible Loyalties: Reciprocity in Intergenerational Family Therapy* (New York: Brunner/Mazel, 1984).

27. E. E. Sampson, "Justice Idealogy and Social Legitimation: A Revised Agenda for Psychological Inquiry," in *Justice in Social Relations*, eds. H. W. Bierhoff, R. L. Cohen, and J. Greenberg (New York: Plenam Press, 1986), 98.

28. M. A. Karpel, *Family Resources*, 219–220.

29. M. P. Atkinson, "Conceptualizations of the Parent–Child Relationship: Solidarity, Attachment, Crescive Bonds, and Identity," in *Aging Parents and Adult Children*, ed. J. A. Mancini (Lexington, Mass.: Lexington Books, 1989), 81–97.

30. M. P. Atkinson, "Conceptualizations of the Parent-Child Relationship."

31. J. Orford, "Control, Confront or Collude: How Family and Society Respond to Excessive Drinking," *British Journal of Addiction* 87 (1992): 1513–1525.

32. J. Orford, "Alcoholism and Marriage: The Argument Against Specialism," *Journal of Studies on Alcoholism* 36, no. 11 (1975): 1537–1563.

33. Contextual family therapy is a resource-oriented, intergenerational approach to family dynamics that holds that trust and family justice are the cornerstones of family rela-

tions. Developed by Boszormenyi-Nagy and Sparks and refined by Krasner, Cotroneo, Hargrave, and others, its proponents hold that there are four dimensions of who we are: facts (genetic, historical, birth order, etc.), individual psychology (the individual's own psychological makeup), systemic transactions (communication patterns, interaction patterns, etc.), and relational ethics (the balance of justice and trust). Contextual therapy is most well known for its emphasis on trust and relational ethics.

34. I found that by asking couples to describe their relationship today, most provided detailed accounts of what was good and what was problematic. In addition, participants were typically asked what, if they could change something in the relationship, would that be. This gave them ample opportunity to discuss problems and concerns and helped me avoid seeing them in unrealistically good terms. Most spouses appeared comfortable in the interview situation and appeared to speak with candor.

35. The search for idealized relationships (marriages or families) has been criticized for suggesting that anything less than ideal is by definition, wrong, pathological, and lacking in resources. The search for the ideal couple enforces the notion that there are only two kinds of marriages: ideal and pathological. This ignores the vast majority of couple relationships, which includes degrees of healthy relating and less healthy relating. It also suggests that relationships are constant, rather than changing over time, with some periods more satisfying than others. Researchers are now attempting to account for the complexities of real relationships rather than idealized relationships. For example, John Gottman's marriage research (1994) suggests that even volatile marriages can be stable and satisfying. Such marriages may not be "ideal," but they may in fact be perfectly good marriages.

Part I

The Gundersons: From Survival to Striking Gold

Love is not love
Which alters when it alteration finds,
Or bends with the remover to remove:
O, no! it is an ever fixed mark,
That looks on tempests and is never shaken

—William Shakespeare, Sonnet 116

Chapter 1

Good Moments in the Midst of Bad

Ken and Cara Gunderson
Married: thirty-four years; four children
Cara: fifty-five years old, semiretired receptionist and bookkeeper
Ken: sixty-two years old, semiretired store manager; sober twenty-seven years
Children: Mara, thirty (nurse); Tim, twenty-five (store manager); David, twenty-four (construction worker); Alex, twenty-three (medical technician)

I met Ken and Cara through a friend of a friend—the way most of the couples who participated in this project came to be involved. From the very first telephone contact, they were anxious to be included in the hope that their participation might help others. In that initial conversation, Ken explained to me that they are both very involved in A.A. and Al-Anon,[1] a fact he felt would enable them to be of particular help. In addition, he suggested that their "situation" was quite different from other people's, and for that reason, their story might be of special value. When I asked him if he could say briefly how their situation differed from others, he just said that they had been through everything—and more. My curiosity was aroused. We arranged a time to get together the following week at their home in northern New Jersey. Because both Ken and Cara are semiretired, the arrangements were easy. I got directions, explained in very general terms what the interview would be like, and hung up the phone feeling curious about Ken's cryptic comment.

THE INTERVIEW

I arrived at the Gunderson's home early on a rainy October morning. As my car pulled into their driveway, I was struck by the quaint appearance of the houses in their retirement community. Simple in design, each town house had its own drive and garage, a designer mailbox in front, and a basket or pot of fresh flowers on the porch. The colors of the town houses were what you might see in

Williamsburg, Virginia. The Gunderson home is antique blue with white trim. A colorful wreath of multicolored dried flowers hangs on the front door. It is clear that neatness, effort, and care are important parts of their life. The neighborhood is not fancy but well maintained and tasteful. The streets were quiet that morning, with an occasional neighbor dashing to their car or out to get the newspaper.

Cara came to the door as soon as I knocked. Tall and slightly plump, she greeted me with a smile. Her clothes were practical—dark cotton slacks and a long-sleeved striped blouse. She wore no jewelry, except a gold wedding ring, and no makeup. Cara explained that she had just begun to clean the house so that I would not see the way she and Ken "really" lived. In fact, my eyes caught the shine of the entryway and kitchen floors, which were highly polished walnut. The overall effect was one of comfort and warmth. Cara invited me to have a seat in their dining room while she did one or two small tasks so that she could concentrate on the interview. She then called to Ken, who was in his garage workshop.

The rooms of the house were small and the furnishings were in keeping with the exterior—modest and tasteful. Like the outside of the house, the dining room was antique blue, with white trim. A white lace tablecloth and blue candles in silver candleholders adorned the table in the center of the room. I unpacked my papers and tape recorders, and within a minute or two, Cara returned with orange juice and tea.

Still smiling as she poured the tea, Cara asked about the interview, and her voice took on a serious and more reserved tone. She explained that she wasn't certain she had much to offer because she felt that their situation was significantly different from other couples'. I thought immediately of Ken's words, which had heightened my curiosity. *"We've been through everything—and more."* I assured Cara that I was interested, regardless of how different their life had been. She looked more at ease, but I noted that her jovial demeanor took a backseat to her more serious side—the side that would be present for the remainder of the morning.

Ken entered in work clothes. I knew from our telephone conversation that he worked part time in a hardware store. Dressed in overalls, plaid shirt, and work boots, Ken was handsome and grandfatherly. Like Cara, he was tall—over six feet—large boned, with silver-gray hair. He greeted me warmly with a handshake. His hands were rough and large, making mine seem miniscule in comparison. Ken looked pleased that I was there and not the least bit uncomfortable. He explained that he had been busy with his avocation—woodworking. And he acknowledged that he had put in the gorgeous wood floors in the foyer and kitchen. Ken's face broke into a grin as he explained that he and his eldest son had laid, sanded, and polished the floors together. Cara noted that she loved the floors and admired them every day. Ken offered to show me around his workroom when the interview was over. I accepted, and the interview began.

Ken took the lead in a hushed voice, telling me that his recovery was a very personal matter. His rule in recovery was threefold: neither to drink, question, nor analyze. *"This is going to sound very selfish. I'm happy that Cara is happy and*

I'm very proud of that—but that to me is just an outgrowth of my not drinking—mine is a very simple program, very personal." His comment immediately made me wonder about how well the interview would go. As it turned out, my concerns were unfounded—Ken proved to have a great deal to contribute. I told him that, although I did want to hear about the personal side of his recovery, first I hoped to learn something about the two of them. Ken agreed, saying he would try to contribute as much as possible. He added, grinning at Cara like a little boy, that he knew she would have a lot to say about their relationship. Cara did not return his smile. We began with their childhoods.

Cara: A Bit of Ozzie and Harriet

Cara grew up with her parents and four siblings in a stable, working-class neighborhood in Cincinnati. Her mother was a seamstress, and her father was a factory worker who never missed a day of work—and always had work. She recalls her childhood fondly. Her parents cared about one another as well as caring about her and her siblings. They lived a simple and frugal life, which focused on church, community activities, and family. Her family of origin is remarkable in that they suffered virtually no major losses or traumas during her childhood—at least that Cara can recall. Cara does have a vague memory of her grandmother's death, a grandmother who had lived with them until Cara was about five years old, and indicates that this is about the saddest event of her memory. Overall, Cara summarizes her life story by saying it was *"a little bit of Ozzie and Harriet."*

Her siblings get along as adults, with the exception of one brother, Nathan, who is distant from the rest of the family. Beyond the apparent discomfort related to Nathan's distance, her memories are of Christmases and Thanksgivings together, occasional trips east to the seashore as she grew older, and a good relationship with both parents. I press her a bit, and she assures me that her family still gets together and has good times, and that she is a support to her siblings, as they are to her.

Cara's parents wanted each of their children to complete high school, which they did. Her brothers were sent to local colleges, and Cara and her sister attended a local business school. Cara learned basic secretarial skills and, after graduation, became a receptionist for a large insurance company. Her memories of this work are all positive—she started as a general secretary but within a few years advanced to become the executive secretary to her division head. Her sister Kate did the same, but eventually Kate returned to school to become a nurse. Two of her brothers completed college, and the third brother, Nathan, joined the military so that he could travel. All of the siblings are either self-supporting in middle-income jobs, or retired. With the exception of Cara and Nathan, they all still live in the Cincinnati area.

Cara and Nathan were the adventurers of the family. After several years of secretarial work, Cara accepted an elderly aunt's invitation to come to Philadelphia to live with her and help around the house. Cara was the first of her siblings to go more than a few miles from home.

Upon arriving in Philadelphia, Cara found a job almost immediately. Her competence combined with her easygoing nature made her a shoo-in for receptionist positions. She reminds me that these were the days before computers, when receptionists and secretaries were respected. Hired by a well-known frozen-food company, Cara was a model employee. But living with her aunt was less than ideal. She recalls that the aunt had really wanted a full-time housekeeper, so Cara was always torn between her responsibility to her aunt and her desire to lead her own life. She remained with her aunt out of a sense of family loyalty and for companionship, as Cara missed her family horribly. After a year in Philadelphia, she made the difficult decision to move back to Cincinnati. But before she had a chance to start her move, she met Ken. Then, everything changed.

One day, while eating at a local diner where Ken was a newly hired busboy, Cara began to talk with him. Several years younger than Ken, she was immediately attracted to him, as he was to her. The banter they exchanged at lunch rapidly expanded to real conversations, the exchange of telephone numbers, and finally, a date. Shy by nature, Cara was attracted to Ken's outgoing personality. He added a spark to her life—a spark that she had longed for. His rough-and-tumble approach to life, the fact that he was less polished, less constrained by rules of etiquette, and so seemingly self-confident, added spice to Cara's comfortable but dull routines. In fact, Ken's lack of education made him even more attractive. He was street smart, and never "put on airs." Plus, he made Cara laugh.

After dating a few months, they drove to Cincinnati one weekend so Ken could meet Cara's family. They both recall that the visit went smoothly. Cara met Ken's mother and his siblings on separate occasions. She knew that Ken had had a difficult childhood and accepted the fact that his life had been quite different from what she had ever experienced.

On the drive back to Philadelphia from Cincinnati, Ken and Cara decided to get married by a justice of the peace to avoid anything large and complicated. The next week they became husband and wife and rented a small, inexpensive apartment in a working-class section of Philadelphia. Cara was relieved to be out from under her aunt's control, and Ken was just glad to be with Cara. Cara remembers this period as a whirlwind of intense excitement, fun, and freedom, and although she often still visited her aunt out of a sense of obligation, her life was now her own.

Ken's Boyhood: "I made my own rules"

Ken grew up in a rough-and-tumble working-class neighborhood. He makes the point that his family life was far removed from that of Cara's. They smile knowingly at the obvious, and it appears that this observation has been made many times over. Ken's father was an alcoholic, and his mother was unable to stand up to him. As a consequence of the father's alcohol abuse, Ken and his siblings lived a life of shame and fear. Ken recalls that his father used to beat his mother *"ungodly."* His mother, he says, believes she *"is on the earth to do the Christian thing but never make waves."* Ken remembers her lamenting, "Where am I going to go with five kids?"

I ask Ken how his father's alcoholism and the abuse of his mother affected him. He looks at me and says three words: *"Not real good."* Again, the grin. *"Before we knew about alcoholism, when me, my brothers, and sisters would walk down the street, people would see us and just turn their backs. At the schools, everywhere we went, we were pieces of shit. Nobody knew about alcoholism in the 1940s—my father kept being locked up . . . he'd get stopped for drunk driving and they'd put* [his picture] *on the front page of the local newspaper!"*

Ken grins, but once again it is more a grin of pain than of humor. *"The abuse that went on in the house, the violence—my father was a professional fighter."* The grin melts into a grimace. He describes with incredulity in his voice how his father would shame the family.[2] *"He'd go to the convent* [of the Catholic school Ken and his siblings attended] *at 8:30 at night and chase the nuns throughout the convent, and we had to go to school the next day!"* Ken's father eventually died from his abuse of alcohol, but not until after Ken and his siblings were grown. Behaviors like chasing the nuns were common for his father. Ken recalls that his father also forced him and his brothers to steal beer for him. It was not uncommon for them to spend school nights stealing rather than studying.

The shame in Ken's childhood was pervasive and carried over into his adult years. When I ask Ken who was there for him, his voice is flat: *"Nobody. I made my own rules. I hurt them when they hurt me—*[but] *I only hurt myself in the end. I'd take care of my brothers and sisters. We'd be on the corner at night. My father, you know, we went through the alley in the middle of the night to steal beer."* To escape the violence that went on inside the house, *"We'd sit on the corner—it's where we had to sleep."* I now understand some of what contributed to Ken's addiction. Its impact on their marriage would be profound.

Marriage: The Good, the Bad . . . and then the Ugly

The excitement of the months of getting to know one another carried Ken and Cara into their first year of marriage. When I ask what it was that made those early times good, Cara smiles and recalls that Ken was *"fun-loving, good looking, and liked to party."* Early in the relationship and in the marriage, they partied together often. As Cara speaks of this time, her eyes light up. She glances at Ken and they exchange a knowing glance. Eventually the excitement of an occasional martini or a cold beer faded for Cara. For Ken, it always seemed "the more the better," and his drinking and partying began to take a different path. Cara started to see that his fun-loving nature was dependent on a party and a drink. Ken also kept leaving jobs—one after another. The story was always the same: an unfair boss, a better opportunity someplace else, poor working conditions. Unlike Cara, who had worked her way up to a position of higher responsibility at the frozen-food factory, Ken was always on the first rung of the ladder. An intelligent man, he found this galling. By their first anniversary, Ken had left three jobs and had been fired from two. On the eve of their first anniversary, he was unemployed. Nonetheless, he continued to party. It was Cara's meager income that supported them.

This went on for several years. At first, Cara was just happy to be married. She felt that it was her duty to support her husband emotionally, and she believed all his reasons for the job changes. In addition, Cara continued to do well at her job and became the receptionist to the vice president of the company. By the time she started to acknowledge to herself that there was a problem, the marriage was four years old and their first child had been born. Mara was a healthy looking infant, but at three months, she was diagnosed with a form of childhood cancer, a disease that, in those days, almost always led to death. Ken and Cara were devastated. Both suffered from the shock, anger, and confusion of the diagnosis and the knowledge that their daughter would likely die.[3]

By this time, Ken was unemployed more often than he was employed. Cara resented that she was forced to work part time, just to keep them afloat. She also felt she had no other choice. During the following two years, Cara and Mara practically lived at the local children's hospital. Cara shuffled back and forth between work and the hospital, doing the best she could. During that same period, there was a wild escalation in Ken's drinking. He also started to dabble in illicit drugs. He lost more low-level jobs, had begun to stay out very late, and sometimes did not come home all night. Cara took over all responsibility for Mara, while she continued to be the breadwinner with her part-time job. She was also the intermediary between the doctors, the hospital, and Ken.

Money was tight, and they literally lived a step away from destitution. Although Cara had not grown up with a great deal of material wealth, she had grown up in a financially and emotionally stable environment. Their life at that time was stressful. I ask Cara what she thought of Ken, and of their situation, at that time. She closes her eyes before responding, as if she must compose herself. *"I wasn't going to Al-Anon then—I think I was focused on survival—financial, emotional—I was very focused on doing for Mara. I was trying to keep it all together."*

Mara's life-and-death situation, coupled with the need to work to put food on the table, left Cara little time or emotional energy to think or respond. She reminds me that, unlike today, she had no knowledge of the facts of alcohol addiction and certainly no knowledge of drugs. In fact, she never suspected at that time that Ken used drugs in addition to alcohol. Cara adds, as if she wants to make certain I don't misunderstand, *"I wasn't dumb—I just didn't know."* Then, almost apologetically: *"I was busy. I never had time to think."* With this, Ken provides some enlightenment regarding how bad it really was for him.

Ken: The Walking Dead

As Ken begins to speak, Cara sits forward awkwardly in her chair and listens intently. Unlike most of the alcoholics I interviewed, Ken stands out as telling a very gritty story. There was nothing respectable about the life that he once led. Ken grins as he begins to speak—almost like he takes some delight in shocking me. *"It was nuts—but I couldn't stay out of jail."* I glance at Cara, but her eyes are unmoving laser beams focused on Ken. She doesn't move a muscle. I look back to Ken. He nods as his lips appear to break into a more pronounced grin. *"Being an alcoholic, if somebody said 'Try this,' I would do anything . . . I used to come home with blood all over me, and I never knew, I never had any idea what happened."* Ken gulps his tea and then continues. *"Yeah. I was violent—guns and you know. I was taking pills—I just took them like candy to take the edge off. I went through a lot of money with that stuff—I'd be down in the neighborhood all night long."*

As Cara nursed Mara, Ken found a home of sorts for himself away from Cara—in his childhood neighborhood; now drug and crime infested. Ken spent his time between jobs and parties sitting in the local bar drinking, making deals, and wasting away at every level. Although his memory is limited on many specific incidents, he knows that at some point he was reduced to doing just about anything that anyone asked of him. In return he got a drink or several and sometimes drugs. He often did not know what he was drinking or what drugs he was ingesting.

He recalls being carried to the hospital one morning, having been unconscious, he believes, for a long period of time. *"Some people found me in a parking lot. These Puerto Rican people took me to the hospital—I don't even know how they got me there. Anything people would tell me, that's what I would do."* Ken emphasizes the word *anything*. I find myself not wanting to know all of the details but ask what caused him to do this, and he responds simply enough: *"I was on a death mission—I was trying to come off the planet."* His drug addiction was so serious he believes he was near death, or at least playing at the sidelines of death. Nonetheless, he still could not stop the downward spiral.

Ken's behavior carried him into worlds that most people only read about in cheap novels or newspaper exposés. He goes on to give more detail about being "in" jail. He grins as he speaks, as if he knows his story will shock me: *"I used to break into prisons for people . . . to bring drugs in—I brought in everything, sides of beef, cases of stuff . . . I was on a death mission for a long time, like all my life. I'd do anything anyone'd ask me . . . there was nothing I wouldn't do. I had no respect for myself . . . I came from neighborhoods where . . . that's how you survive. I'd ask people for money, panhandle—that was at the end—all that stuff. I was walking dead."*

Cara breaks into the conversation at this point to explain that the whole situation had gotten out of hand and her only goal was to survive and to keep Mara alive. I feel like I am in a movie: the lace tablecloth, the antique blue walls, the handcrafted floors, so lovingly polished—drugs, jail, panhandling. It doesn't fit, and I say so. Ken shrugs his shoulders and explains that there is a lot he doesn't even remember. Cara looks pale, as if even discussing this period is almost more than she can bear. She recalls Ken's deterioration as well as her pain: *"He lost a lot of weight . . . and I never in my life would have thought Ken would have done drugs."* Then, in a near whisper, *"That put me to my knees. Ken became a loan shark in a really tough neighborhood—which allowed him to be in a bar all day—and things like that."* Ken adds in a tone suggestive of the obvious: *"I was easy to hire: I didn't want to live."* Once again, Ken grins. Cara shakes her head. *"I remember Ken saying to me* [at the time of Mara's illness], *'God, you're strong. How are you doing it—don't you want to drink?'"* She chuckles at the memory, yet her face looks blank.

What brought this difficult chapter of their lives to an end? Ken recalls one particular incident near the very end. *"I sat in an abandoned house with two lowlifes, six-foot men dressed like women. No heat. No electricity. One chair. I used to meet them every day . . . I was filthy."* Ken drops his head and again mutters, *"I was on a death mission—you just get to a point. I remember just trying to die—just being empty."*

We sit quietly for a moment. Cara is playing with the cloth napkin on the table, twisting the corner over and over again. I don't know whether the look on her face is sympathy or embarrassment or both. I look at Cara and ask her why she stayed with Ken. Cara leans back in her chair and breaths heavily. *"I never did stop loving him. Although basically, I felt the marriage was over, I still, I always liked him. He's a great guy—I saw that years ago—he just never saw it. I wanted to stick around and see if he was going to make it.*[4] *Emotionally, it was killing me . . . thank God it worked out; we are very fortunate."* Her words remind me of an attorney I met who works with the poorest people in a large northeastern city. She refers to her clients as "gems in the trash"—the forgotten people of lost potential, lost hopes, and lost dreams. As I sat there, it struck me that perhaps Ken was one of those gems, and Cara had known it all along.

RESIDUAL RESOURCE: LOVING, LIKING, AND FRIENDSHIP

The vast majority of couples, particularly spouses, reported that loving or liking their partner and considering them to be a friend played a significant part in their remaining in the marriage. In fact, this was one of the most common reasons given for the survival of the marriage. One spouse recalled simply, *"During all that I still loved him."* Another spouse said firmly, *"I knew even in his alcoholism, with drinking, . . . he was the best person in the world. I used to tell him all the time: 'You're such a good person—intelligent.' He was the best. I never did stop loving him—ever—through that time—I was angry, mad—but I never stopped loving him."* An alcoholic surmised, *"Well, I do think that when drinking was occurring, our relationship was difficult in many ways, and it definitely has changed. A lot of that, I do think we loved each other, and I think that that helped to keep us together—I really do."* Another spouse explained, *"I think part of it's chemistry . . . I think whatever it is, love is or relationship is, it keeps us in orbit—it's there, I'm not even sure what it is. I love him, I always loved him, even when he was an S.O.B., I loved him. I couldn't live with him, but I loved him—and I always got the feeling he felt the same way about me."*

Factors like loving, liking, and chemistry, are typical residual resources that held couples together through the worst of times. They are part of the reserve that enables couples to survive periods of transitory unfairness and deteriorating trust. Most couples marry because they care about their spouses. Even as alcoholism deteriorates the relationship, these residual resources keep them bound at some invisible and often, to outsiders, incomprehensible level. Other recent research on couples and alcoholism underscores this point.[5]

Although love kept Cara in the marriage, it could not prevent or contain the destruction. In fact, Ken and Cara got farther apart than either could have imagined during their dating days. Love and friendship were not enough to halt the destruction. What did help to stop it?

For about three years, things appeared nearly hopeless for Ken and Cara. Mara survived against the odds, and that was a tremendous relief. Yet Ken's life was in shambles, threatening Cara's and Mara's lives as well. They could barely pay their rent, they were in debt, and essentially lived lives of quiet desperation. Cara recalls that the stress was constant. It made her pull back from friendships and live a life dominated by watching Ken struggle, praying that things would get better, and caring for Mara.

Many spouses talked of leaving or of being on the verge of leaving. Interestingly, thinking about leaving was sometimes a response of *caring* and not simply of anger and disappointment.[6] As one spouse explained, *"I was ready to leave at that point. I was ready to say 'This is over.' Not because I didn't care about him, but because I was being forced to watch him commit suicide and it wasn't good for me and it wasn't good for my children and I wasn't going to do it any more."* But in the final analysis, they usually remained. Why? One retired teacher passionately told me, *"I've always looked at it as maybe because we did like each other—even in the worst of times we had some good moments—we had some good moments, too. I couldn't look back and say it all hurt—there were low periods but it just wasn't all bad."* In addition, several spouses talked of being bound because of the financial realities of their situation. This was usually true with wives who had children and felt that even if they had wanted to leave the marriage, they could not support themselves and their children.

Ken shakes his head slowly as if in disbelief. Cara continues in the same deliberate manner. *"Ken used to come into the building where I used to work. I must have weighed about 100 pounds by then, I was so devastated by everything that was happening. Just worrying, was he going to die today? I was consumed by it."*[7] By this time, it was obvious to other people that Cara was struggling. She had lost more than twenty pounds and was often distracted at work. A coworker suggested she get in touch with Al-Anon and A.A. Cara took the advice and, to this day, relies on Al-Anon.

Cara and Ken's situation deteriorated even more as Ken kept reaching new lows. Cara volunteers a revelation in a clipped voice. *"We were divorced and then we got remarried after he got into A.A."* She speaks rapidly, as if speaking the words in as little time as possible makes them less painful or the situation less real. I look at Cara and ask what made her take the step of divorce, but I should be looking at Ken. Cara twists the napkin several times before she speaks in slow, deliberate cadence: *"I did not initiate the divorce. Ken did. But what happened was, as I said, things got very very impossible."* She pauses and then adds with a slight smile, *"Ken was a loan shark; he was the shark with a heart! This allowed him to be in a bar all day."* In fact, Ken drank until he simply couldn't take any more. When it got to an "impossible" point for him, he announced to Cara that he was leaving. Why exactly, he doesn't know. Cara provides a brief answer. *"He, well, I don't want to get into this story, but . . . he was completely off the wall."*

THE DIVORCE

"I really hit bottom then emotionally and physically," Cara explains. *"I was completely depressed . . . during this time I really held on to Al-Anon like it was a life preserver and went to a lot of open A.A. meetings."*[8] In fact, Cara did a great deal more than go to Al-Anon meetings. With Ken gone, she organized her life around work, Mara, and Al-Anon. Although depleted and depressed, she found her way and started to put some order into her life for the first time in years. What did she think about Ken during this time? *"I probably cared more about him after we separated than when we were living together and the drinking. Because I wasn't having to put up with his behavior, and, although the money was tight for me and Mara, I wasn't earning much, at least I had control of what I was earning—it wasn't going for booze."*

I recap my understanding of events to make certain that I am following the correct sequence. Cara's expressions are noticeably flat. The smile that greeted me at the door ninety minutes earlier is gone. Before moving on to their reunion, I ask about her thoughts at that time and even suggest that some people might say that she was weak or "dysfunctional"—perhaps "codependent," for not leaving the marriage herself. Her voice at once becomes stronger, almost strident. Her flat affect drops away, and her cheeks flush. *"I felt that if he was drinking, there was no future for us even though . . ."* she hesitates and then says with emphasis, *"I did still care for him. I wasn't going to subject our daughter to that, and I might as well tell you that if he started drinking tomorrow—that would be it! I would not live through that again."*

As Cara finishes her last sentence, the telephone rings and she goes to the kitchen to answer it. I turn the conversation to Ken and ask him to tell me about the divorce. He shifts his weight uncomfortably and rubs his finger on the side of his orange juice glass and appears to study it. *"Well,* [before the divorce] *I think we became more distant and of course, I started chasing other women. She became colder, naturally, and I could justify, then, for me to go out and look for something else* [other women], *and that was another thing for me . . . and I was always drunk. I began to drink around the clock: morning, noon, and night, and then of course we would argue and I'd go off on a toot and pack my suitcase."* And he reiterated, in case I hadn't understood, *"We did get a divorce."*

Ken's mood now appears to be more in line with Cara's expressionlessness. His grins are temporarily replaced by a somber intensity. *"We did break up, and I was the guy who did it,"* he confesses. Although Ken has been very straightforward, I clarify the fact that they were divorced and not simply separated. *"Right, a divorce. Then I remarried Cara. But first, I really went down hill. To tell you the truth, I don't know how I survived. I have trouble really remembering how it worked."*

KEN: A MOMENT OF CHOICE

Sometime early in the divorce, which lasted only about eighteen months, Ken moved to Richmond, Virginia, because he had a cousin there. Under the wing of his cousin and desperate, he took odd jobs, stumbled into A.A. (he doesn't remember how he actually got to a meeting), got sober, and stopped using drugs. His memory is limited, but he recalls: *"My head began to clear up a bit, and I asked myself, 'What the hell am I doing here?' . . . so I went through a major depression for six months. I would feel all the guilt and remorse . . . mostly, for my wife and daughter—in fact, that was all of it."* While in Virginia, Ken remained employed and lived in a rooming house. His life consisted of work and A.A. meetings; sometimes two and three meetings a day. Beyond this, he recalls almost nothing about that time except his limited contact with Cara, which occurred *"only in court when she was trying to get money out of me."*

Cara returns with a fresh pot of tea as Ken is finishing what he has to say about the divorce. She silently takes her seat, but Ken stops speaking as if to protect her. I suggest we take a break, as the morning has been long, and offer to come back another day. Both Ken and Cara say they are fine with continuing on. As I pour more tea, Ken brings out a few of his woodworking projects. They are exquisite vases and boxes. Ken talks of how his woodwork has added an important dimension to his life. We each take several cookies and go look at Ken's floor. Cara is as proud of Ken's skill as he is. The beauty of the floors is such a contrast with the story they have recounted.

NOTES

1. The A.A. and Al-Anon programs are described in the appendix.

2. In recent years, shame has been identified as a source of psychological and spiritual bankruptcy. Researchers have shown that shame is highly correlated with addiction, especially for women alcoholics (C. Bepko and J. Krestan, *Too Good for Her Own Good: Breaking Free from the Burden of Female Responsibility* [New York: Harper & Row, 1990]). Batshaw defines "toxic shame" as an "all pervasive sense that I am flawed and defective (J. Batshaw, *Healing the Shame That Binds You* [Deerfield Beach, Fla.: Health

Communications, 1988, 10. He suggests that shame is at the center of all addictions, and that it is shame that keeps addictions active. At the same time, Kaufman (1992) notes that a sense of shame is crucial to the development of identity, self-esteem, and intimacy. He distinguishes "good" shame from "bad" shame by suggesting that good shame amplifies our awareness, whereas bad shame captures and dominates us. Certainly, Ken Gunderson's upbringing may have facilitated development of an excess of bad shame. According to Kaufman, once shame is internalized the person must build up defenses in order to protect himself from further pain and suffering. Some of these defenses include rage, to keep people at a distance; contempt, to maintain distance and to elevate one's self above others; power, to gain maximum control; the striving for perfection, because there is no internal sense of being adequate; and blaming others, in order to shift blame away from oneself.

3. A diagnosis of childhood cancer made thirty years ago was usually considered a death sentence. V. C. Peckham, A. T. Meadows, N. Bartel, and O. Marrero, "Educational Late Effects in Long-Term Survivors of Childhood Acute Lymphocytic Leukemia," *Pediatrics* 81 (1988): 127–133.

4. The majority of female nonalcoholic spouses said they would end the marriage if their husbands returned to drinking.

5. J. Harper, "Recovery for the Relationship: A Treatment Model for Couples with a Recovering Chemically Dependent Partner," *Alcoholism Treatment Quarterly* 7, no. 2 (1990): 1–21.

6. This should not be read to suggest that anger and disappointment were absent. They were pervasive for the majority of couples during the active drinking phase and often in the early recovery phase.

7. To be consumed by alcohol/the alcoholic is indicative of what has been called an alcoholic marriage. Alcoholic marriages are organized around alcohol.

P. Steinglass, L. A. Bennett, S. J. Wolin, and D. Reiss, *The Alcoholic Family* (New York: Basic Books, 1987).

8. "Open" and "closed" A.A. meetings are described in the appendixes.

Chapter 2

"It's a Two-Sided Thing"

No voice is without value, no witness without reality.

—Maurice Friedman, *The Healing Dialogue in Psychotherapy*

After approximately twelve months of going to A.A. meetings and trying to clear the fog in his head, Ken contacted Cara on his own. By this time, he had started to send her some money to help support Mara. Because Ken had been sober for nearly a year, Cara was willing to see him. They met for several visits on weekends. The visits went well, so Ken moved to New Jersey, got a job, and they began to *date*. He recalls that it was at this point he started to *"come alive."* Ken remembers wandering around his apartment shortly after moving to New Jersey: *"I just walked through the hallway with all these tears. He* [Ken's sponsor] *said that I just thawed out. You know, cause I never felt anything. Love, hate, anger: I never felt nothing. Somewhere along the way people in A.A. started describing my feelings. I never heard somebody who felt like I did on the inside. It was a very slow awakening. I felt like I was coming in in the middle of a movie."* Finally, he was beginning to feel and to come alive.

Ken and Cara dated for nearly a year. They spent weekends together and had dinners mid-week. Ken contributed almost half of his meager salary to Cara and Mara. Although Cara smiles at this memory, she says it made a difference. Why? *"Because he was trying."*

A MOMENT OF CHOICE: UNCONDITIONAL LOVE AND EXONERATION

In fact, Ken's trying meant a great deal to Cara. Cara looks directly at me, almost as if she resents my pushing her on this. *"I guess,"* she hesitates and begins again, *"I guess I felt more compassion. I hate to use a term as corny as unconditional love but it just seemed to be there. It seemed to be, whatever you want is OK, whatever you are is OK. . . . And I know that drinking could happen again, but I don't think about that."* I ask Cara about her anger at Ken for all he had put her and their daughter through. She waves her hand slightly, *"I gave it up."*

Cara is not the first spouse to use such words. Another spouse said, *"I see the alcoholism as a short time period in my life that just passed. I don't blame my husband at all for the alcoholism, and don't make him feel guilty about that. We've talked about it, and I've let that go."* Another alcoholic, explaining the same general thinking said, *"You see, we decided we are going to live together till we die, so we are going to make every effort to be mutually, unconditionally, as accepting as possible."*

What these spouses are describing is the process of exoneration. Exoneration simply means to free from blame. Terry Hargrave provides a detailed analysis of this process.[1] Distinguishing exoneration from full forgiveness, or "relationship reconstruction," he suggests that exoneration does not demand responsibility by the wrongdoer but it brings about a reduction of blame.[2] Boszormenyi-Nagy and Krasner distinguish exoneration from forgiveness by noting that with forgiveness there remains an assumption of guilt. With exoneration, this assumption is dropped. Rather than a framework of blame, there is an appreciation for the other's limits and efforts.[3]

Exoneration enables spouses to stop filtering everything in the relationship through a prism of personal pain and rejection.[4] One spouse noted, *"I didn't feel the criticism and judgment and the anger. I realized later it was just full-blown alcoholism—it wasn't even rational. Criticism that I took to heart was not even rational."* Likewise, Cara was choosing to stop filtering everything through the prism of divorce, perhaps humiliation and despair. Instead, she found the capacity to offer unconditional love. Through exoneration of Ken, what Cara calls "unconditional love," she was "turning toward" trust building—the core of relationship reconstruction. It is likely that this was possible because of her sustained love of Ken. Although exoneration was not part of the healing equation for all of the couples, it was a salient element for many.

Cara shifts the conversation to the money Ken contributed at that point—about enough to pay for their milk and bread. Plus, Ken had immersed himself in A.A. On the nights he was not with Cara and Mara, he was at an A.A. meeting or he was babysitting so that Cara could go to an Al-Anon meeting. Yet, it was Ken's efforts that Cara noticed. Like many spouses, she thinks effort counts for a great deal. As long as there is effort, there is the ability to be hopeful, to have faith that things will improve. Hopefulness is a resource in relationship as well as a characteristic of many resilient individuals. Hopefulness can infuse a relationship with energy, liveliness, and a vision of the future that is defined by the expectation of good.

Ken and Cara dated for only a short time before they decided to get remarried. Cara moved to New Jersey, and they started life together once again. During those first years, Ken and Cara had three more children—all boys. Ken's job as the manager of a local hardware store eventually enabled Cara to give up her secretarial position to be a full-time mother—an opportunity she had always hoped for. They had to scrimp and save to do this, but they both felt that the children needed her at home. Although the changes in their relationship were gradual, and not always smooth, they were moving in a positive direction. Both of them depended on A.A. and Al-Anon a great deal. Ken proudly notes, *"A.A. particularly taught me to talk to other people—that's how I learned to communicate—Cara always could—and I think A.A. taught me what to say, how to express my feelings, and how to listen to somebody else's feelings and where they are coming from. I never did that because I was always too obsessed with myself and my drinking. I learned it was a two-sided thing."* In fact, Ken's talking to other people, expressing feelings, and going to A.A. brought about a very significant change for both Ken and Cara. Together all of these changes helped to rebuild trust between them.

BUILDING TRUST: TALKING THE SAME LANGUAGE

I ask Ken to try to help me understand what happened when he and Cara got back together. Ken worked hard to stay sober, to keep the job he had landed as the manager of the family-owned hardware store where he is still employed, and to be a parent to their expanding family. He believes that the A.A. and Al-Anon programs helped them. Ken explains, *"We can talk the same language. I think one of the big strengths is we are both working the same program. I think it helps a lot because we talk about things even if we have different opinions about them. It gives us sort of a common area for getting this stuff out and getting it out on a very honest level. You know, not game playing. We're using the honesty we've learned in the program to get this stuff out and talk about it on an honest level."*

Cara nods her head in agreement. *"We started to talk the same language—get an understanding of things a lot different for ourselves, and it was very good.* [Early on] *it was a nice period of talking the same language, we believed the same things. It was a nice period of just growing."*

By the time most spouses reach the point of sobriety, their marriages have been severely damaged. For many, the chasm that separates them seems to be able to be bridged by the use of a "script" telling them what to say, think, and feel and how to conduct their relationship. A.A. and Al-Anon provide such scripts. Although some couples do not embrace A.A. or Al-Anon, they were especially helpful to Ken and Cara. Helping couples find a common language, a set of words or phrases to share, some guidelines to live by, seems to be a major contribution of the A.A. and Al-Anon programs.[5] Cara recalls, *"I think the biggest relief was being able to say the word* alcoholic *and acknowledge it. Yes, that was it. We could work on that and we could talk about it—we could talk about program kinds of things."*

BUILDING TRUST: ALCOHOLISM AS A DISEASE

I ask what else made a difference for Cara. She again twists her napkin between her fingers. *"I understood very easily that it was a disease—my father was a diabetic. Right away I just equated it with my father's diabetes. Once I got an understanding of it* [from that perspective], *I could have compassion for Ken and see the difference between him and the disease."*[6] I press Cara to help me understand how accepting alcoholism as a disease helped change her feelings. She thinks for a moment and says, *"I realized it was an illness and I realized it wasn't something he got up every day and said 'What can I do to ruin everybody's day, today?'"*

The idea that alcoholism is a disease is often debated. Some claim that this labeling removes responsibility by suggesting that alcoholism is akin to cancer or cystic fibrosis. However, for the spouses interviewed for this book, the notion of alcoholism as a disease seemed to be helpful. It reduced the anger of the spouse and enabled the spouse to feel compassion toward the alcoholic. For wives of alcoholics in particular, the idea seemed not only to be accepted but welcomed. It was almost as if they were driven to find something to help them see the humanity of their alcoholic spouse.

BUILDING TRUST: FINDING A VOICE—CARA

I say that I am interested in learning about the two-sided part that Ken had mentioned earlier. How did that happen—what else had to change between them? Ken and Cara had literally lived two separate lives as a divorced couple. How does a couple move from divorce to re-creating a relationship? Cara and Ken look at one another. It is Cara who responds. *"Oh, I've changed in a lot of ways. I'm not subservient the way I used to be. I speak up for myself. If Ken said something* [previously], *I would agree with it, and I would go along with it, and I don't do that anymore. I speak what my mind is . . . I've gained the insight and courage to know that I have a right to say what I feel. You've got to remember, I was on my own for almost two years and I learned to become very independent, and once you learn that, you don't relinquish that easily."* Cara offers an example by referring to the telephone call she took right before we took our tea and cookie break. *"That was Mara who just called. She is trying to find a time when she can come and visit, and she wanted to come one week in February—a week prior to when we are going to take a trip. I'm willing to accommodate her up to a point but not to the point that I will put so much of a burden on myself that I won't be able to handle it. I sort of had to do some fast mental gymnastics with her in weighing all the pros and cons while on the telephone. She didn't like it. I'm sure she didn't like the fact that she's going to have to come at a time other than February—I told her March would be better than February."*

I ask Cara how this is different from times past. She shakes her head to suggest disbelief. *"There would have been a time that I would have been terribly upset about having to tell her that March would be better, and I would feel some rejection. Now, it doesn't bother me nearly as much to say, 'Hey, this is the way things are.' I've changed also in that I don't try to do everything like I did before. I was always, if you wanted to come I would say 'OK, come,' and I would bend myself inside out. I would tear myself apart in order to accommodate other people. . . . I am more of a whole person."*

D. C. Jack suggests that "silencing the self" may be an adaptation, at least in part, to try to maintain a relationship with a significant person.[7] However, the outcome is that the adaptation, the silence, not only fails to maintain the relationship but diminishes the person who silences him or herself in the process. Jack suggests a constellation of behaviors used in attempts to maintain relationships: excessive pleasing, helping, and self-silencing.[8] All of these, when carried to extremes, result in confusion, rage, and depression.[9] This selfless giving is a failure to respond to one's own needs.[10] This is what happened with Cara.

Cara is now able to consider the needs of the other people in her life, and at the same time, she is strong enough to take care of her own needs in the process. She displays that ability in her telephone conversation with her daughter. No longer willing to give to the point of depletion, she offers Mara alternatives that ensure that they both get what they need. Ken listens intently as Cara speaks. I ask Cara what she meant by being a *"whole person."* She was a mother, wife, and had worked at a job that she took pride in—wasn't that being a whole person? She shakes her head emphatically. "*My relationship was that I had no identity whatsoever! My whole identity was wrapped up in Ken. Before Al-Anon, if we sat there and he said 'We're Democrats,' I'd say, 'OK, we're Democrats.' And if he changed it five minutes later and said, 'No, wait a minute, I think we're going to be Republicans,' I'd say, 'OK, we're Republicans,'*" Cara shakes her head again as if she can't believe herself. *"I was absolutely totally enmeshed in his personality, and I totally lost my whole identity."*

BUILDING TRUST: FINDING A VOICE—KEN

I ask Ken about Cara's ability to express herself. Like Cara, he answers my question with a story—a story about his middle son's braces some twelve years into sobriety. "*You know, I used to go along to get along—that sort of thing. I had Mara in braces—Cara took my middle son, David, to the dentist and came home and made the announcement that the dentist said David should have braces. I looked at Dave's mouth and he had straight teeth. I was sober at this time, maybe ten, twelve years, and Cara said the doctor said David should have braces. I said, 'I think it's really ridiculous.' Mara I can understand, Tim, maybe, but David, I don't understand—and I don't need another payment plan at this moment.' Cara was dumbfounded—she said, 'You don't understand—the doctor told me when he is in his late thirties or forties he could develop an overbite or have an overbite that could take surgery and could possibly cause gum disease.' I said, 'I hope he has a dental plan at work and when he's forty-three years old, he'll have to address it—but at eleven years of age—no braces!'"* Ken recalls this interaction with Cara as a kind of epiphany. *"I discovered that when I talked, I felt better. When I got it out, I felt OK. I wasn't bad, I was repairable."*[11] I ask Ken why he feels Cara was dumbfounded. *"She was stunned because I had an opinion on something that was a given. . . . The guy who was drinking would make needless compromises on matters that he thinks are important—the guy who was drinking would compromise anything to keep the peace. Before, I would compromise anything to keep the peace and that was probably a turning point in my own thinking—I'm allowed to say 'No.' I'm allowed to say 'Hey, I like the red car or I don't like white cars.'"*

Cara describes her own reaction to this incident. *"I don't remember an argument over it. I remember thinking, well, he's right. . . . I had to depend on myself so much I guess I thought that all of the decisions that I made for the children were right."* She pauses again, then says a bit tentatively, *"I was the protector of all people. You know, stopping drinking didn't stop all the problems—it didn't change personalities by any means. You know—neither his nor mine. Our personalities are the same."*

Both Ken's and Cara's words describe a process of self-delineation. Self-delineation is one's capacity to define an individual, autonomous self while in the relationship with another person.[12] This process was frequently highlighted during many of the interviews. For most couples, becoming a whole person involved a personal transformation (self-delineation). The most common form of self-delineation described by alcoholics and spouses of alcoholics was finding one's "voice." This meant having opinions, expressing those opinions, and considering their own needs rather than simply keeping the peace at any price. For many wives of alcoholics, self-delineation took the form of a new career, a job, or returning to school. Such actions were important developmental steps.[13]

In the absence of self-delineation, an individual abandons not only him or herself but also his or her spouse. Without a voice, there is no "other" for the spouse to be in a relationship with. It is like pushing at air: There is nothing that pushes back. As Cara so eloquently describes it, she changed colors as often as a chameleon. When she talks of shifting from being a Democrat to a Republican at Ken's whim, Cara is describing her abandonment not only of herself but of Ken as well. This abandonment is the abandonment of her truth, of her responsibility to *be* who and what she is. But in abandoning herself, Cara also abandons Ken, because she fails to be there to hold her ground, her side. Ken may have been demanding and obnoxious—you can picture him drunk and shifting from the Democratic to the Republican Party on a whim—but Cara's collusion is as noteworthy as Ken's shifting identity.

Ken's and Cara's ability to hold on to their respective sides underscores a basic and necessary tension in close relationships. This is the paradox of simultaneously being a separate individual while living in true connection with others. Psychologist Carol Gilligan has referred to this push-pull between self and other as our "paradoxical truth."[14] The challenge is to know ourselves as individuals and separate. But we only do this insofar as we live in connection with others. "We experience relationship only insofar as we differentiate other from self."[15] By Cara not having her own voice, not taking a stand, she effectively cuts herself off from true connection, and from true identity. S. A. Mitchell observed, "There is no 'self,' in a psychologically meaningful sense, in isolation, outside a matrix of relations with others."[16]

Ken and Cara both learned to speak up. Variations of the phrase, "I say what I mean and I mean what I say," were heard repeatedly over the course of the interviews. For them and the other couples interviewed, the ability to know what they want, think, or feel is often a new experience; to voice these thoughts, is even more unusual. Whenever these or similar words were spoken, it was with a kind of forcefulness that emphasized that this ability to say what they mean and to mean what they say would never be taken away from the interviewees. By making such a statement, the individual seemed to be reinforcing a personal determination not to be swayed from his or her hard-won ground. Family therapists, psychologists, and philosophers suggest that knowing and speaking one's own mind are requirements of entering into an intimate relationship with another person. Doing so is the basis of forming and maintaining trustworthy relationships; not doing so is fundamentally dishonest. For Ken and Cara and the couples they represent, "speech with meaning" is one aspect of finding their own identities and bringing who they really are to their marriages.[17]

Ken provides evidence that the loss of voice is not the domain of women alone. Men as well as women silence themselves. Several of the men in this study described a similar process of finding their voices. Often, like Ken, they spoke of remaining silent to *"keep the peace."* In other words, they took a passive role to keep their spouses from having to respond to their needs, opinions, or concerns. Ken, like Cara, struggled to express an opinion that was uniquely his. The stereotype of the male alcoholic in particular is belligerent, loud-mouthed, and critical. Yet, in many cases, men still tell a story of fear, *"keeping the peace at any price,"* and *"stuffing it down"*—of *"silence at any cost."*

Like Cara, Ken first realized his right to an opinion and then slowly exercised this right. His description of saying "No" to his son's braces—a fairly benign topic—is symbolic to him of the effort involved in knowing his side and being able to express it. Hearing his own voice make a real contribution is as dramatic as the blind person who undergoes surgery and suddenly sees light when the bandages are removed. At first he sees a blur, but then he sees detail. Disbelief is mixed with, and eventually replaced by, elation. For Ken, it is as if he had been deaf and was hearing his own voice for the very first time. Expressing opinions—even on something so apparently trivial as a set of braces, is an important step in finding a balance between caring for himself and caring for others.[18]

In Cara's description of her response to the telephone call from Mara, she is essentially saying that she now makes choices on her own behalf and that these carefully considered choices make her life better. She factors in her own needs and her own limitations. Failing to do this, Cara will become a victim, and only she will be responsible for her victimization. Cara considers her daughter's feelings and is sensitive to them, but in the end she makes a choice by including her own needs and concerns as part of the equation. She offers her daughter an alternative date to visit. In this way she acknowledges her daughter's wishes while honoring her own at the same time.

Both Ken and Cara use their voices to effectively say to each other, "I am here. I have an opinion. And that opinion is important. No longer will I silence myself to suit what are, or what I think are, other people's needs." In particular, expressing feelings is an important aspect of building trust.

BUILDING TRUST: EXPRESSING FEELINGS

Still not totally satisfied that I understand what brought Ken and Cara to the point where they are today, I ask them to try and explain what happened *between* them. Cara says that the fact that Ken started to express his feelings made a huge difference—she says it was like "striking gold." *"It made me understand his moods better. If he would not say anything, and if he would be really quiet, I would think, 'Oh boy, what did I do, why is he this way?' Now, if he has a bad day he'll come home and talk about what's going on or what's bothering him, which is even better. If he is angry he can talk about anger—it's so much better when you can talk about feelings. Before, he would never let me know what his feelings were."*

Cara's eyes have become more alive in the last few minutes—her enthusiasm is apparent. I ask if this is easier for her in some way, and she responds with certainty in her voice, *"Yes. Oh yes. Much easier. Because when somebody stonewalls you, it intimidates you. You don't know where they are coming from. And when somebody will talk about their feelings, well, then you have a basis for give and take. You get something going. But if he stonewalls me . . . we go nowhere."*

But, it wasn't only Ken who didn't know his feelings. *"I didn't know what my feelings were,"* Cara explains. *"I always thought I was the communicator, that I could express my feelings but I didn't know what my feelings were. . . . I could talk but I couldn't communicate."* I ask Cara what the difference is. *"My feelings, how I felt. I didn't know what they were, I didn't know that it was OK to say, 'I'm feeling really angry because of something.' I just shut down. In my family there was no shouting and yelling: silence was the way anger was expressed."* She continues, *"Now we can share again. These things just keep you closer, really and truly. It's amazing how when you can communicate and share troubles and griefs, it does bring you closer.*[19] *The difference between now and before is Ken may, you know, present something to me that he wants to do. Rather than argue with him, what I will do is present how I feel about it. Not in an argumentative way. I won't rant and rave and carry on. I will say how I feel about it, so we will hear one another out, and if I feel very strongly about it, you know, that I don't like it or vice versa, somehow we come up with a compromise, yeah, a compromise."*

Ken looks downright proud as he hears Cara talk of how he has changed. I ask Ken if he sees this the same way. Ken nods an acknowledgment. *"When I was young I didn't have a drinking problem, but I was still an introvert and I still didn't talk. I didn't know how to talk to somebody, didn't know how to express my feelings. I didn't want to express my feelings. I would never let anyone get close to me. Never. I always had that wall."*

Today, Ken does more than simply express his own feelings. As Cara explains, *"He listens more to how I feel now, and he is very changed from being somebody who never really shared. It was like a 360-degree turn. Since he became sober, he really can talk about his feelings. We can communicate better in that we can talk better. Before that, he would clam up about things and he would refuse to talk about them."*

Ken and Cara's ability to express their feelings to each other allows them to see what influences and what motivates each other. In short, they have come to know who the other is. Although it was a change for both of them, it was a particularly difficult and profound change for Ken. The combination of a traumatic childhood and drug and alcohol abuse effectively cut off Ken's feelings. Some people claim that immersion into alcohol or drugs is, at least in part, an attempt to dull whatever feelings and memories one has.

Before we take another break, I ask Ken and Cara about the painful feelings from their past. Although I understand that Cara *"gave up"* her bad feelings, I still wonder if they have ever discussed some of those painful times, the old wounds. Cara shakes her head no, and Ken just looks passively at Cara. Being aware of their daughter Mara's life-threatening childhood illness, I ask how they dealt with that. Cara begins, *"Well, when our daughter was sick . . ."* Ken interrupts, a slight sound of agitation in his voice, *"She personalizes this stuff."* Cara responds, *"See, now that was the most hurtful thing. When Mara was a baby, when she was sick, you know, I spent many nights at Children's Hospital with them telling me she wasn't going to live."* Cara's voice quavers. *"And my husband was out drinking—you know, to me that was like—you know—I couldn't believe that! That was a very very hard time, and I think that after that, it was like every day I woke up questioning, is this where I want to be—is this what I want? Can I go on this way? He didn't even realize that. He didn't even see it that way. His whole thing was, 'Well, I'm out earning a living to pay her hospital bills."* Cara rolls her eyes with great drama. *"I care,"* Cara laughs a laugh of disgust. *"Well, I couldn't—you know, that was, that was the hardest part."*

The mood is tense. As in so many interviews, the pain of the past is just below the surface. In stories about children—their illnesses, births, deaths, any tragedy—there is great poignancy. Ken, for the first time during the interview, seems frustrated with Cara. His voice is defensive. *"That wasn't an excuse, that was the reality. I mean, I came down* [to the hospital]. *Cara would personalize that lack of support. She personalized that. . . . In retrospect it was a kind of per-*

sonalization saying, 'Oh gee, Ken can't handle these types of things.' It was bull. Ken can handle it. . . . Within my family, those amends occurred as they were done and subsequently, all my family really wants is a healthy, full Ken. That's what they want. They don't want somebody beating their chest and saying, 'I want to discuss with you the hurt of August 6, 1975.'"

But it was hurtful, I suggest, as I look at Cara. It is Ken who responds. *"It was hurtful. Don't get me wrong. The hurt was there. The action occurred and that was reality. But was the thought behind it? The intention was not there."* But, I suggest that it played itself out in Cara's life like that. Ken hesitates, as if pondering Cara's pain. He responds in a soft voice, *"But it played itself out as the intention and the action."*[20]

Both sit quietly for a moment. Then, as if to break the silence, Cara interjects, *"You know . . . I did recognize that he was alcoholic and he wasn't doing this on purpose, but in my own emotional weakness, I didn't accept that."* At this, Ken acknowledges the pain he caused Cara. *"She got hurt. If I thought as Cara did, I would have taken my head off."*

I ask Ken about making amends, and the response is telling. Cara speaks for him. *"Ken has never been a talker about things like that. This has all been very private with Ken. I can't say that Ken has sat down to make amends."* She hesitates and, in a voice so soft the tape recorder barely picks it up, she says, *"I'm not saying that I wouldn't like that. That probably would be very nice—but I know that's not Ken."*

Ken looks surprised and states with total innocence, *"I didn't know that."* Cara looks knowingly, and seems to accept his comment as the making of amends. *"I take the amends,"* she whispers.

NOTES

1. T. Hargrave, *Families and Forgiveness: Healing Wounds in the Intergenerational Family* (New York: Brunner/Mazel, 1994).

2. Hargrave suggests that there are two salient aspects of exoneration: insight into how relational damage occurred and understanding why the damage occurred. "When we exonerate a family member . . . we are not proclaiming the person trustworthy for the future. . . . Exoneration makes the wrongdoer less powerful because the victim is able to prevent the destructive situations from occurring again" (T. Hargrave, *Families and Forgiveness,* 46). Exoneration functions to leave the victim with a reduction of blame and the possibility to begin to see the victimizer with new eyes.

3. I. Boszormenyi-Nagy and B. R. Krasner, *Between Give and Take: A Clinical Guide to Contextual Therapy* (New York: Brunner/Mazel, 1986).

4. B. R. Krasner and A. J. Joyce, *Truth, Trust, and Relationship: Healing Interventions in Contextual Therapy* (New York: Brunner/Mazel, 1995).

5. Several nonalcoholic wives did complain that A.A. and Al-Anon were helpful initially but less helpful for long-term relational growth. This is not to suggest that A.A. and Al-Anon are not helpful in the long run for many couples.

6. The idea that alcoholism is a disease is often debated. A brief discussion can be found in the appendixes.

7. D. C. Jack, *Silencing the Self: Women and Depression* (New York: Harper-Collins, 1991).

8. D. C. Jack, *Silencing the Self.*

9. This is true of symmetrical relationships such as marriages where it is expected that partners have approximately equal power. There is an expectation of fair give-and-take. However the same standard does not hold in asymmetrical relationships where there is unequal power. When a child is expected to give in the manner of an adult, as if they had power equal to their parents, the child is at risk for developing a skewed sense of what they owe and what an adult owes them.

10. D. C. Jack, in *Silencing the Self,* found that the women in her study tended to maintain an "either/or" image of themselves in relationship: Either they could subordinate themselves in the relationship (silence), or they could act with authenticity (express who they are) and thereby risk isolation. A woman may remain silenced and in a state of depression "rather than grapple with an unknown self that will, perhaps, destroy life as she understands it. She may feel depression is a necessary price to pay for the survival of the relationship she values." (Jack, 1991, 146–147).

11. The idea that alcoholics are not irreparable seems to be important. Their guilt and remorse or their awareness that they had damaged the relationship, was noted by most, male and female alike. Some form of self-exoneration or exoneration by their spouse helped to lift the burden of guilt and remorse. Most spouses in the happier marriages were able to see the goodness in their alcoholic mate, or at least to believe that they were more than their disease. Cara seems able to see both the disease side of Ken and the side that has markedly changed and is kinder, more open, and makes efforts to contribute to the relationship.

12. Self-delineation differs from individuation and differentiation in that self-delineation is not simply an individual stance, it is a relational one. For example, Ken Gunderson's finding his "voice" is a form of self-delineation because it is relational and not simply individual—it enables Cara to know who he is and what he thinks. The complement of self-delineation is due consideration, the consideration of another person. Self-delineation and due consideration must exist in tension in order for there to be a true relationship. Psychologist Jane Buhl (*Intergenerational Inter-Gender Voice,* 1992) proposed a typology of self-delineation and due consideration based on her research on relationships between mothers and their adult sons. She suggests that self-delineation includes self-disclosure, acts of self care, direct address of other, direct address of conflicts, and making claims on other. Due consideration includes listening/responding to the other, acts of care directed at the other, acknowledging/crediting the other, imagining the other's side, and eliciting the other's side. For a thorough explanation of self-delineation and due consideration, see I. Boszormenyi-Nagy and B. R. Krasner, *Between Give and Take*, 1986.

13. The tendency to seek out a job or profession is corroborated by Wiseman's 1975 study of wives of alcoholics who remained in their marriages.

14. C. Gilligan, "Do the Social Sciences Have an Adequate Theory of Moral Development?" in *Social Science as Moral Inquiry,* ed. N. Haan, R. N. Bellah, P. Rabinow, and W. M. Sullivan (New York: Columbia University Press, 1983).

15. C. Gilligan, "Do the Social Sciences Have an Adequate Theory of Moral Development?" 47.

16. C. Gilligan, "Do the Social Sciences Have an Adequate Theory of Moral Development?" 47.

17. S. A. Mitchell, *Relational Concepts in Psychoanalysis: An Integration* (Cambridge, Mass.: Harvard University Press, 1988).

The term *speech with meaning* was used by philosopher Martin Buber, who eloquently described the requirement of true relationship. See his *I and Thou*, *The Knowledge of Man*, and *Between Man and Man*.

18. This balance has been referred to as the ethic of relationship (M. Cotroneo and B. J. Hibbs, "Ethical Discourse in Families," *American Family Therapy Association Newsletter* 46 (1991):11–14. It has been suggested that the ability to care for both the self and the other is indicative of a morally mature person. Vivian Rogers (1983), in writing about adult development, suggests that the single most important struggle of adulthood is the tension between functioning autonomously *and* relationally. In other words, investing in oneself and investing in others.

19. L. C. Robinson and P. W. Blanton, "Marital Strengths in Enduring Marriages," *Family Relations* 42 (1993): 38–45, reported that closeness in relationships was enhanced by the shared experience of joy and pain. "Times of adversity afforded some couples an opportunity to support one another and to pull together" (p. 40).

20. During this brief interchange, Ken shifts positions from suggesting that the problem was Cara's "interpretation" of events—her "personalizing"—to acknowledging the very real pain of that abandonment. He is able at this moment to see from Cara's perspective. This is a moment of acknowledgment of Cara's experience.

Chapter 3

Not Perfect, But Very Good

> *Of the multitude of hopes and yearnings we experience, these two seem to subsume the others. One of these might be called the yearning to be included, to be part of, close to, joined with, to be held, admitted, accompanied. The other might be called the yearning to be independent or autonomous, to experience one's distinctness, the self-chosenness of one's directions, one's individual integrity."*
>
> —Robert Kegan, *The Evolving Self*

Ken is again grinning as we begin to bring the interview to an end. I ask each of them to tell me about their relationship these days. Ken immediately responds: *"Today, it's a oneness—just part of you. Twenty-five, twenty-six, twenty-seven years ago it was a one-sided street. It was all self-centeredness. It was one of those fakery type of things. You did things not because you wanted to but because, well, that's what you have to do. 'Oh yeah, I have to get Cara a present for Christmas.' Today, those things just don't exist that way. It's just something you do together. Back then, it was just like bouncing off a wall. What you did, it made no sense. It was like throwing a lot of balls against a wall and they just bounced off. You never knew what was going to happen. Today it's just something that runs together, for the most part. It's not perfect, but very good. Everything is great. Part of why we get along is that she does respect some of my opinions, and I think she also goes along with me on some things that she is not totally comfortable with. I do the same thing. I think respect for the other guy, mutual respect* [is what makes it work]." Ken leans back in his chair and looks satisfied with himself, and then clears his throat to speak again. *"The war is over, and we came out of hell."*

RECOGNIZING DIFFERENCES

Cara nods her head in agreement. Her voice is less tense, and it is softer. *"I think Ken and I have a good marriage primarily because we do love each other. We want our marriage to work and we're committed to family. We enjoy doing the same things. We enjoy reading, we enjoy bowling. Maybe we accommodate each other. We are not cut out of the same mold. There are always going to be differences. Now every once in a while, important differences come up and we are to the point where we can sit down and we can talk about that. Sometimes we reach an agreement—sometimes we don't. Sometimes I have to accommodate him, and sometimes he has to accommodate me. But basically I think we have a good marriage. . . . I think one of those strengths is we recognize those differences, and we respect those differences."*

"You see," Cara continues, *"I went into the marriage with certain preconceived ideas of what marriage should be. Well, I thought that marriage was sharing. Marriage was more or less two people compromising on things. I have never to this day been able to figure out whether it is Ken's Scandinavian background, but there are certain things that are just his way, and you don't deviate from them. Maybe it's that male alcoholic piece."*

RESIDUAL RESOURCE: DETERMINATION

Again, Cara emphasizes the fact that she considers the marriage to be a good one. I notice she does not say "great." *"I think we have a good marriage, better than any other time. I think the only reason, or one of the reasons, we have a good marriage is that I have to say to myself when certain things come up, 'How important is it?' So, therefore, I feel I am willing to try to bend more to try to keep the relationship healthy."*

I ask Cara if she thinks this is an incongruity—to "bend more" while expressing feelings more and being more determined to protect her own needs. She considers my question before answering. *"I try to be really considerate of the fact of his disease; even in sobriety I feel that there is a certain thread that runs through the personality of an alcoholic that is different from other people."* I am a bit uncomfortable with Cara's direction, but Ken seems at ease and she indicates that they have discussed this many times. I ask Cara what that thread is. *"Oh, I think alcoholics are very self-centered people. I've told Ken that."* Cara looks directly at Ken and he nods in acknowledgment. *"They are very self-centered, and they are very selfish to the point where it is almost a juvenile or infantile thing. They want to have things their way. They are open to compromise but only up to a certain point. I often say to Ken that when God made alcoholics he put one part in backwards—it misses. It's like something doesn't mesh, and you get this aberrant behavior."*

Ken smiles in acknowledgment. My initial discomfort dissipates as I realize Ken seems to agree with Cara. Identifying an "alcoholic personality" is a way for Cara to understand, to live without too high an expectation. Although I am hesitant to push too hard and to have Cara feel as if I am second-guessing her, I ask her if there is a conflict for her between having a good marriage and Ken's "alcoholic personality." Cara speaks once again in a slow rhythmic voice. *"Every once in a while I dig in my heels and I simply say this is the way it is. I state what I feel and I've learned with Ken, I state what I feel and I say what I mean. Then, I turn around and walk out of the room. I don't wait for an argument because in the end, I will not win that argument. I know that. Sometimes I get a response, and sometimes I don't get a response. That is OK as long as I can say how I feel to the other person. If they choose not to respond, then I can accept that, but at least I have been able to say what I need to say. That has been very freeing. I don't have to stick around and listen to a lot of—I don't want to say abuse because that's a strong word—but I don't want to get into a rebuttal about it. I know that from my past experience, if I walk out and leave the room it is much more productive."*

I ask Cara what happens when she walks out. *"He will think about it, and I sometimes find that if he does blow up, he may get all pushed out of shape, as we say, but then he will go to a meeting and he will come home and will have been fed something that will get his thinking straightened out. He will come home and he will be a different person."* Clearly, the war is over, but occasional skirmishes continue. What Cara realizes is that a certain amount of conflict still exists. She is realistic and understands that relationships, at least hers and Ken's, is not perfect.

"What about when the two of you stay in a disagreement—do you feel that generally you won't win that?" I ask. Cara responds immediately, *"No, because Ken's attitude is, 'well, I don't want to talk about that. We're not going to talk about that.' So I get cut off. I had asked him when we were married the second time to go into counseling. He has refused to go to any kind of counseling. He said A.A. and Al-Anon are enough for us. Frankly, I don't think they are. As I said, I think we have a good marriage. When I look around at other marriages, I'd say we have a good marriage."*

The term *alcoholic personality* is used quite often in conversation about alcoholism. The idea of an alcoholic personality is not new. Usually this label refers to impulsivity, immaturity, and dependency. There is no scientific evidence that all or most alcoholics share one type of personality. However, this does not mean there is not a constellation of attributes that are common among alcoholics.[1] Cara's comment that Ken has an "alcoholic personality," and therefore simply cannot do better than he does, seems to help her gauge exactly what she can expect and what she cannot expect. It provides her with a way to understand Ken. One of the prominent themes presented in G. O. Higgins's book on resilient adults is the ability of these adults, often brutally abused as children, to accept rather than deny their victimization, but also to refuse to be defined by it. In part, this is the outcome of understanding their victimizer. One person interviewed stated that although she could not forgive her abusive parent, she planned to truly understand him so that she did not have to continue blaming him.[2] Likewise, Cara *understands* Ken. She knows what she can expect from him and what she cannot. Thus, his "alcoholic personality" serves as a reminder to Cara that she must find ways to satisfy herself and not hold Ken wholly responsible for keeping her happy.[3] It also provides an explanation for why certain aspects of her relationship with Ken are at times disappointing. But for all of the imperfections, the "mistakes," the marriage is still good.

BEING A REALIST

"But Ken's more receptive to my feelings now." Cara pauses, as if she is uncertain whether she should go on, and then continues in a steady voice. *"Again, I don't know if this is alcoholism or typically male, but I find he is more apt to want to talk about his feelings than my feelings . . . but he is not able to* [always be responsive to me]. *I understand. He has certain limitations, so, therefore, I cannot expect any more from him. I think he is trying his utmost. If I didn't believe he was trying, I don't think I would be in the marriage. He's doing the best he can, but sometimes his best doesn't quite fulfill my needs. But that's the way it is, and I'm a realist."*[4]

Judith Wallerstein and Sandra Blakeslee concluded that the couples they interviewed about their good marriages were also realists. "No one denied that there were serious differences—conflict, anger, even some infidelity—along the way. No one envisioned marriage as a rose garden, but all viewed its satisfaction as far outweighing the frustrations over the long haul."[5] One of the spouses said to me with equanimity, *"It isn't that grand bouquet you're looking for. I mean, you're not going to marry a Prince Charming. But life doesn't promise palaces."* Cara put it this way: *"I love this man—so, therefore, that's what you live with. If I had wallowed in the past I would have raked up a lot of old resentments about things that had happened in the past and it could have wrecked the marriage for me, for us. As far as the things that happened in the past with Ken, I put those to sleep, and I don't dig the old skeletons out of the closet. That's counterproductive to me. I want to get on with my life. I don't want to wallow in that muck. I wish it had been different. I wish my life had been different. It wasn't. That was the way it was so, therefore, I guess I have to accept that and go on."*

Although both are proud and relieved that they have survived the "war" and that they can now be like normal people, Cara clearly still wants at least a bit more. What does she do with her disappointment? In part, she becomes, in her own words, a "realist." According to *Webster's New World Dictionary,* a realist is a person who faces facts or sees people and things as they really are or really appear to be.[6] Cara takes delight in the pieces of the marriage that have so greatly improved and developed, but her delight is tempered by Ken's shortcomings. By viewing herself as a realist, she is able to accept his limitations rather than attack him for them. I ask Cara what she does when her needs are not quite fulfilled. She hesitates once again and appears to think about her answer. *"Well, I guess I read my Al-Anon literature. I guess I get depressed sometimes. I go to meetings—that's where my support is."*

Cara stops speaking, and I turn to Ken. I do not want this to become a therapy session, but I also don't want to ignore Cara's comments. I ask Ken what he thinks of what Cara is saying. Ken says, *"I'm not big on probing up wounds or whatever—because I don't think it's very healthy. She, as I say, she's always been supportive."*

Cara nods her head. *"It's really funny. He is trying to do that with me. I'm going through some hormone problems, and he is trying to be supportive with me. He's trying to be that way about it, because he's on the other side."*

She clears her throat and continues. *"We have a lot of luck on our side."* And then, as if she is worried that I might not have seen this, *"He was hard-core, Karen. To sit down in a restaurant, to be like normal people—little things in life, I look at all that, all the time I am so grateful. It's what "normal" people take for granted. I think keeping things you've been through close to you makes the world look different."*

After seeing Ken's workroom, I head home through a driving rain and think about what I heard and what I have seen. I am grateful for the "window" they have opened—perhaps only partially, but it is indeed, an opening. As I drive on, I think about the ways in which Ken and Cara's relationship resembles many of the other couples I have spoken with. Like so many others, their relationship has liabilities. But it also has abundant strengths and resources. They are still, after thirty-four years of marriage and twenty-seven years of sobriety, in love. Their lengthy and ongoing process of rebalancing their relationship is remarkable. They are happy, grateful, and, as Cara says, lucky.

Ken and Cara's relationship survived in part because of Cara's ever-present love and affection for Ken. In fact, of all the people I interviewed, Cara's ongoing, unwavering love stood out. Even in the worst of times, this helped to sustain them. But beyond love, what helped them to build a more trusting relationship? Certainly, Ken's decision to return to Cara and Mara after their divorce was an important factor. Cara's decision to offer Ken unconditional love following his return to the marriage helped to facilitate the changes necessary for building a strong, albeit imperfect, relationship in their second marriage. Unconditional love enabled Cara to access her compassion for Ken. It provided both of them with the possibility of growth. They each described how expressing their feelings enabled them to get to know one another in a new way. As Cara said, being able to express her feelings was like striking gold for her. They were supported further by their mutual involvement in A.A. and Al-Anon, which provided them with a common language. After so much had happened between them, the language of recovery served as a starting point for them to be able to talk to each other, and then became a significant ingredient of building trust between them. Perhaps the most outstanding change was the fact that both learned to assert their own opinions, to have a voice. Rather than being what they thought the other wanted them to be, they each learned to have a side. No longer will they remain silent.

Yet, speaking for one's own interests means that, inevitably, there will be conflicts. They have different ways of handling such situations, and the end result is not always what they want. Cara is sometimes depressed, and she turns to her Al-

Anon literature when she feels she has no place else to go. But, as she says, she is a realist. She has learned to accept what is good and to accept the fact that part of being a couple means that they will inevitably have differences. For both Ken and Cara, the war is over, and they savor the good times—even though they are sometimes punctuated by very real dissatisfaction. Ken and Cara have gone from being "hard core" to being "like normal people."

NOTES

1. A. M. Ludwig, *Understanding the Alcoholic's Mind: The Nature of Craving and How to Control It* (New York: Oxford University Press, 1988).
2. G. O. Higgins, *Resilient Adults: Overcoming a Cruel Past* (San Francisco, Calif.: Jossey-Bass, 1994).
3. The risk here is that Cara may limit Ken in some unintentional way by suggesting that he has permanent limits that he cannot overcome. Although some might ascribe to this kind of thinking, it is worth considering the possibility that in the long run this might limit their relationship. However, Ken seems to accept what Cara says.
4. Cara's realism has a sharp edge to it. Being a realist seems to have benefits but can also serve as a means to "contain" or define another person unfairly. In this case, one wonders if her realism acts as a kind of double-edged sword with the capacity to help but also to harm.
5. J. S. Wallerstein and S. Blakeslee, *The Good Marriage: How and Why Love Lasts* (New York: Houghton Mifflin, 1995) 329.
6. *Webster's New World Dictionary,* s.v. "realist."

Part II

The Royers: Endurance

Independence is a footbridge, not a dwelling place.
—Martin Buber, *Between Man and Man*

Chapter 4

Never Expecting Anything

Dave and Peg Royer
Married: twenty years; three children
Peg: forty-six years old, paralegal
Dave: fifty years old, house painter, owner of "Royer Paints"; sober fifteen years
Children: Jeanne, twenty (college student); Tamara, eighteen (high school graduate, traveling in Europe); Mark, seventeen (high school senior)

PEG

Peg and Dave Royer have found independent lives, but like ships passing in the night, they are hard pressed to find one another. Although Peg would like to "meet" Dave, Dave has found contentment in other places. Prisoners of their own anger, fears, and blame, they are blind to a better way of relating to one another. They serve as a stark, if unfortunate, reminder of marriages that endure with little or no growth or healing between spouses. Their residual resources are nearly, but not altogether, extinguished. Their moments of choice include misjudgments, unfortunate decisions that neither seems willing or perhaps capable of reappraising. Thus, it is no surprise that instead of building trust between them, Peg and Dave provide a glimpse of how trust can be repeatedly diminished, leaving spouses drowning in blame and despair. The resources that still exist between them are tenuous. Left inactivated, they do neither Peg nor Dave much good. The marriage is in a state of stagnation in which the options for a different way of relating become more and more limited. How did they get to this point? What potential, if any, is there for resurrecting their relationship? And what would be required of them to make resurrection a possibility?

THE INTERVIEW

I had gotten Peg and Dave's names through a friend with ties to A.A. As always, I asked that they be interviewed together, although it could be alone. My initial contact was with Dave, who agreed that they would be interviewed. When I called to confirm the interview time, Dave explained that Peg was willing to be interviewed initially alone and, after that, along with Dave. I spoke with Peg the next day, and she voiced her hesitation about being interviewed at all. Dave's alcoholism had not affected their children, and, thus, she feared she had little to offer. She explained that one child was in college, one in Europe, and one a sports star. When I assured her that my primary interest was not the children, but the longevity of their marriage, she agreed to the interview. We met the next day.

The Royer's house is in a transition area, on the border between middle- and working-class neighborhoods. Like many streets in Philadelphia, theirs is tree lined, with sycamores in front of every other home, postage-stamp sized front and backyards, and every house with an identical front porch. It is November, but the Royer's porch is crammed with the remnants of summer: lawn furniture, a bicycle, a half-wound hose, watering can, and some rubber flip-flops.

Peg answers the door dressed in a navy skirt and sweater, with a strand of pearls around her neck. She is middle-aged, of average height, and a bit stocky. My first impression of her is that she is "tired." Her hair is blond and streaked with gray. Barely reaching her shoulders, her hair is kept off her face by a navy headband that pulls all but her bangs back and gives her face a harsher appearance than is flattering. She has high cheekbones, and her complexion is unusually smooth and creamy, although the skin that frames her eyes is wrinkled. Peg is nervous, but welcoming. She speaks initially in short sentences, jumps from one topic to another, and giggles nervously. Throughout our time together, her giggles will mix with tears as she recounts her life with Dave.

The living room is small and extends in an "L" shape to include the dining room. The two windows, one facing an alley that runs behind all the houses on their side of the street, are darkened by thick drapes, giving the room a heavy, closed feeling. Directly beside the dining room is the kitchen. It is also small, but the bright yellow walls provide some sense of space and light. The living room and dining room walls are covered with brocade wallpaper and family portraits of all sizes and shapes. I spot one of Peg as a teenager: She appears to be carefree, with wide-eyed expectation. It is a look that says, "My life is in front of me, and I greet it with open arms." The wedding picture on the mantle highlights the same features: She is attractive, vibrant, and full of the hope of a new bride. On the mantle next to the wedding photograph are several baseball, basketball, and soccer trophies. Directly under the stairway to the second floor is a large aquarium filled with tropical fish. A fire burns in the fireplace.

Dave comes in the back door shortly after I arrive. He is tall and heavyset, with dark graying hair around his ears and a bald spot on top of his head. Unlike Peg,

Dave moves with a bounce, which makes him seem younger than his fifty years. He is in his work clothes, which are spattered with paint. Knowing I have come to meet with Peg, Dave introduces himself and then immediately excuses himself to get cleaned up for an A.A. meeting. Peg says in a matter-of-fact voice that Dave is a professional indoor house painter.

With this information dispensed, Peg offers me a cup of hot apple cider, which I readily accept. As she heats and then pours the cider, she describes her childhood, her speech remaining tinged with nervousness. Raised in this neighborhood, they live only a dozen blocks east of her childhood home. Dave was raised within a dozen blocks the other direction. Peg has six living brothers and sisters, and all but two live within walking distance. The two who are not within walking distance have relocated to "Jersey." One sister was a drug addict who was killed in a tragic accident that Peg later reveals was a murder.

Both Peg's parents were alcoholics. She makes the point that she was devoted to both of them and that they did not fit the common stereotype of alcoholics. Her father worked at a local business and repaired cars on the side. Her mother did sewing and ironing for people in the neighborhood, to make "milk money." Neither, she points out, was abusive. They were devoted to each other, childlike, and in some ways, irresponsible. Alcohol, according to Peg, was simply part of the fabric of her family life. She recalls that her parents' drinking made their house "the place to be"—it was unpredictable and chaotic. The neighborhood children loved the fact that her parents were like children themselves—playing ball in the living room and having a barbecue in the backyard at the drop of a hat, any time of year—rain, shine, or in the middle of a snowstorm.

As the eldest child in her family, Peg feels that she got more attention from her mother than the younger children did. Her mother encouraged her to take risks, to be different, to question her life. Peg credits this added attention as helping to build a career and a life for herself. She believes that the fact that she was out of the house at an early age and ahead of her siblings was a circumstance that protected her from the full effect of alcoholism, which her siblings had to endure. As the eldest, she was expected to take care of the others, to maintain a modicum of order in the house. Being expected to play this adult role often gave her a sense of accomplishment, of being in control. Yet maintaining order was also a source of frustration, because it was usually impossible to do. Peg holds no conscious grudges for being given such adult responsibility.

All the brothers and sisters, with the exception of one brother, who is an alcoholic, see each other at Sunday dinners and for virtually every holiday. All of the cousins (Peg and Dave's children included) get together every Thursday night for a spaghetti dinner. Peg describes this with obvious pride in her voice, and, for the first time, her nervousness seems to be gone.

While describing their three children, she points to photographs of them that also crowd the mantle. She pulls several of the most recent photos, including high school graduation pictures, off of the mantle for me to inspect. The eldest, Jeanne, is a sophomore at a local college; she hopes to become a physical therapist. Born with one leg shorter than the other, Jeanne has spent a great deal of time in the local children's hospital. Peg sees her as stronger because of her struggle with her disability, and she feels that Jeanne's interest in physical therapy is a direct result of it. Tamara, their "rebellious and bright" daughter, is traveling in Europe with a friend before attending college on a scholarship. The expression on Peg's face is enough to let me know that she is both proud that Tamara has chosen to follow an unconventional path and that she is not altogether comfortable with the traveling. Mark, their son and youngest child, is a sports fanatic with true skill and ability. According to Peg, he is also a typical teenager: he loves basketball, skateboarding, soccer, and baseball, and excels at all of them. He has little interest in school and hopes to join Dave in the family painting business after high school graduation. Peg holds out hope that he will receive a sports scholarship to college. She would like to see him study business before going into the painting business, if he truly wants that to be his life's work. She worries that he is "too much like Dave." When I ask what that means, she says only that Dave doesn't always know what's best for himself, but he thinks he does.

As she returns the photographs to their rightful places on the mantle, Dave pops his head in the living room and waves good night. Peg simply reports with no particular emotion that this is typical of Dave: home from work, change clothes, and out the door for a meeting or time with friends.

Peg explains that money has always been tight for them. In part, she says Dave is too nice a guy. He gets to know his customers and can't find it in himself to charge the going rate for his work. He listens to their stories about the costs of weddings, the need for college tuition, the need to help out a relative's family, and he charges them less than he originally planned. She hesitates as if deciding whether it is safe to say what is on her mind, and then she adds that they have all paid the price, literally, for Dave's favors to others.

Peg, clearly annoyed at Dave's lack of business sense, took the initiative to return to school. She attended a program to become a paralegal, graduated almost fifteen years ago, and has a good job with a large law firm in center city Philadelphia—the kind, she says, with *real* wood floors and *real* oriental rugs. Although she has been working for years, and loves it, she is frustrated that the family still seems to struggle financially. However, she confides in a slightly hushed tone, that she recently inherited a small "nest egg" from a favorite uncle who never married. This is changing her life in small ways: She has money for better haircuts, treats herself to lunch out once a week, and is planning a vacation to the Pocono Mountains with a group of her high-school girl friends. She then adds, a bit wistfully, that Tamara is probably the smartest of the five of them—she is having some fun and not worrying about her future.

Peg seems more comfortable with me after providing an introduction to her family, so I turn on the tape recorder. With this, she begins to speak noticeably slower and her eyes well up with tears. *"Well, maybe I can give a little more back-*

ground here. I was married previously. Like I said, both of my parents were alcoholics. My previous marriage was to a person with just a lot of problems."

Married right out of high school to a *"neighborhood guy,"* Peg says that it was never a real marriage. Ed was never home, spent a lot of time with other women, gambled excessively, and left Peg after a three-month "non-marriage." Ed was not an alcoholic, but his problems were nonetheless, pervasive. Although the divorce was painful, Peg feels that it was really the best outcome possible, because it moved her to attend several Al-Anon meetings to try to begin to understand the impact of addictions like gambling and alcohol. Being left alone at the age of eighteen motivated her to create her own life.

Peg got a job, moved into a room in a rooming house and slowly increased her income until she could afford an apartment. Well liked at work, she was promoted, and eventually a supervisor encouraged her to take a class at the local community college. Peg discovered a new life and new sense of freedom and direction. At the end of the semester, she decided she would get her associate's degree, thereby becoming the first member of her family to finish college. An average student, her determination carried her over the rough spots, and within four years, at the age of twenty-five, she completed her associate's degree. Her success was the talk of the neighborhood. Today, she says that she still does not understand what enabled her to take a step like going to college. She feels that her degree restored her self-confidence, which had been shaken by her marriage to Ed. She also credits her own college experience with giving her the conviction to encourage her children to get a college education.

At about the time she graduated, Peg was introduced to Dave at a neighborhood Fourth of July picnic. She smiles as she recalls the clothes they were wearing (blue jeans and a halter top for her, jean shorts and a black T-shirt for Dave) and what they ate at the picnic (lots of hot dogs, grilled corn-on-the-cob, soft ice cream, and beer).

Peg averts her eyes as she continues. She was feeling old and says with no apology that she was looking for a husband. *"When I met Dave, I knew he was a an alcoholic. Well, first I thought he was crazy, then I thought he was an alcoholic. I found out the reason I thought he was crazy was because he was drunk a lot of the time. Anyway, I knew he was an alcoholic."* Still, Peg found him fun to be around, and this made her feel younger.

Dave liked people, and he made Peg laugh. Although she loved the life she had created for herself, she also longed for a family and a traditional life. Dave seemed to offer all of that. Although she recognized the risk of marrying Dave, she was drawn to him. Her response was to take a strong stand. *"I said to him, 'I absolutely cannot get involved in a relationship with you because I can't do this again* [get involved with an addict again]*.'"* He said, *'No problem, I'll quit.' He was basically "dry" when we married."*

Initially, they both worked and, thus, lived more comfortably than most of their friends and family who had factory jobs and small businesses. They rented a house around the corner, and Peg took on the combined tasks of wife and working woman. She recalls some feeling of disappointment in Dave's commitment, or rather lack of commitment, to the house. It seemed that most of the household tasks fell to Peg. She took over the finances, the household decisions, and the day-to-day running of their lives. Dave was consumed with his work and social life, two areas Peg was not involved in.

Although there was little time available for the house or simply being together, Dave always made room for a get-together with friends. He had friends from high school, from the service, and from his daily activities. She smiles at the memory of Dave bringing home total strangers for dinner. A few had even spent the night, even though neither Peg nor Dave knew anything about their backgrounds. At first Peg welcomed his friends. However, she soon saw that his spending time with friends not only meant no time left for her, but it inevitably led to the consumption of large quantities of alcohol. In fact, his abstinence did not even last through their second month of marriage.

Peg's response was to encourage Dave at least to slow down his drinking. He would try for a while, but soon a long-lost service buddy would appear on their doorstep, and, before she knew it, Dave and his buddy would be out visiting every tavern within a three-mile radius. If her anxieties about Dave were moving into high gear, her own life felt much more secure. Peg liked the feeling of earning her own money, of having a house, of looking like a young married woman. Yet when Jeanne was born, Peg decided to stay home and be a full-time mother. Jeanne required extra time and attention because of her disability, including trips to the orthopedist and the physical therapist. Jeanne's care required a great deal of organizing and keeping details straight—not one of Dave's strengths.

It had been a wrenching decision for Peg to stop working, but she wanted to give Jeanne all the attention she needed. Once more, Peg was putting her trust in a man who, like her first husband, seemed more controlled by his addiction than drawn to their relationship. Nonetheless, she did what she felt was right for Jeanne, as well as what was expected of her as a wife and mother.

Jeanne's birth seemed to be a catalyst for Dave to control his drinking more strictly. He spent the next three to four years limiting his consumption, always with the goal of quitting. He allowed himself to drink only at bars and occasionally at family get-togethers. During that period of time, Tamara and Mark were born. Peg and Dave went about their busy lives, still spending little time together. Yet, Peg remembers it as a relatively satisfying time. But soon after Mark's birth, Dave's behavior and Peg's life both took turns for the worse. Dave's drinking escalated. Peg's job of nagging Dave became a full-time occupation. She encouraged Dave to quit. He promised, repeatedly, only to "do better."

If it weren't for the problems related to the alcohol, they lived a relatively conventional and quiet life. Dave's drinking was more like Peg's parents': It made him fun and outgoing, unpredictable and childlike. *"The worst that he would do was he would come home and play soccer in the living room and make a big party attitude out of things. That was the worst Dave would do at that time. But I still felt that there was a problem and that he was drinking too much. I felt like it was my problem so I went and got some more help."*

Peg's occasional visits to Al-Anon helped for a while. Eventually, the pressures built and Dave became more difficult. When he attempted to do what Peg requested, he drank, and the more he drank, the more his temper started to show. Peg's hopefulness began to dwindle. Time was rushing on, and Dave could not stay sober.

The tension built to a peak during the year after Mark's birth. No longer easy-going, Dave was angry and critical. Peg's anxieties were understandably high, and she felt that once again she had married the wrong person. She put more pressure on Dave to stop drinking for once and for all. Finally, he refused to even try.

Peg's response was to get more involved in Al-Anon, even though she resented it. She made some friends there and had a sponsor she liked well enough. Eventually, with the encouragement of Al-Anon members, she just stopped pestering Dave. *"There weren't major confrontations because I already knew from my first husband that arguing with an addict was not a good idea."*

Peg notes that she was extremely nervous about their financial situation. Raised with little material wealth and having become accustomed to controlling her own money, she found the situation nearly unbearable. Dave was bringing home less and less with each passing week. He became unpredictable and could not be counted on for such simple responsibilities as buying milk at the local supermarket. His repeatedly broken promises and open hostility had made Peg lose faith that Dave could ever stop drinking. The enjoyment she had once taken in his spontaneity now turned to resentment. She also started to back away from Al-Anon. She was discouraged by the hands-off attitude and the apparent calmness of others, when she knew she was seething inside.

In addition to her resentment, Peg's loss of faith also led to self-recrimination. She blamed herself for marrying another addict and for ending up in a predicament that she knew she should have, and could have, avoided. Peg felt that there was no one to blame but herself. Her self-esteem plummeted and she became depressed. Her depression was made worse by their constantly precarious financial position. Eventually, Peg decided to return to work. Jeanne was in elementary school, Tamara was three years old, and Mark, almost two. By that time, Peg and Dave had been married nearly six years.

Although she remembers those years as primarily nonconfrontational from her side, she recalls one incident that was especially upsetting. She had returned to work only two weeks earlier. On this particular morning, their baby-sitter, a grandmother from the neighborhood, had called to say that she was ill. Dave's work was slow, so he agreed to stay home with the children. Peg was not comfortable with this arrangement, but none of her sisters could take over on that particular day. Feeling that she could not call in sick after only two weeks on the job, she left for work, leaving Dave as the baby-sitter. Late that afternoon, after leaving work early because Dave did not respond to her phone calls, she returned home. *"I came home, and he was drunk: passed out on the living room floor. You know, Mark was there—he was only two years old, and he was still in his pajamas I had left him in that morning! Thank God that was the beginning of the end. Dave didn't want that to happen any more than I did."*

For Peg, as for other spouses of alcoholics, the alcoholic spouses' repeated failures to act responsibly and to do what has been promised erodes the relationship. More than alcohol consumption per se, the fact that the alcoholic is not dependable or trustworthy causes the spouse to despair. The good feelings of hope and expectation, of building a relationship, are usurped by the day-to-day reality of broken promises. Peg states, *"As far as damage to the relationship, I would say that the breach of promise, to not stop drinking, that was hard."*

MOMENT OF CHOICE: SEEKING HELP

Like many of the spouses interviewed, Peg saw alcoholism as a disease. Her exposure to it during her early life, as well as her intermittent involvement with Al-Anon made it easy for her to see it this way. However, as she pointed out, *"By the same token, having the intellectual understanding, it was still tough emotionally to deal with."*

Peg's college success was not enough to hold at bay her sense of impending doom and self-loathing. What she recalls most about that period is being overwhelmed with the children, fearful, and filled with anger at Dave for not holding to the promise he made before their marriage. He had had plenty of time to prove that he could keep his promise. Apparently, he could not. Yet, as she recalled the sense of abandonment she'd felt when Ed, her first husband, had left her, she also felt a sense of outrage. The outrage competed with the self-recrimination and self-loathing in Peg's mind. *"Our relationship wasn't very good by then. I never felt he was there for me anyway, so I'm very independent. I never depend on him for anything—I never expect anything. I decided I better get myself to a place where I don't have to be dependent on anybody, because it sure didn't look like being dependent on people would work out."* Peg's words are indicative of the diminishing trust she has in Dave. To never expect, to never feel one can depend on others, is the result of repeated failures of trustworthy relating. Peg's outrage and desperation once more moved her to take action.

After finding Mark still in his pajamas and Dave passed out drunk, Peg took the advice of a friend and confronted Dave with the seriousness of his drinking. To her surprise, Dave agreed to enter a rehabilitation hospital. With Dave in rehab, Peg faced the fact that she was still seething from her first marriage, which had left her angry and insecure. Now, with this man she once truly loved, she felt abandoned all over again.

Peg, now quietly sobbing, recalls that after waiting five years for Dave to get sober, she was told by the rehabilitation center that she could not expect Dave to be attentive to her for a long time to come. *"So when he was in the rehab, I went to a number of the family groups. I guess I was pretty angry for a while, because he was receiving a lot of help, a lot of understanding, and it was like here I am, left still with the kids and everything. He was getting nurtured all along, and I still wasn't getting anything—and they told me in those group sessions you really can't expect to begin to think about a relationship with him, he can't even think about you for about another five years—that's a lot. You know, I'd waited the last five years for something to give here, and now I've got to wait another five years to be able to think about working on a relationship?"*[1]

Discouraged with the family program and Al-Anon, angry with Dave, and furious with herself for being so dependent and trusting, Peg enrolled in a four-month, intensive paralegal program. She believed this would be her ticket out of her situation and into complete independence. In addition, they needed good health coverage and benefits for Jeanne's disability, which Peg believed she would get as a paralegal. She borrowed money from her sister to pay the tuition and to keep the family afloat, begged another sister to baby-sit, and started school within weeks of her decision. *"I threw myself into school. Anyway, it took the focus off of problems. I felt like I am smart and I can do it; I can accomplish."* By this time, Peg recalls, *"I didn't care if he got sober. Really, I didn't care. I was so completely disgusted and fed up . . . but he took to the rehab like a duck to water."*

During Peg's paralegal program, Dave attended early morning A.A. meetings as well as evening and weekend meetings. His life was divided between the children and A.A. There was little energy for housework, or much of anything else. Peg was satisfied with the arrangement because of her single-minded goal of completing her program. As long as the children were well cared for, she was satisfied. In addition, she recalls that she had all but given up on Dave: *"I didn't want to get hurt again. I didn't want to go through this any more. I was just steeling myself like a big fence around me. I functioned but I wasn't loving. I had resigned myself that this is my life."*

Although Dave was good with the children, she says that she "thinks" she remembers that he was physically violent toward her for a brief period after leaving the rehab. *"He dried out and his nerves were frayed and I don't know if they healed. I think he has dead brain cells. I had to stay out of his way, because he did hit me. Well, I think he hit me before he was sober, too."* Peg pauses and then continues, *"Yeah, he did."* Her sobbing stops, and I note how matter-of-fact she is as she tells me this information. I recall another wife who said in an equally matter-of-fact voice, *"A few times he tried to kill me . . . just because he had all this anger."*[2]

Dave returned to work as Peg completed her paralegal program and immediately got a position with a law firm. Dave seemed energized about his business, and he had great plans for his success. Peg felt good about completing her program, but she was exhausted from caring for three small children and being out of the house at work all day.

With her income, Peg again hired their "neighborhood grandmother" to care for Jeanne, Tamara, and Mark, with her sisters pitching in when necessary. Life was busy for everyone. Both Peg and Dave seemed more content, but they continued to spend little time with each other. Peg's life was a series of tasks: work, housework, and baby-sitting while Dave went off to A.A. meetings. In a defeated tone of voice, she remembers her life this way: *"Getting up, getting dressed, getting ready for the baby-sitter—getting to work."*

A MOMENT OF CHOICE?

In addition to tending to her job and family, Peg read a multitude of self-help books, and she made time to enroll in a psychology class to try to untangle the web her life had become. What did she learn? *"I realized I was pretty good compared to all the cases in the psychology book. My professor wasn't big on counseling. He taught us it is a waste of time. He taught us you can help yourself. He said, 'if you are afraid of something, just keep trying it over and over again until you conquer it.'"*

Influenced by her feelings of abandonment and anger, armed with her professor's advice, and fed up with Dave and Al-Anon, Peg stopped going to her Al-Anon meetings altogether. *"We all have problems, but you hear so many stories there. I realized I don't enjoy listening to everyone's hard luck story. So I didn't pursue it any further. It used to be that that program was set up that you were supposed to go along with everything, and I'm not that type. I go my way. I'm not an Al-Anon person."*[3]

With her phrase, "I'm not an Al-Anon person," Peg highlights her view of the marital problem as rooted in Dave rather than in their relationship. *"I felt A.A. would be good for Dave. I didn't like the results for me. The way I felt was—I didn't cause this, why should I have to suffer? I think I had to change, but I didn't like it. No way. I didn't like it. Everything had to be perfect for Dave, and I'm not a perfect person. I mean, why should I have to stop having a cocktail once in a while? Why should the other person be penalized? That was part of the program I could never understand—that the sober person had to suffer."* Although other spouses began to see their own roles in the problems of their relationships, Peg was adamant that Dave and her troubles had nothing to do with her.

In addition, Peg struggled with Dave's increased involvement with day-to-day decisions around the house. The changes in Dave, which many spouses would have welcomed, were not welcomed by Peg. *"He was a little more watchful—maybe a little more dominating. He had his own full faculties once he was sober, so things I would do before would bother him, things that would never have bothered him before. That was difficult, that he was taking control not only of his own life, but taking control of the whole family."* Dave started to play with Jeanne, Tamara, and Mark. He slowly took an interest in their friends and their lives in general. Peg recalls, *"It was too overpowering for a person like me. He was the dominating factor, and for a dominating person to start dominating more—it was just too overpowering for me."*

"MISSING THE MARK"

However, Peg's own life, her independent life, flourished. Today, she has many friends, works full time, volunteers one day a month at the local Red Cross, and has recently become involved in the auxiliary of the local firehouse. She takes great pride in her own successes and is grateful that Dave's alcoholism forced her to take steps to become her own person. At work, she has consistently been given raises and has taken on more and more responsibility. She worries at times that she does too much and exhausts herself, just to avoid truly facing her life with Dave. Again, she becomes momentarily tearful. *"I seriously, over the last two or three years, thought, 'let's forget it.' Unless I just don't know when to give up. Uhm. I question that sometimes. The problem is, sometimes there is no emotional attachment at a healthy level. You know what I'm saying? In other words, we kind of keep missing the mark. We keep waiting to make contact with each other and that's kind of the way it is."*

RESIDUAL RESOURCE: PERSONAL INSIGHT

Peg wipes a tear from her cheek with the back of her hand. Her lip quivers, and she continues on. *"I think everything for me comes out as that abandonment thing. If I tell you I am angry, then you may not like me then, or you are going to reject me, or you are going to storm out of here or whatever. I don't know, but I'm afraid the bottom line for me keeps being I'm afraid and I won't have anyone there for me."* Peg laughs halfheartedly and asks me if any of this makes sense. I nod my head affirmatively.

Peg alternates between anger at Dave and anger at herself for her own perceived inadequacies. Her vision of Dave slowly emerges: *"He is very content but just wants more. He just wants to keep it on the track it's going, and I'm shaky. My problem is that I'm terribly afraid of being hurt and abandoned."* Peg giggles softly while more tears stream down her face and asks rhetorically: *"How can you walk around and be in a relationship for twenty years and still have a fear of being abandoned? It's like that hurt and wounded child. . . . Because my first husband had left me, just walked away, I, you know, really didn't want the second marriage to fail. I wanted to do everything correctly. So I drove myself nuts trying to please somebody who could not be pleased."*[4]

Over the next hour Peg unleashes a barrage of feelings about Dave. It seems as if they come to her almost faster than she can get the words out. Her tears and giggles congeal into a strident cacophony of anger. *"It's very easy to get lost in this shuffle of people who all they do is make their needs known to you. I was raised in that way. I married into it. And I was raised to solve the problems—to react, to take care of the situation. It serves me very well in my career. I work with difficult people* [lawyers], *and I am just terrific with that: anticipating peoples' needs, all that kind of stuff. . . . And I think that still goes on today."*

The struggle to find a balance between pleasing others and doing for herself plagues Peg. As the interview goes on, it is clear that she can articulate what she wants, but is unable to make it happen. In her mind, Dave is mostly to blame. *"You saw him—he's a big, physically big person, and his reactions are loud and verbose, and, you know, I tend to be kind of the opposite. He is constantly complaining and confronting, so to me he never looks vulnerable, like a lost puppy; he always looks like a volcano."*

It is striking that, on the one hand, Peg has a career, friends, and enjoys many activities in her life. She is *independent,* a term, which, to many, connotes success. In fact, she is remarkable in many ways. She has on two occasions (after Ed left her and when Dave got sober) enrolled in and completed school, when few of her friends or family received any post–high school education. She also has insight into her own life and what shapes it. Yet, on the other hand, she cannot behave independently with Dave; with him she is shackled by her sense that she should be able to make things all right for other people. Rather than disrupt the volcano, Peg tries to placate and please Dave.

From an early age, most of us are taught to give to others, to act selflessly. But the flip side of acting selflessly is depletion. The alternative is saying what we need while considering the needs of others. As B. R. Krasner and A. J. Joyce write, "People are schooled to please . . . the notion that it is better to give than to receive. But the fact is that one *has* to receive in order to continue to give. Sometimes though it seems easier to disengage than to risk the consequences of the spoken word."[5]

Peg goes on to describe how she tries to be totally balanced: juggling house, family, and career. She stays up late into the night trying to make the house run smoothly. She puts in overtime at work to assure herself that she will never be in danger of being fired. As far as the children are concerned, she is grateful that Dave is an attentive father, but she finds that the demands of teenagers are almost as unrelenting as toddlers' demands. From her view, she gives and gives and gives, with little to show except a sense of independence—that she can do it on her own. Depleted, Peg hears every comment as a judgment of her own worth. Unable to gauge what is reasonable, she retreats into her pent-up rage. What Peg describes is the "stone wall of unbearable weight and excessive limitations. . . . It is at the moment when people intuit that they can give no more without getting in return. When we perceive ourselves as giving without sufficient return, the very fabric of day-to-day existence unravels, and meaning disappears."[6] As M. Cotroneo notes in writing on what shapes and reinforces abuse in families, "When we do not experience another's concern for us, we tend to withdraw from the attempt of reciprocity in order to 'take care of ourselves.' We pull back to one-sidedness and trust is diminished."[7]

Peg has hit the stone wall running. Her ability to find the energy to invest any more in the relationship is nearly extinguished. Dave's selfishness, according to Peg, is his underlying problem. As an example, Peg tells of a recent incident involving a trip to the airport to see Tamara. With Dave's truck in the shop for new brakes, Peg had to drive across town to pick him up at a work site. He wrote very explicit directions, which she followed, only to find they were incorrect. As a result, Peg was lost for over thirty minutes. This left them with little time to get to the airport and see Tamara. She describes the scene when she finally arrived at Dave's work site: *"Dave picked up right away that I was frustrated. You see, before I would have come in and pasted this smile on my face—the perfect little wife . . . but that day I said, 'Yeah, I'm pissed off. You gave me the wrong directions.'"* Peg is crying. I prod her to describe what happened next. *"Dave looked at me and said, 'It's on you. It's your problem.'"* There was no apology forthcoming. Peg smirks, *"Dave was always a great manipulator—and now I know when I'm being manipulated."*

RAGE

What is the outcome of these feelings and these interactions for Peg? *"Rage. I think I don't let it out as much. I turn it inward on myself, and I have more depression. And I'm angry. Unfairness in our relationship makes me have a lot of rage or what I perceive as being unfair—what he expects for himself, he expects maybe much more of me than he expects of himself. You know, it's never OK for me to make a mistake. It's never OK for me to waste anything—never OK for me to be outside the absolute perfect mold of the absolute perfect person—nothing is to ever be broken."*

She pauses to compose herself and then says in a more controlled voice than I have heard for the past hour, *"In the past I used to break things. I used to take it out on the children. More often nowadays I just get very despondent—because I start to believe—believe that I am wrong. So I get very down on myself and turn that internal and get depressed. Sometimes I scream back. I feel very wrong. That I'm a wrong person. That I don't do enough, that I don't do things well, that I'm a wasteful spendthrift, ruining the ecology or whatever Dave's concern happens to be that day."*

Peg holds herself accountable to Dave's standards. Although she can hold her own in the work world, she is knocked around at Dave's whims, and each pillorying leaves her a bit more bruised, a bit more vulnerable, less trusting. When it comes to Dave, she feels judged and judged harshly. Peg uses the back of her hand to wipe tears from her face and then adjusts her headband. Surprisingly, she admits that she is hurt because Dave's behavior toward her has softened a bit in recent months. Why? Her explanation underscores the lack of trust between them. *"I think he knows any time I could leave* [because of my inheritance]. *I could leave if I wanted to. Before he knew I couldn't leave. We had the three children and I was dependent on him, so he'd kick me around."* Peg dabs at her cheeks and eyes. *"I think his relationship with his father—it was like a real hell house they grew up in, with a father who demeaned their mother—he would actually call*

Dave's mother 'stupid.' Dave wouldn't call me stupid, but he intimates that I have a stupid idea. I used to fight back a lot more than I do now. It's almost like I'm resigned to it and it's not going to make any difference. I used to say to Dave, 'You're treating me like your father treated your mother, and I'm not going to take it.' I was pretty fiery, but I'm just kind of worn down."

Although Peg no longer fights back, she still has the capacity to understand some of Dave's behaviors. The fact that she recognizes the "hell house" in which Dave grew up suggests that she is still capable of empathy and compassion. Even though she is enraged and bitter, the ability to factor in Dave's experiences is a resource that under the right circumstances might be activated to bring about change for the better.

In order to shift the conversation, I ask her about attempts she has made to lighten her burden around the house. Because Peg handles their finances, she has been responsible for savings and planning for the future. Peg finds this task burdensome, mostly because she feels the weight of responsibility for making a poor decision, and she feels that she doesn't have much financial savvy. In order to balance out this area of their lives, she insisted that Dave open an IRA as a way to get him involved in financial decisions. She directed Dave to their local bank around the corner. *"He went down to the bank to open an IRA—the guy who was there, the vice president, a friend, told him to go home and ask his wife! This is defeating my purpose. He's supposed to go to the bank and find out how to do this for himself."*

Peg straightens her headband yet again, smoothing her hair behind her ears. In a voice that is notable for an absence of emotion, she solemnly adds, *"I think I run around as fast as I can—as hard as I can. I try to do it all the way he wants it done. Until I crash, and then I either cry for three days straight or lock myself in my bedroom. I completely withdraw. We're very dependent on each other but very independent. There is no emotional availability for each other. Even though we're present with each other, we never meet. So I just chug along not thinking about it. I don't know how to get close to him—I can't get in there. I see other couples who work things out together and talk things out and I say, 'Yeah, that would be nice.'"* At this, Peg's shoulders sag; her body language reflecting her sense of discouragement.

Blinded by her disappointment and rage, Peg cannot even entertain the possibility that Dave might make a genuine effort to interact with her. Even when he inquires about her, Peg hears it as an insult. *"I can tell when he has a group assignment or whatever from A.A. He said he wanted to hear about my day and I said, 'Is that your assignment for the week?' He never probes for how I feel."*

Peg's eyes seem to focus on the photographs on the mantle—or on nothing. Her hands come up to her face and she cradles her cheeks as if to hold up the weight of her head. I ask her why she stays—the children are about grown, she has a job, a small inheritance—what keeps her in the marriage? Peg shrugs. *"It's sad. I don't even know if I still love him. I care what happens to him. It's been coated for so long I don't know what I feel toward him. I'm kind of numb."*

With this she shrugs and then slumps in her chair. *"I just chug along and don't think about it. I think he's doing the same thing. I'll threaten every once in a while that I'll look elsewhere—'I won't put up with this.' And he'll say, 'You're not going anywhere—where would you go? You can't even afford a roof over your head.'"* At this point, I question Peg about the violence and find that she has never said a word to Dave about it. Why? Because she doesn't want to *"throw it up to him. I just don't want to throw anything up 'cause I don't think he knew what he was doing. And it's a disease. Besides, I don't seek emotional satisfaction from him that much. I don't think he has it to give."*[8]

Unlike Cara Gunderson and many others who talked of their underlying continued love, Peg's love is "coated" with what she sees as long-term, repeated failures of effort and consideration on Dave's part. Although Dave is sober, their relationship is largely defined by blame and disrespect. According to Peg, Dave has little respect for who she is. Although he does not necessarily verbalize his apparent disdain for her, Peg feels it as a powerful and relentless force.

RESIDUAL RESOURCE: A SHRED OF HOPEFULNESS

In a final moment before the tape recorder is turned off, Peg sums up the state of her marriage in a sad, slow voice of near defeat. *"Like we don't really talk about our relationship. We don't have that kind of close communication. There's nothing one-on-one, heart-to-heart. I don't know whether or not it will happen. You know, that little fairy tale vision in your mind of how two people can know and grow with each other? I don't know if that will happen. Every once in a while there are little glimpses—maybe something will develop sooner or later."* Peg stares into the fire in the fireplace and speaks wistfully. *"I keep waiting for that to happen—you know. I put my five years in. . . . Is it my turn now? Dave's been recovering ever since 1981, and the relationship never really has recovered."*

And then, as if I might have misinterpreted what she has told me, *"It's definitely a struggle. I've filled my life with other things—I don't really take time to think about how much I might be hurting as far as leaving the relationship goes—and I don't know if the relationship's possible with Dave—I don't know. You know, I've just kind of gotten numb to it. We never go out, the two of us. It's just not something we do. If we do, we just talk uncomfortably about the kids, but that's about it. There's no closeness. It's covered over. It's crusted right now. We usually don't get into long, involved conversations. I make a comment, he makes a statement, sometimes a sarcastic statement back: 'Well, what did you expect?' That kind of stops it. And you know, I'll try to tiptoe in again till I get stopped again."* Peg smirks: *"Even my sister said, 'You've GOT to give him credit, he's not drinking and THAT takes A LOT of courage and an AWFUL LOT of strength, Peg. You've GOT to give him credit.'"* And then, with equal amounts of dismissiveness and anger, she continues, *"I DO. Can we go on now?"*

NOTES

1. It is Peg's recollection that she was told in the family group that Dave could not even think about her for five years. Whether or not this is exactly what was said at those meetings, it is what Peg understood.

2. Spouse abuse is prevalent in the general population. Most abuse is committed by men against women, but in some cases women are the abusers. Physical abuse is just one kind of domestic violence. Domestic violence can also include psychological, sexual, and property abuse. It is estimated that violence is experienced in a full one-third of marriage relationships at one time or another (M. Struass, R. Gelles, and S. Steinmetz, *Behind Closed Doors: Violence in the American Family*) (New York: Doubleday, 1980). There have, however, been distinctions made between relationships in which violence is routinely used to control a spouse and those in which violence is not a central aspect of the relationship.

3. It is not uncommon for spouses to attend Al-Anon meetings during the crisis period of alcoholism, only to end their involvement once the alcoholic has attained sobriety.

4. Reference to "wounded child" from Peg's reading of psychology books refers to the popular notion that the traumas of childhood are perhaps the primary obstacles to a happy and satisfying adult life.

5. B. R. Krasner and A. J. Joyce, *Truth, Trust, and Relationship: Healing Interventions in Contextual Therapy* (New York: Brunner/Mazel, 1995), 23.

6. B. R. Krasner and A.J. Joyce, *Truth, Trust, and Relationship*, 23.

7. M. Cotroneo, "Families and Abuse: A Contextual Approach," in *Family Resources: The Hidden Partner in Family Therapy*, ed. M. A. Karpel (New York: Guilford Press, 1986), 416.

8. Physical violence was reported by two wives. In both cases, the husbands apparently do not realize it occurred. It was not ongoing, but appeared to have occurred during a limited period of time. The wives did not consider it a serious issue at the time of the interviews, rather a brief aberration of the past.

Chapter 5

"I Wouldn't Call It Healing"

"How with this rage shall beauty hold a plea?"
—William Shakespeare, Sonnet 65

DAVE

Dave is relaxed and friendly, almost overly so. We sit in the living room, in mid-afternoon. The house is quiet. The curtains are open, and sun streams in through the rear window. I glance again at the wedding picture on the mantle. The rugged good looks of Dave's youth are succumbing to age. He has gained considerable weight over the years, and the hair around his ears seems thinner than it did the first night I met him. He is dressed in blue jeans and a sweatshirt, and his hands and face reveal his trade: white paint outlines the fingernails on his left hand, and there is a small spot of paint above his eyebrow.

Dave begins by telling me that his life is simple and uncomplicated. In contrast to Peg's initial nervousness, Dave smiles and seems lighthearted, confident, at times, charming. Again, he seems much younger than Peg and less weighted down by the world. The contrast cannot be missed.

THE INTERVIEW

Dave's family also struggled with alcoholism. Briefly, as if he prefers not to think about it, he draws a tragic picture of his parents and his childhood. The elder of two children, Dave remembers his parent's life this way: *"It was a very violent marriage—they were married very young. There again, in sobriety I was able to eventually realize it was two kids trying to raise two kids. They always had their drinks every day. Dad had two drinks a day that we know of, and my Mother probably did abuse alcohol. She was tipsy a lot of times. Booze was definitely a factor there, and I think it did fuel the violence—no question."*

The violence was mostly between his parents, Lucy and Tom. With little money, limited education, and no family support, Lucy and Tom faced life unprepared for the pressures and responsibilities of parenthood. Their frustration, confusion, and despair led to Dave's father's drinking, violence, and womanizing.

Like Peg, who felt responsible for her parents, Dave was also in a caregiving role with Lucy and Tom. *"I was triangled—my father was a womanizer, and, well, I ran scared all my life. I was scared all my life since I can remember. Alcohol took the fear away. Anytime I wanted to do anything, all I had to do was drink. I found that out at five years of age. My father took me to a local bar. He put me up on the bar and wanted me to drink, and I got drunk and danced on the bar all afternoon. I still remember dancing and being drunk and I was just a kid."*[1]

Unlike Peg's loving relationship with her parents, Dave's memories of his parents are quite different. His relationship with his father *"existed, but it didn't really exist—it was not a close relationship. No one ever watched a ball game I played in. My father died when I was thirteen. When I got old enough, he wasn't well. He was sort of a nervous wreck. When he came home* [from work] *he didn't want to be part of anybody or anything. I think that's when my mother got hooked on prescription drugs. I remember he did tell me just before he had this stroke, 'I have everything paid off,' and then he had the stroke and died."*

The death of Dave's father left the family in a financial decline, which his mother was unable to reverse. They continued to live in the same house, but each year, there was a little less for everyone. Although he is not certain, Dave believes that his mother developed a quite serious drug problem. The pressure of being a single parent, of trying to raise two sons alone, combined with an unstable marriage when his father was alive, was more than Lucy could take.

Lucy died several years after Dave graduated from high school, a death that he feels was greatly speeded up by her dependence on drugs as well as the pressures of being a single parent and a lung condition caused by a twenty-year smoking habit. When asked to describe his relationship with her Dave says only, *"She was very domineering, bossy, outspoken—a real pain in the neck to me. Well, I thought she was pretty cruel—she would say cruel things about people."*

In addition to saying cruel things, she confided in Dave about her problems with Dave's father, and then after his death, about her financial concerns and her loneliness. By this time, Dave knew that he could find relief in one place, the place he had been able to find it since that night at age five: alcohol.

A poor student, Dave entered the military after high school graduation. This was a practical solution to having no job or career plans, and his mother's constant concern about a lack of money. Dave thinks that joining the military was also an attempt to control his drinking. Unfortunately, alcohol was a favorite pastime of his friends in the service. Days and weekends off were often spent drinking and searching for women. The discipline of the military was uncomfortable for Dave. He envisioned himself a self-reliant, independent thinker who chaffed at taking orders and being constrained.

Nonetheless, Dave remained in the military for the duration of his commitment and upon discharge, returned to Philadelphia with little money and no job prospects. An old high school friend, Albert, suggested they start their own painting business, which they did. For the first several years, it was touch and go. They were either quite busy, or they had nothing to do for weeks at a time. As a consequence, Dave's income was erratic.

But Dave loved the freedom of having his own business. He could pick and choose whom he would work for and exactly what hours he would work. The solitary aspect of painting appealed to him as well. Unlike the military, where there were always people to answer to and guidelines to follow, painting allowed him the freedom to do things his way. He still drank a lot, but controlled it enough that the business eventually succeeded. Through the experience he learned a great deal about painting and about running a business.

Compared with his childhood and to his time spent in the service, life felt sweet to Dave. When he met Peg, he, like her, was looking for someone he could marry, someone with whom he could make a life and have a family. He liked Peg's independence and her income. Unlike many of the women he dated, she seemed more self-assured and more self-directed. Dave believes that she liked the fact that he had his own business; that he had, like her, pulled himself up by his bootstraps. He talked of making money, of expanding the business, of creating a future.

Peg's request that Dave stop drinking seemed reasonable to him. After all, he controlled his drinking, so why not just stop? He recalled their courtship as fun, but the early years of marriage as stressful. *"It was fine with me, but uncomfortable. You know, wanting to be married and continue the relationship with Peg and not drink* [was hard]. *I knew that Peg had had experience with Al-Anon and she knew what was going on. So I guess I had to hide it a lot. We still got along fairly well, from what I remember.*"

Although their early relationship was stressful, it is important to note that Dave had wanted to be married and that he believes that he and Peg got along overall in the early years of their marriage. It seems that there was a foundation there—although not terribly sturdy—that was at least somewhat positive. This is difficult to decipher in detail because of Dave's limited memory. Many of Dave's responses, especially pertaining to the presobriety years, are eclipsed and vague—based on "what he can remember." This is not dissimilar to Ken Gunderson's difficulty remembering the details of the period of his divorce. Dave offers insights from his perspective about the few years before he entered the rehabilitation hospital. *"I would say the last few years I didn't consider it a drinking problem. The only annoying factor was that Peg wouldn't go out with me as she used to because the children were basically more demanding. The only clue I had that she was going to Al-Anon was I knew she had started to go out on her own at night a couple times a week. I really didn't know and didn't care too much because it gave me time to drink. And I enjoyed sitting and watching TV and baby-sitting. I thought I was doing a good deed."*

Like many of the other alcoholics interviewed, Dave's concern for the relationship was limited at best. As Dave recalls, *"Our marriage was in difficulty but I wasn't aware of that. I guess I really didn't care about that. I was more consumed with booze and women. The daily living thing was completely miserable. Everything I knew was people that drank. People who dropped in would bring alcohol when they came, you know, so eventually it was like torture. I was lost. I was miserable, and I was lost."*

Consumed with booze, Dave barely recalled his promise to Peg that he would stop drinking. As Peg's ability to cope dwindled, he recalls that she threatened him. *"Finally, she threatened that something had to be done about this drinking—that she was going to leave. I said, 'OK, leave.' Again, I didn't care. At that time, work was not going well, the money didn't seem to be as plentiful."*

Peg finally "threatened" Dave again, and this time, to their mutual surprise, he agreed to get help. He opened a telephone book and found the name of a local rehabilitation hospital. Within a few days, he was a patient. *"It got me off the hook. My only concern was to get off the hook. I went to the rehab to get my wife off my back. But mostly, I was just sort of consumed with alcohol thoughts. I was so out of it."* Only vaguely aware of Peg's anger during the final months of his drinking, Dave was surprised at her lack of concern for him once he entered the rehab hospital. *"She came up to see me. I hate cheese. I said, 'Why don't you bring some good food? Bring me some food to cheer me up.' So she brought me sharp cheese! I was furious. 'I hate cheese,' I screamed at her. 'Take that damn stuff home!' Then my counselor said he wanted to see her. So she came up to the rehab and I never saw her as angry as she was after she saw my counselor. Oh she came up there—very tense."* At this point in the interview, Dave's easygoing nature shifts to impatience and annoyance.

What happened when she spoke with the counselor? I ask. *"I don't know what he said, but she just blew up at the fact she was married to a drunk! I'd never seen her that angry. She was out of control—me and this place where she didn't want to be . . . and she was just rigid when she came to see me."* And then with a sarcasm reminiscent of Peg's, he said, *"She did make the remark, 'What do you DO here all day, anyway?' She was extremely angry. She came, yeah, she came O-N-E Wednesday morning—it was all SHE could handle!"*

The easy, friendly exchange at the start of our meeting is replaced with an intensity that makes me want to back up and sit farther away from him. He continues in the same angry tone. *"She said she couldn't take these people talking about being beaten up by their drunken husbands and all this kind of stuff. So I said, 'Don't come,' and that was that. I'll tell you, her position was, 'There is nothing wrong with me—it's your problem.' So we just became, like, I remember a couple of times thinking, this just doesn't seem to be working."*

Peg never returned to the rehab hospital again, until the day Dave was discharged. He recalls that she arrived late to pick him up. All of the other clients who were headed home had been welcomed with flowers, or hugs, or their children dressed up to greet them. But he was left waiting at the front door for what seemed like hours. Their ride home was in silence.

A PREMATURE MOMENT OF CHOICE?

Once back home, Dave baby-sat and thought about his business. He felt abandoned by Peg, even though he had little desire to spend time with her. At the same time, he was relieved that she was in the paralegal program. It gave him time to think, to go to meetings, and to plan his future. Her inability to show any feeling for him made him resentful. I ask Dave if he can have any empathy for Peg's frustration and anger about the burden she must have felt. He responds with the same anger and sarcasm. *"Well, I certainly can't imagine what another person—I can't tell you how Peg felt!"* Dave's failure to try to imagine Peg's position underscores how badly their relationship had diminished. It suggests Dave's preoccupation with his own needs and hurts and his inability to see the world through any but his own eyes. It helps to maintain an "unstable arena with a dog-eat-dog quality."[2]

After returning to his business, which his brother-in-law had handled while Dave was in rehab, Dave recalls feeling even more distant from Peg. They were unable to talk and were rarely ever in the house together. Between her job and outside commitments and his A.A. meetings, seldom did they find a need to interact. In fact, Dave claims that there was no overt conflict at that point. Nonetheless, he was frustrated. He wanted Peg to appreciate his pain, his struggle, his effort. When this was not forthcoming, he sought the advice of his rehab counselor.

Dave recalls this counseling visit as a turning point in his thinking. *"I remember a couple of times thinking, this is really coming apart here. I thought, if you* [Peg] *don't like it, leave. Yeah. I would have been very happy. So I went to* [my counselor], *and he told me, 'Look, you've got to make up your mind whether you're going to get divorced or lay off this. There's no way Peg can handle this. Just that few minutes Peg and I had at the rehab, it was evident.'* [The counselor continued], *'I know she's not going to be able to do it, and you're going to push the marriage right out the door—maybe that's what you want to do. If you don't, you've got to accept that's the way it is. You've got to just realize that's not going to happen.'"*[3]

Dave holds his index finger up and very dramatically points to his head: *"And a light went on and I realized I'm thirty, thirty-five years old here, and have three kids. I can't go off looking for another person. So I cut it out* [pushing Peg to change]. *I accepted the fact that I have a maid. She takes care of me. But as far as discussing anything of real importance, feelings, there is no discussion. 'Cause I recognize that she does not know how to do it. I accept that. That's what it is. I get that part of my life* [discussing feelings] *from my A.A. friends. So that's where it's been for fifteen years. But that year was a real hard year all around. You know, sobriety-wise and A.A.-wise, it went really well. The way I looked at it, it really worked for me."*

I ask Dave if he misses being closer to Peg. He looks at me as if I haven't understood him. His eyebrows rise as he speaks: *"I'm very thankful for my counselor that when I went to him, he clued me right in."* Dave then refers to the A.A. serenity prayer: "God, grant me the serenity to accept the things I cannot change, the courage to change the things I can, and the wisdom to know the difference."[4] Mixed with his anger is a look of pride for recognizing and accepting the lack of potential for his marriage. As I question him further in an attempt to find any evidence of relational growth or healing, he stops me. *"I wouldn't call it any healing in the relationship. There was no support, absolutely no support* [from Peg]! *I don't think the relationship was there for so long because of my alcoholism and her denial. She has the strongest denial system of anybody I ever saw."*

Dave explains that from the beginning, Peg's position was: *"There is nothing wrong with me—it's your problem."* He smiles a smile of contempt and adds as if it is a joke, *"It's a good thing she's not an alcoholic, because her denial system is so strong—she'd be dead. She'll actually tell you that Jeanne's in college, Tamara is in Europe, and Mark is a future Olympic soccer player."* Dave rolls his eyes. *"So that's proof, according to Peg, that my drinking never caused a problem!"*

Dave shakes his head with disbelief. Then he brings up the same example that Peg brought up, involving the directions to his work site before heading to the airport to see Tamara. His version of the incident is similar to Peg's, except when it came to the two of them addressing the mistake. Dave proudly announces, *"Yeah, you see, before* [sobriety] *my stomach would start churning—all kinds of anxiety—*[I'd think] *I've got to make this right. I've got to fix it. God forbid, you might think something's wrong here, where that night I just said, 'It's on her. It's her problem—that's on her.'"*

It is not clear to me what his thinking is, so I ask him, given the fact that he had made a mistake with the directions, why say it's "on her?" Dave looks agitated with me for not understanding. *"I'm responsible for myself. I made a mistake, but her emotions are hers. If she chooses to be pissed off it's on her. I've learned it's NOT all MY responsibility."*

Another example Dave offers is house chores. He described how he and Peg had a recent argument about changing a lightbulb: *"I'm not changing the lightbulb,"* Dave announced to Peg. And then, to Peg, *"Are you?" So it stays burned out for three weeks and no one changes it. Like OK, if you want to curl your hair in the dark in the bathroom, go ahead!"* And Peg? I ask. Dave turns his hands palms up to indicate that she does nothing.

In addition, Dave complains that none of the children or relatives say anything to him about his efforts at sobriety. He longs for acknowledgment, but their "denial" of his reality stands in the way of this. *"They never say a thing to me. I think this all stems from Peg. I think the kids learned that from her. It was just sort of, don't talk about it—push it aside."*

Dave feels left out of the family in many respects. Although he spends time with his children, especially Mark, he feels that, as Peg does, there is little real communication. I ask him if he ever told his children his experience from his side or asked them what it meant to them. Dave shakes his head. His previous anger melts away and is replaced by a look of pain. *"What I'd like them to say is, 'Dad, I'm really proud of the fact that you've done this—we have friends whose parents are drunks, and they haven't done this' "* Dave smiles for the first time in twenty-five minutes. *"I'd love some acknowledgment. I would like that."* Again I press and ask him if that is something he could ask them for. He shakes his head vigorously. *"Well, the answer to that is, it is something you could ask for, but I would not ask for it because then I would feel that if I did ask for it, it would be meaningless. I think too, in their minds, it's like—like, having the measles and that all you do is recover."* Dave snaps his fingers as he says the word *recover.* Just as he is unable to imagine Peg's feelings, he is equally unable to imagine asking for some acknowledgment from his children.

RESIDUAL RESOURCE: COMMITMENT TO OTHERS

As though he believes we are finished with this topic, Dave launches into a list of his children's accomplishments. He follows this up with a description of his various A.A. volunteer positions, especially focusing on his work with alcoholics who have been living on the street prior to their sobriety.[5] He is excited and animated, back to the charming easygoing self he displayed upon my arrival. His commitment to his A.A. activities seems to be a substitute for his relationship with Peg, but his enthusiasm for his children and his volunteer work are as much potential resources as they are indicative of his ability to give to others, to have concern for others. These activities suggest that Dave is capable of giving, of genuine compassion and insight. Dave's interests in his children and his volunteer work have functioned as residual resources in that they keep him in his family context. What he does not get from his marriage, he gets from his children and his commitments outside of the family.

Just as Peg is committed to the upbringing of their children, so too is Dave. In fact, this may be the one area of their lives they cherish and share. Should they ever decide to address the differences between them, their mutual concern for their children might provide a much-needed common ground. Although Dave is critical of some of Peg's parenting, and he feels she has had too great of an influence on them, they both simply light up when talking of Jeanne's, Tamara's, and Mark's accomplishments. Even though Dave is frustrated by his children's failure to acknowledge his efforts in maintaining sobriety, he is delighted by everything else they do.

What does Dave see for the future of their marriage? *"If I didn't want to be married I'd go, I'd do whatever with the children, and I'd leave. So the point is, I don't want to leave. It's been more of a day at a time for me. I don't look backwards very often. I can have an argument about something, I can be upset about something, and I get past it. And the next day, I don't look back there. I don't look behind me. So I think emotionally the relationship has gotten better for me and worse for Peg from the way I look at life, and the way she looks at life."*

I timidly ask whether he thinks marriage counseling could help them, and Dave responds immediately. *"I'm not the one to do that—you know, my head's not screwed on that good. I look at life different. I look at each day different. If we have an argument about something, Peg remembers stuff from two months ago. I don't even remember it. Peg can look back and say, 'Yeah, you said dut dut dut dut dut.' I don't remember that kind of stuff. It's gone. I don't get into all that. I don't store up those same things. I don't store them up and have them get stuck in me emotionally. Gone. Away."*

The remainder of the interview is dedicated to discussion of Dave's many commitments to helping alcoholics. It is indeed an impressive array of volunteer activities. Among his children, his business, and his A.A.-related work, Dave finds satisfaction and meaning in his life. His work as a painter enables him to have flexible hours so that he can respond to fellow A.A. members' emergencies. Most of the people he works for like and trust him, so arriving an hour late or taking a long lunch break to help out a newly recovering person, works easily with his flexible schedule. In addition, he often paints for practicing alcoholics and, over the years, has reached out to many. In a few cases, they eventually joined A.A. His business serves as a kind of traveling bully pulpit to convert those alcoholics who could be helped by A.A.

Before we end, I bring up the IRA incident at the bank.[6] I explain that Peg had said I could raise this issue as an example of the kinds of ways they seem to work at cross-purposes. Dave looks perturbed, but he remembers the incident and responds flippantly, with a sarcastic grin. Then he launches into a monologue about his feelings about Peg's "control" issues. *"What was I supposed to do, go and call the bank president? That's why I threw it* [the IRA information] *in the drawer—I'm not reading all this crap! I make my own decisions. If there is something that I feel is my decision, I just make it. If it is something that involves both of us, then she has a right. I have to decide in my own mind whether it is a control issue or whether it is really a combination. I don't trust her decision about certain things because she has a control issue—I've got to decide where I've got to draw lines. Where is my decision? What is our decision? Then I make the decision."*[7]

I raise the possibility, the "for instance," of some mutual decision making, and Dave balks: *"I wouldn't allow the person who has the big control issue to make the decision. You don't allow somebody who has big control issues to decide what is my issue. I have to decide that. In general, I don't have a big control issue in terms of what she does or what she decides. After a while Peg understood that, once I made a decision, all the ranting and raving in the world was not going to change it. Every time I said the same thing: 'Now, YOU have a choice. I've got to do this. You have a choice to get pissed off at me and rave and ruin the next couple of days, or you are going to accept that I have got to do this.' Like I said, I'm responsible for myself. I made a mistake with the directions, but her emotions are hers. If she chooses to be pissed off, it's on her."*

Dave goes on to emphasize that Peg's real issue is control. *"When she gets distrustful or in her 'shit bag,' it is wonderful to not be guilty. I'm almost indignant, you know. I have nothing to feel guilty about. If you are in a bad place, I'm sorry you feel bad about that, but that has nothing to do with me. 'Cause I was constantly in shame. That's part of the addictive spiral. The more guilty and shameful you are, the more you act out. The more you act out, the more guilty and shameful you are. I am not guilty. I have nothing to hide. I have nothing to be ashamed of."*

As we bring the interview to a conclusion, I ask Dave what might have made a difference. His answer reflects his discouragement with Peg. *"I don't think she has the capability of understanding emotions without her going, now, to Al-Anon. She was taught the way I was. Her mother and father drank and never talked to her about anything of any importance as far as I could tell."* Dave takes a deep breath and adds, *"What I do is, I'm fanatical about A.A. I love to talk about alcoholism—I find it fascinating. What I don't get in the marriage, I get in A.A. One thing Peg has never done, she never said 'Oh, do you have to go to the meeting?' She's been very supportive of that. I told her I said, 'The meetings have got to come first.' But that's OK with her because we don't have this intimate, personal feeling."*

Three weeks later, the night before the interview with Peg and Dave together, I get a call from Dave saying that they have decided that they need to reschedule the interview. In fact, despite several attempts to reschedule it, the interview with Peg and Dave together never takes place.

NOTES

1. *Triangulated* is a clinical term that often refers to a family transactional pattern in which one family member is "caught between" two others. It can take a variety of forms, but often a child is triangulated between his or her mother and father. Triangulation is often, but not always, trust demolishing. One of the most common occurrences is when a child is triangulated during or in the aftermath of divorce. In this situation, each parent may attempt to have the child side with him or her, against the other parent.

2. T. Hargrave points out that it is destructive entitlement that is at the root of family hurt and pain. Destructive entitlement is contrasted with entitlement. Entitlement refers to what a person actually deserves; destructive entitlement refers to an action by people who see the world as their debtor, whereby they seek repayment in inappropriate and destructive ways (Boszormenyi-Nagy and Krasner, 1986). Hargrave notes that destructive entitlement can take different forms, including paranoid attitudes, hostility, rage, and emotional cutoffs. In the case of Dave Royer, it appears that his inability to consider Peg's experience is a form of destructive entitlement.

T. Hargrave, *Families and Forgiveness: Healing Wounds in the Intergenerational Family* (New York: Brunner/Mazel, 1994).

I. Boszormenyi-Nagy and B. R. Krasner, *Between Give and Take: A Clinical Guide to Contextual Therapy* (New York: Brunner/Mazel, 1986).

3. It should be noted that this is Dave's memory and interpretation of what the counselor meant. For Dave to "accept the way it is" between him and Peg could have been intended as a temporary measure or to bring about a temporary truce, rather than as a statement about Peg's permanent limitations and poor abilities.

4. The serenity prayer is also said at Al-Anon meetings. See appendixes.

5. Dave makes no mention of involvement with other women, and I do not raise the issue because of confidentiality. This underscores one of the difficulties of interviewing spouses separately.

6. Peg Royer had given me her permission to raise this topic.

7. Some research has suggested that men tend to talk about decision making as an individual endeavor, whereas women talk about it as more of a mutual function (Mackey and O'Brien, 1995). Most couples make distinctions between big decisions and less significant decisions. Style of decision making also varies by religious orientation. In most research on long-term marriage stability, listening to the other person's point of view (Robinson and Blanton, 1993) is considered a significant positive factor in marriage satisfaction, and lack of communication is one of the most common reasons for divorce (Lauer and Lauer, 1987). Dave Royer's comments suggest that decision making is a separate endeavor for him, one that he largely avoids with Peg.

Chapter 6

Hidden Resources?

Imbalance in the reciprocity of a relationship is never static or stagnant and unless it can be rebalanced, it leads progressively to more explosive tension.

—Ivan Boszormenyi-Nagy and Geraldine Spark, *Invisible Loyalties*

By their own individual accounts, Peg and Dave have a troubled marriage. At first glance it seems easiest to identify the many ways that trust between them has been continually diminished, as both of them provide ample evidence of this. Peg believes that she cannot depend on Dave at all, and she takes a fatalistic stance *("I had resigned myself that this is my life.")* toward her relationship with him. Her rage is turned inward and manifests itself as depression. She complains that Dave never inquires into her feelings, her thoughts. Furthermore, they do not communicate well. Emotionally depleted, Peg now sees Dave more as a volcano than a person. At the same time, she continually tries to please him, even as she announces that his expectations are downright inappropriate.

For his part, Dave seems to relish his anger about Peg's past deeds—even for things that happened fifteen years ago. This anger is so intense he is unable to imagine, even for a moment, Peg's experience of his irresponsibility and breaches of promise. Just as Peg sees Dave as a volcano, Dave reduces Peg to her "denial system" and her "control issue." Similar to Peg's complaint that Dave never asks about her is Dave's complaint that Peg is incapable of talking about feelings. Dave fails to ask for what he wants, such as understanding and acknowledgment from his children, even though he holds them responsible, as though they are the adults and he the child, much like Peg holds Dave responsible for her own compulsion to please him. Like Peg, who has chosen or been forced into independence, Dave functions from a position of isolation. He assumes he knows the thoughts of his family (they think that alcoholism recovery is like recovering from the measles), without inquiring into what their true thoughts might be. Dave carries on an internal monologue that excludes others.

Peg and Dave have been unable to mend their relationship. Recent research on good marriages has suggested that multiple factors may be involved in couples' successful survival of crises. These factors include a realistic acknowledgment of the crisis, recognition that a particular crisis did not cause all of the problems, the ability to distinguish fears about the worst that could happen from what is likely to happen, refusing to blame each other, the use of humor, acting neither as martyr nor saint, and intervention before a full-scale crisis takes place.[1] Peg and Dave have struggled to simply endure. What has hindered the repair of Peg and Dave's relationship?

Their "moments of choice" seem to have guaranteed the least likely opportunity for them to heal their relationship. Peg's choice to do it alone and Dave's early decision to accept his counselor's advice that Peg lacked the capacity for any further insight or understanding effectively brought a premature end to the possibility of rebalancing their relationship.

Given these patterns, combined with the fact that both Peg and Dave feel they have some very legitimate reasons for their anger and pain, is it possible that residual resources still exist between them that could be activated into building trust? If trust can be activated, what might lead to this in Dave and Peg's relationship? What resources, in the midst of all the pain and accusations, might still be available to them, should they decide to seek help? M. Cotroneo notes that although "trust is presumed to be present in all relationships, life experience informs us that sometimes people are unwilling or unable to receive care or to extend it appropriately, signaling mistrust. However, in any given relational context, so long as people continue to interact with each other, resources can be presumed."[2] What resources, then, can be presumed?

It is important to note that Dave claims to be satisfied with the relationship as it is. Given this position, his motivation for getting anything more from the relationship with Peg might be limited at best. On the other hand, he is disparaging of Peg and critical of his children's inability to truly understand what he has been through. There is a longing in his words for more, if not from Peg, then certainly from his children. Although he claims to be satisfied with his life, his anger suggests that it is a satisfaction built on resentment and rejection. Even though he might choose to live out the rest of his life with his anger at Peg intact, the opportunity to salvage more of the relationship with his children might be enough to sway him to assess his family life. If Dave was open to such an assessment, could he tolerate any exploration of his marriage, past or present? His children might be the leverage in such an undertaking. Would such an exploration, if only to address the pain and disappointment, hold any potential benefit for his relationship with his children? If so, is he willing to take such a risk? As it stands, Dave is protected by his anger. He has made a choice to seek refuge in blame, distance, and relationships outside of the family, rather than risk making himself vulnerable in an exploration of everyone's part in the past he shares with his wife and children.

Unlike Dave, who claims to be comfortable with the status quo, Peg hints that she might still be open to one more attempt at rapprochement. She is worn down and discouraged, but for all of that, she still seems to hold out the hope that perhaps something more can happen between them. *"I don't know whether it will happen . . . every once in awhile, there are little glimpses—maybe something will develop sooner or later."* Although her energy is depleted, she still remains open to the possibility of change. This in itself is a resource, for it suggests that her hopefulness is not completely shattered. She could, with her small inheritance and her children nearing independence, leave the marriage. Instead, she stays, ever hopeful that something different might come to pass.

What other resources exist for Dave and Peg? Peg has the capacity to understand some of Dave's behavior in the context of his childhood. She refers to the "hell house" in which he grew up as well as her acceptance of the disease concept of alcoholism. Information gleaned from these fleeting moments of an interview with a stranger suggests that given the appropriate arena, Peg still maintains the capacity to have some measure of compassion for Dave. Like Cara Gunderson, who learned that Ken's alcoholism was a disease, just like her father's diabetes was a disease, Peg still seems willing, after all the disappointment and pain, to see Dave through a lens that is not strictly focused on pathology. Although this may seem like a small, almost inconsequential resource of the relationship, it is out of such seemingly tenuous resources that relationships are sometimes able to take hold and grow. It would take the courage to risk honoring the connection that exists between them to move beyond the stagnant impasse that holds them both captive.

Peg is clearly held at arm's length by Dave's dismissal of her. In fact, there may be little she can do in the short run to change this. But what she can change is her tendency to keep trying to please him. This is within her control. It is striking that it is Peg who identifies the vicious cycle of continually trying to please Dave as the thing that keeps her angry and exhausted. Certainly, if Peg and Dave's relationship were ever to improve markedly, Dave's attitudes toward Peg would need to change. This might be more likely if Peg would stop trying to please Dave. Her tendency to "measure" herself by Dave's yardstick triggers Peg's self-flagellation, with Peg being both the person doing the whipping and the one being whipped. For, although Peg rails against Dave's demands, she also tries to meet them, holding at bay one possibility for building trust. Her comment *"we never meet"* is almost like a self-fulfilling prophecy. How can they meet if Peg fails to state her own expectations, to stand up to Dave, to create her own "yardstick," rather than attempting to live by his?

It was striking that, when asked to imagine what life had been like from Peg's perspective, Dave responded immediately that, of course, he could not do that. As in the case of asking his children to listen to the story of his past, Dave's imagination fails him and leaves him stranded and alone. The bitterness with which he speaks these words is indicative of his own pain and timidity. In fact, he makes fun of Peg's belief that the children escaped the effects of his drinking, suggesting that Dave may suspect that his actions have had consequences. If this is the case, it might serve as another common starting point for changing their relationship. Treated more like an adult than a child by his parents, Dave probably knows little about asking for consideration from others. It seems easier for him to hold others at a distance than to ask them for what he wants or to ask what life is like from their point of view.

In addition, Dave bolsters himself by using labels to talk about Peg. Her "disease," he notes, is denial and control. Instead of trying to imagine her suffering, he condemns her. This labeling is a weapon, which Dave uses to maintain his distance from Peg and from the possibility of his own compassion. Instead, he offers compassion to strangers. Although this is an admirable use of his time and energy, it highlights the tendency of people to seek comfort outside of their families rather than do the hard work required to strengthen their own family relationships.

What other resources are available to Peg and Dave? Recall that they liked each other when they first met. In fact, Dave could make Peg laugh. They are both clearly dedicated to family and seem to share a common work ethic. These shared characteristics are resources that could be utilized. Peg and Dave have many individual resources at their disposal. Both work hard, both are determined, and both have friends—indications that they are capable of sustained relationships. Just as Peg has insight into Dave's childhood suffering as well as her own motivations, Dave also has insight about himself. He understands that his parents were *"two kids trying to raise two kids."* Certainly there are limits to insight, but it has been referred to as an initial step in forgiveness.[3]

Although they are unwilling or unable to change at this time, Dave and Peg do have resources available to them, should they ever choose to invest in their relationship in a different way. For example, and perhaps most important, they have children whom they both clearly care about. In addition, they both have similar childhood experiences, which include parentification and alcoholism.[4] Should they ever wish to explore their pasts together, surely the common aspects of their difficult childhoods might function as additional resources. From this they might come to see, as Peg already intuits, that each of them has brought aspects of their parents' marriage into their own, as all couples do. The resources are there. The question is: Is there enough left between Peg and Dave to enable them to address the deep wounds that help to maintain their rage, so that they can begin to activate trust?

It may be that Peg and Dave do not have the desire or the inclination to try for anything different. Their wounds may be too deep and too familiar. But should they choose to address their relationship, it is clear that resources exist for them to find a better way. If they cannot explore the possibilities for themselves, perhaps they might do it for the benefit of their children so that Jeanne, Tamara, and Mark can understand what has shaped their parents' marriage.

Peg and Dave Royer represent a minority of the couples interviewed. Most relationships continue either to grow or fail, but Peg and Dave are at a relational standstill. Couples at relational standstills are those whose marriages endure but do not grow and develop. Although there is some individual healing, there is little or no healing between spouses. Compared with Ken and Cara Gunderson, who have found a new balance in their marriage that not only enables, but facilitates, individual growth in conjunction with relational growth, Peg and Dave live lonely and isolated lives. Both are independent, yet, entrapped by their blinding rage. In contrast, the next section introduces Mike and Ann Bertolino. Like Peg and Dave, Mike and Ann experienced difficult childhoods. Yet, Mike and Ann have been able to take the resources available to them to strengthen and resurrect their relationship. They have made a commitment not only to their own development but to the development of the relationship as well.

NOTES

1. J. S. Wallerstein and S. Blakeslee, *The Good Marriage: How and Why Love Lasts* (New York: Houghton Mifflin, 1995).

2. M. Cotroneo, "Families and Abuse: A Contextual Approach," in *Family Resources: The Hidden Partner in Family Therapy*, ed. M. A. Karpel (New York: Guilford Press, 1986), 416.

3. T. Hargrave, *Families and Forgiveness: Healing Wounds in the Intergenerational Family* (New York: Brunner/Mazel, 1994).

4. *Parentification* is a clinical term usually used to describe a circumstance in which a child is treated like an adult. For example, if a four-year-old were given responsibility for the care of a two-year-old on a regular basis, this would be parentification of the four-year-old. Generally, parentification is considered unhealthy. If parentification were to exist because of an extreme emergency and for a limited period of time, it would not necessarily be considered destructive and might even be seen as an opportunity for the four-year-old to participate in a way that is positive for his or her development. Parentification was originally described by Boszormenyi-Nagy in the 1960s. It is considered destructive when it depletes the child of resources and trust reserves.

I. Boszormenyi-Nagy and B. R. Krasner, *Between Give and Take: A Clinical Guide to Contextual Therapy.*

Part III

The Bertolinos: Passion, Volatility, and Devotion

But every married person knows conflict-free marriage is an oxymoron.

—Judith Wallerstein and Sandra Blakeslee, *The Good Marriage*

Chapter 7

Finding a Soul: Two Survivors

Mike and Ann Bertolino
Married twenty-eight years; one child
Ann: fifty-two years old, art therapist; sober thirteen years
Mike: fifty-six years old, journalist; publishing executive
Child: Michael, twenty-three (geologist)

Ann and Mike Bertolino live in a stately four-story home on a tree-lined block of center city Philadelphia. The small front and back yards are enclosed by black decorative wrought iron fencing that matches the railings outside the second- and third-story windows. The front gate stands ajar. Mike greets me at the door and apologizes that Ann, caught in traffic on her way home from work, will be another twenty minutes. He escorts me through a sky-lit corridor carpeted with oriental rugs, the dominant color of which is deep red. The walls are white with black and white photographs hung every foot or so. All of the photographs are of their son, Michael, taken at various ages. Mike explains that the photography is Ann's work. We enter a modern kitchen—white walls, shades, countertops, and appliances warmed only by rich wood floors and a few color portraits in black frames on the walls.

Mike is tall, over six feet, and wiry. At fifty-six, he has the gangly appearance of a marathon runner. His glasses are tortoise shell with rather thick lenses. His clothes are a cross between business and academic fashions: khaki slacks with a somewhat rumpled oxford cloth shirt, bow tie, and multicolored wool vest.

We make small talk for the first few minutes—how refreshing the fall is after such a steamy summer. I comment on the beauty of their house, and Mike asks if I have any interest in seeing what the rest of it looks like. I say yes, and he walks me from top to bottom. Each room is filled with items collected during their travels abroad—Turkish rugs, Chinese ceramics, Belgian lace, Indonesian batik. Their belongings magnify the natural beauty of their home.

A journalist by training, Mike is an executive for a large publishing company. Although today he shuttles between Philadelphia and New York, much of his career has taken him and the family overseas to live and travel. It seems that if they haven't lived in a particular country, they have at least traveled through it. Mike is enthusiastic about his travels and their extensive collection of goods from around the world, but his pride is most apparent when he points out Ann's photography. Mike reminds me of a grandfather showing off photos of his first grandchild. He describes Ann's progression from being official family snap shot taker, through taking a course at a local community center and several workshops, to now, where she has an occasional commission to photograph the families of their friends and relatives. Mike comments that Ann is such a talented person, it is a shame she can't acknowledge her talents more herself. With this, we return to the kitchen and a pot of freshly brewed coffee.

In the bright whiteness of the kitchen, and surrounded by Ann's photographs, Mike questions me about this project while he prepares a tuna fish sandwich for Ann. I explain that my interest is in how relationships change and develop, rather than simply how individuals change. He asks questions about the kinds of people I have interviewed and what I believe I have learned. Mike's interest seems piqued. As I respond to his questions, I notice the precise way he makes the sandwich—the pickles and onions are thinly sliced and then diced just so; each lettuce leaf is washed individually and patted dry; the bread slices cut to identical widths. When the sandwich is ready, Mike takes a seat and apologizes, noting that his curiosity is an occupational hazard. Just as he adds that their marriage has been a *"real adventure,"* Ann walks in the door.

Ann is dressed in a crisp black linen suit and a cream colored silk blouse with a striking gold pendant at her neck. She is petite—perhaps five feet two inches and under 100 pounds. Her forceful body language and her clothes convey an almost regal air. Her skin is freckled and ruddy, and her red hair is cropped short and tight around her face, framing her emerald green eyes. She greets me with a firm handshake, apologizes for being late, and explains that she had an emergency with a patient who was just brought into the hospital. She says that she loves this part of her job—helping people who are terrified and alone. Late and with only the tuna sandwich for dinner, she is gracious and polite.

Ann is an art therapist, working primarily with people who have sustained brain injuries. Although her work combines art and therapy, she finds herself more drawn to the counseling side of her work. With a playful smile, she suggests that people get into her line of work for one reason: They grew up with a lot of "baggage."

Ann suggests that we go ahead with the interview—and adds that Mike loves to talk so much that, at some point, she'll "escape" to the bedroom to change, and we'll never even know she is gone. She adds that Mike, after all, is the more talkative of the two of them; she is *"the listener."* Mike glances at her with raised eyebrows and an inquisitive look I cannot interpret. He hands her a glass of milk with her sandwich and offers her some coffee as well. He then places his hand on her shoulder, and she responds by reaching up just briefly and touching his fingers.

THE INTERVIEW

Ann takes a bite of the sandwich. She half closes her eyes as if trying to recover from the rest of her day and focus on the interview. She says that life could be worse—at least she is sober. Like most of the people I interview, Ann has no questions for me. If she is anxious about the interview, she doesn't show it. Instead, she says that to understand her and Mike and what helped them stay together, I need to understand that they are survivors. Ann explains, *"We had to pick ourselves up by the bootstraps. We always had a volatile marriage, but I know we just loved each other."*

From the very beginning of their relationship, Mike and Ann struggled. The volatility of that struggle flashes on and off again throughout their interview, mostly in the form of sarcasm, which includes correcting the other. Although it was initially uncomfortable for me, it became clear that, for Mike and Ann, this verbal dueling is a regular part of their relationship. Also, I noticed that, for each instance of dueling, there was an instance of equally powerful praise of the other person.

Ann and Mike met in New York. Drawn to each other immediately, they found much in common: art, literature, movies, and people. Ann was attending graduate school for her master's degree in fine arts. Mike was working for a large newspaper as a reporter. Ann's life and world at that point was art. Her friends were all artists and, for the most part, barely surviving financially. Mike's world centered around the newspaper business. Mike and Ann's dating revolved around parties and candlelight dinners, with intense debates that were fueled by many bottles of wine to keep them going into the wee hours of the morning. In addition to dinners with friends, Mike often had work-related dinners and receptions to attend. The alcohol was bountiful, and Ann enjoyed hobnobbing with the wealthy, powerful, and famous.

Both Ann and Mike were invested in their own budding careers. Ann admits that she was attracted to the glamour of life with Mike, and Mike found that Ann's world was a welcome relief from the deadlines and rush of his profession. Ann was supported by a very modest research grant on art restoration. Mike, although not making a great deal of money, seemed wealthy compared with Ann. Before long, they were spending all of their spare time together, and within six months they were married. Mike's parents and Ann's mother approved: Both Mike and Ann had the right credentials in their parents' views. Ann was educated, and her natural elegance gave her the look of a person of means. Mike was articulate, educated, and could introduce Ann to a world of travel and interesting people. She was the sensitive artist, he, the powerbroker. Looking at the two of them, theirs seemed an outstanding union.

Mike: A Background of Ruthlessness and Wealth

Mike grew up in a wealthy suburb of Philadelphia surrounded by all of the trappings of the American dream. His father's family had come to the United States as poor immigrants from Italy. They were skilled in building and woodworking, and managed to develop a relatively prosperous construction and contracting business. When Mike was a young adolescent, his father expanded the business to include real estate. This proved to be the investment that shifted them from economically well off to wealthy.

Mike's parents put all of their energy and resources into trying to enter the privileged class. According to Mike, they were financially successful but relationally destructive. In his words, they were a *"very dysfunctional family."* They became the ultimate conspicuous consumers—they bought more things than they knew what to do with, kept moving into bigger and more impressive houses, and always looked for ways to appear rich. Mike and his siblings, all academically talented, attended private schools and sat side by side with children who came from historically wealthy families. But Mike felt that they never really fit in. In fact, he longed to be *"a regular guy."*

Unfortunately, the trappings of Mike's life were just that—trappings. His father's power and wheeling and dealing made Mike resentful. Mr. Bertolino's work kept him away from the family much of the time. Mike feels that the pull of yet another deal, another few dollars, another scam, was more important to his father than Mike and his siblings. The disdain in Mike's voice is palpable. *"My father was kind of ruthless. He was a big business tycoon, and he learned to be that way."*

As a college student, Mike had a great deal of contempt for business. He saw it as a cutthroat way of life. His choice of journalism as a career was a deliberate move, a 180-degree turn away from the evils of his father's way of life. Mike holds himself stiffly as he talks. The veins in his throat bulge and his jaw tightens. He recites a litany of failure to support, offers of money and pills to make everything better, and more acquisitions to prove status. After several minutes of talking about his family this way, Mike's voice softens and he adds that when he got older he had more insight into his father's issues. *"He said something to me which gave me a better understanding. I asked him, 'What did you do to have fun when you were a kid?' He said, 'Well, it was the depression time. We had to take care of our families.' I guess it was a hard time."*

Mike struggles throughout this part of the interview to find the benefits of his childhood, for they are always mixed with the disappointment of a boy who desperately wanted his father's time and affection but instead was given fancy summer camps and private schools. *"I have memories of my father not being there. He was always free to send me on vacation to interesting places. I guess that's what I had."*

He recalls that at one time they owned three homes: the one they lived in, their summerhouse at the shore, and a third house in New York. Although they spent all of their time in the Philadelphia area, Mike's father had this need to acquire more and more. Mike shakes his head, and the veins in his neck begin to stand out once again. He sums up his father's life in one brief sentence. *"All he did was make money."*

Mike's father left all of the child care to his wife, a task that Mike feels she was uniquely unqualified to handle. He pauses briefly. *"You know, he was very selfish, and my mother is interested in herself too. For example, my mother would never think of going to a store and buying anybody a present. She pulls it* [something] *out of a drawer."*

"Because?" I inquire. Ann chimes in, *"She has free rein. She is not giving in the sense that she would think about a present that she would want to go buy for somebody, to take the time out in the day to actually go out and do that. It's more that she'll go to her drawer and give something to someone that's* [used and] *hanging around."*

Mike's mother also came from a poor immigrant family. Her parents worked long hours in factories to try to raise three daughters and give them a better life. Mike explains, *"As I understand it, there was a lot of emphasis put on work, and little on emotions or good feelings. I think my grandparents had a marriage which did not involve love. It was more a marriage of survival. In fact, I recall my mother telling me once that I was so fortunate because her parents had nothing material to give her and that I had everything because I had material wealth."* He pauses. *"I'm not sure she had much of a role model for being a parent or a wife."*

Although Mike's mother constantly accumulated things for herself—jewelry, trinkets, knick-knacks, and every household item imaginable—she would not, and to this day will not, spend her money on other people for birthdays or Christmas. This is true even within her own family, with her own children and grandchildren. Furthermore, according to Mike, *"She lies. She's always lying. And she uses people by paying them off."*

His words about his mother are harsh and unedited. Yet, as he did with his father, Mike seems to search for the one shred of evidence or the one insight that enables him to absolve his mother of some of the pain she inflicted. In this case, Mike lays some of the blame for his mother's behavior on his father. *"She came second to making money for my father. Maybe that is why she is the way she is today."*

Not only did Mike's father run a cutthroat business, Mike feels that his parents deliberately attempted to make him and his siblings financially dependent on them for life by giving the children excessive amounts of money. Although Mike has been able to control his finances and live on his own income, his sister and brother have been manipulated by their parents' financial dealings. Mike holds his parents at least partially responsible for the way his brother's and sister's lives have turned out. *"My sister is just a mess—she lives down in Alabama and was just devastated by my mother and father, by how they treated her. She was in a mental institution. She's a mess. She's had three failed marriages and one husband ended up OD'ing and he died."* Mike feels that he is fortunate in comparison to his brother and sister, both of whom have struggled with eating disorders and substance abuse.

Mike has very limited contact with his siblings, as they inhabit worlds so disparate from his own that it is difficult to bridge the gulf between them. His brother and sister serve as reminders to Mike of how fortunate he is: He has a career, a family, a beautiful home, and his own money in the bank. He feels safely removed from the world of manipulation and greed that his parents created for him.

Even as an adult, Mike always felt misunderstood by his parents. *"They never really sat down and talked to us about serious things. In a way they weren't serious people. Some of it was feeling I never grew up in their eyes. They never really regarded me as a freestanding individual. I mean, Ann still reminds me of how angry I was with my parents. We would go visit my mother, and there we were, thirty-five or forty years old, and she would still be making my favorite sandwich spread, and it just made me furious! I always just sort of felt like we were the twins. Ann and Mike, these children dressed up in adult clothes."*

Mike's voice is disparaging and sarcastic. He practically spits out the words. When I suggest that making sandwiches for them sounds like a loving gesture, Mike can barely control his emotions. *"I don't think so, I don't think so. You see, it's a control thing. We're her little objects—her possessions. There is always a price to pay, always an ulterior motive."*

Ann looks at Mike as she fills in the story: *"Mike's father was actually there more than his mother. If pushed against the wall, Mike's father would come through for you more than Mike's mother. She doesn't have the ability to really enter* [a relationship or] *anything."*

Ann and Mike are in agreement on the manipulation and ruthlessness of Mike's parents. When Mike adds, on a positive note, that he did benefit from his upbringing in that he went to excellent schools and traveled and met interesting people, Ann chimes in with her own positive and telling memory. Ann remembers visiting Mike's parents in those early years. *"One of my attractions to Mike's family was the way they drank. I mean, you'd go over for lunch on Sunday and drink for three hours before you ever got to lunch. I thought that was wonderful!"*

Mike adds the caveat that his family drank, but not compulsively. In fact, the pressure they felt to be part of a world to which they didn't really belong motivated them to drink more than they wanted to. Both of his parents believed that entertaining was a way to move up the social ladder. As the years went on, extravagant parties were part and parcel of their existence. This suited Ann just fine.

Ann suddenly looks less comfortable. The spotlight is now on her. She takes off her linen jacket. The cream colored silk blouse underneath sets off her brilliant green eyes even more. She shifts her weight from one side of the chair to the other and plays with the crust of bread left on her plate. The seconds seem long and heavy; I wait for her to speak again.

Ann: Searching for a Soul

As Ann begins to speak, her regal demeanor dissolves in front of me. She slides down into her seat and appears to be even smaller. *"Someone said, 'thank goodness you're only an alcoholic and you're not an axe murderer,' because I have a very strange family. It's nobody's fault, but very difficult circumstances."*

Ann bites her lip and then continues on in a barely audible voice. *"My mother died in childbirth and lots of our family split up. My father was ill* [with something like multiple sclerosis] *and couldn't manage. My brother and I were adopted when I was two and a half."* Ann glances at Mike as if his presence is necessary for her to go on. *"It was just one sort of devastating loss after another."*

The adoption of Ann and her brother when she was two and a half and he, four, involved a long-distance move and then every few years, a move to a new job location for her adoptive father's career. Although she and her brother had no other biological siblings, they were cut off from contact with any extended family. Their adoptive parents had two natural children, who became playmates to Ann and her brother. Ann recalls her three siblings, her own brother and her two adoptive sisters, as early confidants. But seven years after the adoption, Ann's brother was killed in a freak car accident. Her recollection is limited. For her, *"there was tremendous pain, tremendous grief."* Yet she does not recall her adoptive parents grieving for any length of time. Instead, she remembers that the message then and throughout her life was don't talk about it and it will go away. As life rushed on, Ann turned her grief inward. *"There were lots of* [geographic] *moves. . . . I was just very insecure and desperate to please and neurotic. I had no center, no soul. I literally didn't know who I was."*

Aside from her brother, Ann has never been in touch with any of her biological family. Her voice is a whisper, and the tape recorder barely picks up her words. The ruddiness of her complexion is washed away by a white translucent mask that fades into the cream of her blouse. Even the pupils of her eyes appear to be several shades lighter. In addition to constant moves, life with her adoptive mother was not easy. *"My mother was the controller of information. There was a lot of jealousy when we* (Ann's two adoptive sisters who were close to Ann's age) *got along and excluded our mother. She wanted to be in control of what happened."*

Ann feels she was always distant from her adoptive parents while growing up. She felt like the outsider, the intruder. Ann spent hours as a youngster imagining her real mother and what life would have been like if she had lived. She wondered about her father but never asked about him. To Ann, it was a taboo subject. She believes that these childhood fantasies of her real parents sustained her. They also helped to protect her from her adoptive mother's difficult personality. She describes her adoptive mother as rarely happy and always wanting to control every situation. This caused a split between her and Ann at an early age. This split would not be resolved until Ann became a young adult. Ann recalls that as a child and as a teenager, *"I never told her anything. If you planned something in that household it would never come about. If you looked forward to anything you could be absolutely certain it wouldn't happen."*

Whatever the "plan" was, Ann's adoptive mother seemed to make certain it ran amuck. Everything, from shopping trips to plans with friends for overnights, happened at her mother's whim—or was prevented from happening at her whim. Ann recalls one such event. *"Every year we would write down the things we wanted to do at camp. We had a catalogue of camps and farms in Vermont we'd choose from, but never did we get to go to any of them."* Even so, Ann and her siblings would each go through this routine. *"There was always a reason we didn't get to go. We went through the process of picking a camp out, but eventually we didn't—we said, 'No, never mind.'"*

In addition to her mother's need to control all events, from large to small, the family moves were devastating to Ann. She recalls a move every couple of years, with each move requiring constant adjustment, trying to fit in, to make new friends. Ann always felt like an outsider, someone desperately trying to be liked and accepted.

On top of this, as Ann and her siblings reached adolescence, Ann's mother became less trusting of them. It seemed Ann's mother's drive and stamina were used primarily to control the children. Ann tells of her mother driving around the neighborhood looking for them, then forcing them to go home. Ann recalls that her mother usually found them listening to music and innocently talking to friends at the corner. Regardless, they were forced home where their mother felt they were safe. Ann and her siblings were constantly under scrutiny. Eventually, as with the annual nonselection of summer camps, she and her sisters just gave up and stayed at home. Rather than pulling her and her siblings together as they got older, it seemed that their mother's behavior just pushed them apart. In fact, it is only recently, since their mother's death that they are coming back together to talk about the past and to offer each other support like they did as young children.

When asked about her adoptive father, Ann has little to say. He was not a very powerful force in the family. Her parents would argue fairly often and then not speak for long periods of time. She recalls that her father would retreat to the basement. *"He didn't want to have anything to do with fighting. He was jumping ship."* Ann thinks of her adoptive father as *"an idea man. He had lots of ideas but he didn't have the personality or the ability to follow his ideas up for himself. In my mother, he had someone who had the drive and tremendous stamina."*

The one thing Ann's father did do for her was encourage her interest in gymnastics when she was about ten years old. Although not a star, she liked the camaraderie and the fact she could get lost in her own world. It was gymnastics that helped to maintain what little sense of self and center she had, and it was her father who she could depend on for a ride, for the money to pay her dues, and for moral support.

As Ann neared high school graduation and was preparing to leave for college, her father died suddenly of a heart attack. It was a period of great stress, loneliness, and confusion for all of them. Ann's mother, however, seemed to gain some kind of inner strength during this time. No longer able to depend on her husband and with the children just about out of the house, she became focused on her own life. As Ann recalls, she threw herself into her own career. A longtime antique collector, Ann's adoptive mother decided to take the life insurance money and do what she knew and loved. *"She got a shop and she became an expert in her field. She had an art and antique gallery, and she had it in a very wealthy area of upstate New York. We would have liked her to have had her own business or be so committed to it while we were growing up. It would have taken the pressure off of us."*

In a reversal of what would be expected, Ann's mother eventually served as a kind of role model for Ann. *"She was a real believer in what women could do. In fact it's funny that for so many years there were these mixed messages: 'You can do what you want to do, but don't do it too much or you're going to get sick.'"* Now finally, with Ann beginning college and her mother so immersed in making a go of her business and her own life, the messages took the empowering form of "You can do it!"

Early in college, Ann's life changed in two other fundamental ways: She became interested in parties and art, in that order. She still struggled with unrelenting feelings of emptiness and being an outsider. To fill the void, and to mask the fact that she was fundamentally shy, she became a *"party animal."* She recalls, *"It was a wonderful feeling at first. It was very freeing. It helped me kind of change my personality and become popular and do the aggressive things I really wanted to do. I set out to become popular. That was my main thrust."* To help this along, she always made sure that she knew where the biggest and loudest parties were going to be held. *"I had very little self-confidence but* [once I started to drink and party] *I immediately became very popular. And too, I became aggressive and a party animal. It was a great feeling."*

Not only was it a great feeling, but it changed her life in a very fundamental way. *"Basically, after that I was never connected with people who didn't drink."* She was known around campus as the person who always knew where to go to get the most beer, where to find the best party, and where to meet the most people. Alcohol and parties gave her a way to unwind, to flee her own troubling feelings of isolation and insecurity. Alcohol became a companion of sorts and an outlet for her pain.

Although alcohol had not been part of life for her family, she made up for that lack in college. Like many an alcoholic, she did reasonably well in her courses, and no one ever asked if she had a problem with drinking. In fact, Ann continued to think of alcohol as her friend, the one thing she could always turn to. Unlike her active childhood imagination, the gymnastics, or even the art (which she felt she was good at but not outstanding), she absolutely excelled at drinking and partying. Good looking, energetic, and smart, she had no trouble attracting boys.

During this time, Ann remained in contact with her mother, and, despite Ann's use of alcohol, their relationship improved. In fact, the more success her mother experienced, the more she was able to encourage Ann. *"She would say, 'Don't worry so much—you can do it.' She really believed in me as an artist. Actually, in the later years, I called her all the time."*

Hints of Ann's ruddy complexion are back, and her voice is strong and confident once again. After graduating from college, Ann moved to Boston and spent time working in a museum and continuing to immerse herself in the worlds of art and drinking. Her true interest was watercolor, but at her mother's suggestion, she learned photography. She loved photography; it offered her another avenue for expressing her shy personality.[1] From behind the camera, she could observe others and, to some extent, hide. Although she believed at the time that she was developing her art career, in actuality she was spending more time drinking with friends than on her photography.

Although she did not recognize alcohol as a problem in her life, she did recognize her lack of discipline. Not knowing where else to turn, Ann decided that graduate school was the answer. She applied to art school in New York and was accepted.[2] It was then that she met Mike.

Before we discuss their meeting, Mike goes to the second floor and retrieves a watercolor of Ann's—a beautiful painting of a Boston street—and he proudly shows it off. Ann seems embarrassed, saying, *"Miiike"* in a long, drawn-out way. But Mike's pride in her work is not to be contained. He speaks enthusiastically about the quality of her work for several minutes.

Ann and Mike: Passion and Volatility

Delighted to be out of Boston, Ann settled into graduate school in New York City. She and Mike met early in her first semester at a cocktail party near New York University. Both passionate and driven, they were attracted to one another immediately and soon married. How did their marriage begin? Mike laughs as he recalls, *"We couldn't communicate at all. When we went on our honeymoon, we were mixing gin and tonics."* As she has done throughout the interview, Ann chastises Mike by saying his name very slowly in a clearly sarcastic tone. This time she says it even more slowly than before. *"Miiike."* Mike continues, *"We got married. We were both strong willed and rather spoiled."* Ann explains, *"I can remember we started fighting on the plane to France for our honeymoon."* Mike clears his throat with great drama and says sarcastically, *"Some of us started fighting."* The mood shifts. It is now uncomfortable. Mike grins impishly, and Ann smiles at the innuendo. Again, she responds, *"Miiike,"* like it is a warning for him to watch what he says. Ann continues. *"We always had a relatively volatile relationship, and the alcohol fueled that and masked the underlying problems. It made it impossible to work on the problems."*

The happiness they experienced while dating ended abruptly. As Ann and Mike begin to talk about their early marriage, the feeling in the room changes. The conversation is no longer an easy exchange of information; they correct each other and reprimand each other for not getting the story just right. Ann continues to roll her eyes at Mike and pronounce his name in that long, drawn-out manner. It is a sign of disapproval: He doesn't quite have the story right, or he is making it sound too negative or simply too embarrassing. Mike's response to this seems belligerent, because he ignores her and continues without acknowledging her words. He has clearly heard this tone many times before this interview.

John Gottman's research on why marriages succeed or fail suggests that one type of successful marriage is a "volatile" marriage. Although volatile marriages were long considered pathological, Gottman suggests that many couples in long-term marriages are in volatile, nonpathological relationships that are very stable. These marriages are characterized, like Ann's and Mike's, by bickering and passionate disputes.

One of their underlying problems, as Ann and Mike see it, was poor communication.[3] They simply disagreed on most decisions. While dating, their interactions were social, their debates, although fierce, always ended in laughter and one more glass of wine. Big decisions had to do with which restaurant to go to, what kind of wine to order for dinner, or which art exhibit to attend. As a married couple, their decisions became more weighty and directly affected their lives in significant ways. The decision making was problematic. They both agree that whatever Mike wanted, Ann wanted the opposite, and vice versa. Ann volunteers: *"I was not marriage material—I really wasn't. I had no idea about a relationship with anybody. Hum, I think I want to couch all of this in sort of a general comment about our marriage today, which I think we both think is a good one."*

Mike looks up at the ceiling as if debating whether he should speak or keep his silence. Ann looks at him, and as he brings his face down and makes eye contact with her, he begins to speak in a soft and tentative voice, as if he is making a confession. *"We drank too damn much. Several nights a week. When we went on our honeymoon, I was mixing those gin and tonics at ten in the morning!"* But if he sees this as a problem now, he certainly didn't at the time. Mike shrugs his shoulders. *"It was just what we did."*

When they returned from their honeymoon, Mike went back to work and Ann to school. Although Mike's work as a journalist appealed to Ann, the reality, according to Mike, was long hours, hard work, and lots of competition. Unlike the period in which they dated, after they married, they began to see less and less of one another. Mike was out of town a great deal, and Ann was wrapped up in her artwork. The lonelier Ann felt, the more she drank, and the more she drank, the less Mike wanted to be with her in social situations. Several years passed. Ann recalls, *"We were living totally separate lives. We were in New York for all those years—but traveled back and forth to Europe due to Mike's work. We were always just about ready to go or just getting back from a trip, so I never felt like I was anchored anywhere. I mean, it was an exciting life, but I didn't feel that any one place was base. Our life was very transitory."*

Ann became jealous of Mike's work, and he became somewhat impatient with her. In an attempt to improve their relationship, Ann started to occasionally travel with Mike. She hoped that spending more time together would make the relationship stronger. This in-town, out-of-town life took a toll on Ann's artwork, but nothing like the toll her drinking took on it. Her drinking increased steadily over the next two years to the point of drinking daily, while Mike's drinking tapered off. According to Mike, he simply had too much work to do to drink. He was rapidly climbing the career ladder and given more prestigious assignments, more responsibility, and more money.

Mike found Ann's drinking discouraging. Yet no one, not even Mike, approached Ann to suggest she had a problem with alcohol. Like so many people in the interviews, both Mike and Ann remind me that it was a different era. It was the 1960s, and drinking was not only accepted but encouraged. In fact, it was often frowned on to *not* drink alcohol at a party or social affair. And, as Ann reminds me, she functioned. To outsiders, she took care of an apartment, went to school part time, traveled, and socialized. She felt she was charming and that the alcohol made her more comfortable and interesting to Mike's colleagues and to the occasional politician or dignitary they hosted.

Then, unexpectedly, Ann got pregnant with their first and only child. At her doctor's suggestion, she stopped drinking for the duration of the pregnancy. She gave birth to a healthy baby boy, Michael, but resumed occasional drinking within a month of his birth. By this time, Mike had been promoted several times and he was on the road more than he was home. Ann recalls: *"It was very difficult. I was so overwhelmed all of the time and Mike was hardly there. I was sleep-deprived and depressed. Here I had this beautiful child, but I was just not able to respond very well."*

Ann controlled her drinking so that she was able to care for Michael and to convince Mike that she had her drinking under control. In reality, her child-care skills were probably adequate at best. To complicate things more, Mike was transferred overseas. With a six-month-old and a few belongings, the Bertolinos moved to Asia, a world unknown to all of them.

They had live-in servants who took care of Michael and cleaned their spacious apartment. This relieved the pressure on both Ann and Mike. It also freed Ann to drink more. However, Ann felt more and more cut off and, lacking her center, more and more desperate. Being away from her artwork and her growing relationship with her mother, she found herself adrift as never before. Although drunk much of the time, she was aware enough to know that she was a disappointment to Mike.

Mike focused even more on his work and gave up drinking completely. Ann never slowed down. By the time Michael was out of diapers, she could barely get enough to drink. Scared and lonely, she retreated into her bedroom. Mike shakes his head as he describes it. *"You were so bad. I mean, we had gotten to the point you were not any longer dangerous. You just sort of retired to the bedroom, scurried around a bit. You weren't driving a car, so you could do whatever you wanted to do."*

"Two Boxers"

Once again, Ann responds with her characteristic, *"Miiike."* The tension in the room is now palpable. Doing whatever she wanted meant being in bed or being at the local club, which was frequented by the international set. At the club she could socialize and act as if she were part of the human race. She knew that Michael was in good hands, so there were few constraints on her time. Still, she hated being overseas and started to blame Mike for her life. She deplored the local weather, the language she couldn't speak, and the loss of privacy she suffered because of the ever-present servants. She hated every part of her life. She glances at Mike and says contritely, *"I recall letting you down on a number of occasions. During that year, which was a terrible year, I would stay sober for a few days, then drink again. Mike would say 'drink less,' and I would say 'well OK, I'll try,' but even if I drank less I got drunk. It had really deteriorated into two separate lives—me at one end of the apartment and him at the other end. We were kind of tightening into our corners at that point. It was like two boxers in the ring. I don't think he could stand me, but we were just kind of together."* I ask Ann what she thought about or got out of those years, and she replies, *"I met interesting people and traveled. Yes, Mike enabled me to drink all I wanted to and lead the kind of life I loved."*

The boxer analogy is *apropos*. Ann's anger would erupt into rages, wherein she would scream and verbally attack Mike. *"I would go months without really speaking to you,"* she says somewhat apologetically. *"I would be offended by something and in a rage and would literally go months . . . and I would forget what I was angry about."* Although Mike usually walked out, at times the two of them would get into shoving matches. The shoving matches never progressed to anything more violent, but it was disturbing to both of them.

Both agree that Ann's inability to make decisions, muddy thinking, and lack of manners were a greater concern in a foreign country than perhaps they would have been in the United States. She would readily argue with anyone of authority and on occasion was known to flirt with various of Mike's coworkers and colleagues. Michael's nanny, a patient woman who simply adored Michael, had taken over all outings and almost all at-home play. Although Ann played with Michael, she never realized that the nanny was supervising her behavior as much as she was supervising Michael. Between the nanny and Mike, Michael was a well cared for and happy child. Fortunately, their stay overseas was about to end.

By the time they returned to the United States, Michael was a talkative preschooler, Mike was near the height of his career—and Ann could barely get off of the airplane alone. Ann recalls Mike saying that he was *"close to divorce—that I was risking Michael's life."*

RESIDUAL RESOURCES: RELIGION, SURVIVORSHIP, AND TRUST

Mike explains that Ann was almost never alone with Michael. Although she was usually supervised by Michael's nanny, Ann's rage and anger had begun to flare out of control. Ann's eyes close while Mike talks about this time period. Mike remembers, *"I felt really beat. Remember, we're Catholic so I think that entered in to my thinking too. Plus,"* as they had reminded me earlier, *"it was a different time, a different generation. We did what we were told. We thought marriage was for good."* He laughs and adds, *"It* [the marriage] *was bad, but we thought it was good."* Ann seems to force a smile in response to Mike's comment about the marriage being bad, but thinking it was good. She does not correct him.

For many, the residual resources of commitment to marriage vows, to family, financial considerations, and religious mandates all intermingled with loving and liking their spouses. One spouse reflected, *"He provided very well, and I loved him and I still love him—there were some good things in our relationship, and there still is in that we balance each other out in different ways. He was an exciting kind of person to live with. I am more stable, more steady—so we balanced each other out nice in a lot of ways, and that worked."* Another spouse said, *"Well, I have to be perfectly honest—the main reason why this marriage didn't end was because of our religion: Catholic. That was so ingrained in me, that* [divorce] *was not part of it."*

What else held Mike and Ann together? In addition to the fact that they were Catholic and raised with the conviction that marriage is forever, they shared their status as survivors. As Ann explains, *"I didn't want us to be like my adoptive parents who lived with problems and went through months and sometimes years without speaking to each other and not working on anything. I didn't want that to happen. . . . We wanted something different. We're survivors, like I said. We wanted more than our parents had."*

Even though Ann eventually established a nurturing and supportive relationship with her mother, the losses she experienced as an infant and as a young girl make it impossible for her not to consider herself a survivor. Mike has never had a satisfying relationship with his family. In comparison to his siblings, both of whom live on the fringes of society, Mike is a survivor as well. The unfortunate circumstances of their early lives give Mike and Ann a unique bond. They understand difficulty and struggle. Thus, it is not surprising that Mike says that even when their marriage was bad, they thought it was good. In part, this may be an outcome of both of them having grown up in homes that, in many ways, did not provide comfort. Not having experienced comfort in their families of origin, they are less likely to know when that part of their lives is missing.

Mike and Ann also trust one another, and have since they met. Ann explains that trust from her point of view. *"Mike would never take advantage of me—and that was very unusual—almost all men I had known before I met Mike would lie to me . . . and he never had any of that quality."* In addition, they are both passionate, "spoiled," as they say, and volatile. They also shared interests—travel, study, and books. Finally, like most couples, they are united as a family by a shared devotion to their son.

Back in New York, Michael was enrolled in school and continued to do well. Like many alcoholics, Ann almost ceased to be a presence in the house. Her attempts to control her drinking were not successful. She and Mike settled into a yearlong period marked by increased drinking on Ann's part and greater distance on Mike's part. But, unlike previous years, when she would often retreat to her bedroom, she now ventured out of the house. Ann recalls, *"I was always out of the house—and Mike was very busy with the newspaper, too—seeing colleagues. There were always people coming through, and there was never any release from any of that. People from other countries, other papers—he'd be out at night through dinner."*

A FINAL NIGHT OF DRINKING

Ann's artwork, like everything else, had fallen by the wayside. Feeling the physical effects of excessive drinking as well as the distance between her and Mike, Ann thinks now that she saw the end of her drinking career coming.[4] She recalls one particular night of drinking that scared her enough to convince her that her drinking was a deadly problem. She had gone to a business dinner with Mike—the exact occasion, she doesn't recall. She does remember the following morning. She woke up in someone's car, on a street near Columbia University. She had no idea where she had been or who she had been with—if anyone.

Mike listens to this but looks a bit uneasy. It is my experience that talking about a very private matter in front of a stranger often adds to any sense of embarrassment or disbelief and to the realization of how bad things really were. He interjects with a hint of resignation and humor in his voice to clarify the situation for me, *"Like I said, it was bad, but we thought it was good."* Mike reminds me of how gradual the development of all of this had been. In a brief summary, it sounds dramatic, but over ten years or more, the drama was not so apparent to them.

RESIDUAL RESOURCE: ACCEPTANCE

Ann's description of Mike and herself as two boxers provides an image of the marriage from her perspective. I am struck by how Mike seems more or less to accept whatever Ann does—be it poor behavior, verbal taunts, or lack of responsible parenting. Among the couples I interviewed in which the wife was the alcoholic, it was striking how husbands tended to accept the situation more easily than wives accept their husband's alcoholism. Mike explains his feelings about Ann's long-term drinking: *"She had been drinking all along. It was more or less a given and to some extent had ceased to be a source of friction. I didn't like it. When she drank she felt it made her interact more effectively with people, but it seemed to me less effective. It interfered with our relationship as well as with other relationships we had. It's very difficult to communicate with someone who has had a lot to drink, and she was dependent on it. If we were in a place where she couldn't get something to drink, that clearly was somewhat of a crisis."* What did this do to Mike? *"Well, it left me to some extent retreating. I can, when I'm in a situation I can't handle, I can go off and get to work. . . . If we were losing it* [the marriage] *or whatever—but I could see she was drinking more and more."*

Mike's acceptance of Ann's drinking actually functioned as a kind of resource for them. It seems to have eliminated some of the buildup of anger and resentment that Mike might otherwise have felt toward Ann. This is not to endorse the idea that a spouse should offer a blanket acceptance of alcoholic behavior, but to acknowledge that in this case, what some might construe as "passive," "wrong," or as a symptom of "denial" probably held the Bertolinos together.[5] However, Mike and Ann share a similar past, a passion for their work and their opinions, interests in common, and concern for their son, Michael. In short, there was no indication that Mike and Ann still did not love each other, and love each other passionately. Whatever Mike's response was to Ann's drinking, it took shape, in part, out of the adoration he has for her.

BUILDING TRUST: ALCOHOLISM IS A DISEASE

I ask Mike about his own drinking at this point. *"I always felt that I didn't understand. There was always something that would tell me 'don't drink this drink.'"* If Mike was able not to drink, he was also able to understand some of Ann's struggle as well. *"Now cigarettes, I had an awful job stopping smoking, which I thought I would never do. I think if you put a box of chocolate candy next to me, I would finish it. I'm only saying this because it* [alcohol] *never had any control over me. When I could see Ann falling into this trap she was falling into, it was really discouraging."*

Like many spouses who learned that alcoholism is a disease, Mike was able to equate it with his own struggle to stop smoking and with his urge to eat chocolates. This provides an emotional "nerve" through which he can identify with Ann's struggle, with her addiction. Through identification, Mike is able to feel this nerve, to experience in some small way what Ann's struggle was like. Similar to both Peg Royer's and Cara Gunderson's ability to see alcoholism as a disease, Mike is able to equate it with his own cravings and tobacco addiction.

Ann returned to their apartment after waking up in the car at Columbia University. Scared, dirty, and confused, she somehow knew to call A.A. But she would not get sober for another year. Over the next twelve months, Mike and Ann remained distant, and their marriage became more verbally volatile than ever. Neither seemed to know what to do.

Ann attended A.A. meetings sporadically. She remembers attending a few meetings but little else from that year. Mike recalls that Ann *"raged"* at him, without mercy. In the midst of this, Mike was unexpectedly offered the opportunity to relocate to Philadelphia and work for a well-known publishing house that was expanding into a variety of areas. Growing tired of the newspaper business and the constant traveling that it required, he was ready to try his hand at something new.

"MY MARRIAGE IS HORRIBLE"

Within a few months, they moved. Ann recalls little of the move. For a brief period of time, she drank even more heavily. She recalls, *"I thought the marriage was pretty much over and this was the way it was going to be. I thought that the move here would perhaps change something, but I had no idea what or how. That year I had a lot of just kind of drinking disasters. I would drink with people I didn't like or even know—I didn't have my network of people who would take care of me* [like she did in New York]. *I was very frustrated, and I was extremely jeal-*

ous of Mike's network in the news business. He could just step out of one office and into another with interchangeable colleagues. Me, I had absolutely nothing. I had to start totally over." And, as an understatement: "*In hindsight, if I had gone into A.A. in New York I would have been further ahead.*"

They bought their current house in an upscale neighborhood near the historic district of Philadelphia. A live-in college student cared for Michael, who had started to show the effects from Ann's drinking and the moves by misbehaving. Mike worked long, hard hours, which kept him away from Michael much of the time. The transition from journalism to publishing was an unexpectedly difficult one for him. Having proven his skill in journalism, he was surprised by the anxiety he felt in having to prove himself again. In addition, Ann was miserable. "*I remember saying to people,*" she laughs, "'*my marriage is horrible, and my life is horrible.' All I could think of was I was horribly miserable. I walked around in my bedroom saying to myself, 'if you don't stop this drinking you are going to have to really go to A.A.'—a fate worse than death!*"

ANN: A MOMENT OF CHOICE

Michael's teachers began to call Mike at work to report that Michael seemed to vacillate between withdrawal and anger. They were also concerned that such a bright boy was struggling academically. Calls of this nature, combined with Michael's growing independence, scared Ann. "*I remember what happened the night before I went to A.A. Michael was in fifth grade, I think. I had just made this big pot of gazpacho, which I didn't really feel like making, but I made it any way. My idea was, well now I won't have to cook dinner tomorrow night. Then somehow I found out that everyone was going to be going out the next night—a meeting, a school play, I forget. So this particular night I was feeling put upon because I had made the gazpacho and it turned out they were both going out. I remember feeling absolutely . . . I was like in a rage and we were all in the kitchen . . . and I started screaming and yelling and probably hitting you.*" Ann looks directly at Mike. She stops speaking and shakes her head at the memory. Her voice rises, and she speaks as if this incident occurred earlier today. "*Michael was there, and I just felt like I wanted to take the pot of gazpacho and throw it through this plate glass window!*"

Ann points at the window behind her. Her arm is shaking and her cheeks are flushed. What, I ask Ann, was the rage? "*I was frightened. I felt so furious, I ran upstairs and slammed the bedroom door and went and sat in the shower. I just sat there and I remember sitting there thinking, this is immoral. This has to stop. Then I felt like . . . that it wasn't someone else's fault, that I was wrong, that I was wrong, that I was wrong to do this, and then I felt this wonderful feeling of calm. It was the wonderful thing that happened to me; this calm. And I knew that I wasn't going to get on with my life again unless I stopped drinking. I knew it, I just knew it.*"

After a moment's pause she continues. "*I remember feeling like there weren't any grown-ups in this house anymore. There were two kids, Mike and Ann, and no one to take care of them. I didn't know who I was. I had this sort of persona, but I remember one of my most horrifying experiences of drinking was of emptiness, as though I had no insides, virtually no physical insides."*

I notice that Mike is looking at Ann with what I can only describe as compassion. He says nothing. Ann entered A.A. the following day.

NOTES

1. Several alcoholics spoke of being overly shy and introverted. Shyness is considered one aspect or manifestation of shame. It can be as little as a bother or as great as a debilitating condition. In *Shame and Pride: Affect, Sex, and the Birth of Self*, D. L. Nathanson says of shyness: "It is a way of keeping a profile so low that no one can reduce it. It says to a world we see as probably shaming that we aspire to no height from which we can be dropped . . . shyness is shame instructed by fear" (1992: 329–330).

2. Some readers may be surprised at Ann's ability to function to the point of being admitted to graduate school while drinking heavily. In fact, it is not uncommon for alcoholics to lose friends and family because of their excessive drinking but maintain their work/career status.

3. Communication may well be the most overrated aspect of couple relationships. A disproportionate amount of time has been spent analyzing deficits in communication style and developing methods of communication skill training. The underlying problems in a marriage are rarely communication styles alone but are, more often, complicated and underlying forces. The emphasis on communication style is likely related to the fact that we can observe how people communicate. Unlike fears or loyalty to family of origin, communication style is more apparent and more amenable to intervention.

4. For details on the physical effects of excessive drinking, see the appendixes.

5. It is important to note that one could assign a pathological label to Mike. Some might label him as being in denial. Although Mike might benefit from exploring his relationship with Ann as well as his relationship with his parents, it is unclear that a label such as denial would be helpful.

Chapter 8

Getting Closer by Inches

All actual life is encounter.

—Martin Buber, *I and Thou*

Like many couples, Mike and Ann both agree that the changes were so gradual that it is difficult to untangle the threads of their life together, and more difficult to suggest a cause-and-effect relationship. Both agree that the first major change occurred in Ann.

Ann accepted A.A. wholeheartedly. Early in sobriety, she scheduled her days and evenings around meetings so that she could attend as many as possible.[1] She recalls that she attended for months without speaking up. Instead, she listened to the stories of others, each one containing a description that somehow sounded like her own experience, her own thinking, a version of her own life. She was able at last to begin to feel that a flicker of her center, or her soul, was finally coming to life. In addition to meetings, she slowly began to unpack her cameras and dabble in her old love—photography.

Most importantly, she started to get to know herself. *"Through A.A. I'm talking about to know yourself—to be honest about your imperfect humanity and your wants and your needs. To be open and honest even though you are uncomfortable. To let someone know you, rather than to be playing this role. One can't do that until one knows oneself, and you can't know yourself as defined by your role and by culture and by time—it takes a lot of inner work."*

BUILDING TRUST: "KNOW THYSELF"

Part of coming to life for Ann was finding the ability to accept her limits, to accept who she was, to not feel so defined by expectations (her own or others'), real or imagined. Although she feels it sounds a bit corny she began to like or love herself, perhaps for the very first time.

Several months after she had started going to A.A., Ann received a call from Michael's school. Their son had gone into another slump. Mike and Ann were in conflict over it. Eventually, Ann went to the school to speak with Michael's teachers. *"I went over to school and asked if Michael should go into therapy. They said 'no.' But I came home and thought, well, maybe Michael doesn't need therapy, but I do."* Soon afterward, Ann entered intensive therapy. At the same time, she began to read everything she could on psychoanalysis and psychotherapy, from Freud to Jung, to Carl Whitaker, to Abraham Heschel. Mike praises Ann in a deadpan voice, *"Ann knew more than Freud."*[2]

Ann loved therapy and was doing well in A.A. But, in the first six months of Ann's sobriety, Mike left for a business trip to Europe. During his absence, Ann decided to separate. Ann recalls wanting time alone, *"Just to think and work things out, to see whether I wanted to stay in Philadelphia. To just figure stuff out in sobriety."* Mike recalls, with little emotion, *"I had gone to Europe, and Ann didn't want to go. When I was there, she said she was moving out. When I got back, we just left it that when we wanted to see each other we would see each other. We essentially began dating—and that really put a new perspective on it."*

Ann needed time away from Mike to sort out her life, to devote more time to getting to know herself and Michael. She and Michael, now a sixth grader, moved into an apartment that was within a mile of their house. After Mike returned from Europe, they each spent time alone with Michael. This gave Ann the opportunity to spend time by herself and to focus some attention on Michael. Separated for almost a year, Mike remembers it as Ann's time for reassessing *"the whole thing. Remember, I hadn't had the same kind of trauma or transition or whatever you want to call it that Ann had. So I had been, you know, much more stuck in the rut."*

Mike supported Ann financially during their separation. Therapy forced Ann to face her sense of emptiness and the resultant repercussions. *"All that related to a terrible insecurity and a lack of connection to myself. That is what therapy has done for me. It's a very long, slow process with no quick fixes. In my case, I think my childhood experiences contributed to all this. All of this is a reflection of the terror I have always lived with, the absolute terror."* For her marriage, Ann believes that the therapy was essential. *"Only if you know who you are and have a sense of self, can you have a relationship."*

BUILDING TRUST: "HE LISTENED TO WHAT I SAID"

The separation gave Ann and Mike a chance to be together in a less intense way. *"During that year we'd talk, we would have dinner. I'd have him over to dinner with friends at my apartment.* [One day] *Mike said, 'I think we better decide now whether we are getting a divorce or whether we are going to try and put our marriage back together.' We decided that I'd move back into the house and we'd try it out."*

Ann remembers thinking only that *"Mike had changed a lot at that point. He really wanted to sit and talk. He listened to what I said."* Mike temporarily slowed down his career, his pace, and reached out to Ann. In addition to his continued financial support, he also listened to what she said and showed that he wanted to be with her. Ann clearly responded to his efforts to reach out to her. Much had changed, and quickly. Michael was doing better in school, and Ann felt better about herself and about her relationship with Mike. Because of these factors—sobriety, her own therapy, separation from Mike, and reading all she could on psychology—Ann came to the decision to return to school and complete her master's degree. She decided to get a degree in art therapy rather than a master's in fine arts, so that she could combine her interest in psychology with her love of art. She also felt that this would give her a career on which to focus. She chose to work with people having brain injuries, a choice she has been pleased with. Mike, as he always would be, was behind her the whole way.

BUILDING TRUST: "I'M NOT GOING TO BE AN APPENDAGE"

Ann is very clear that she was motivated to build her career largely by her own pain. *"I was very jealous,"* she recalls of Mike, *"because I felt I was working very, very hard, and no one was recognizing anything I was doing—no one. He was everywhere, and in great demand, and I was like an appendage. After I got sober, I decided, I'm not going to be an appendage."*

Ann did well in school, and her career itself has brought her a great deal of satisfaction. Her most important accomplishment came early in her first job. Seeing a void in children's literature, Ann wrote and illustrated a children's book on coping with a parent who has a brain injury. Mike recalls, *"By that time she had really come to grips with the whole problem and had really begun to change. She was better able to assert her own—who she was and what her needs were generally. In a lot of ways I had realized that I admired her a lot more because a lot of things she simply hadn't been able to do earlier. In the process, I got more interested in her as a person. Now she is less predictable. You know, a person is fairly predictable if you know that every evening they will be sitting around drinking. They are more or less out of it."*

With this, Mike runs up to the third floor once again, this time to get a copy of Ann's book. As he shows it off, he recalls his joy at again being able to discuss ideas with Ann. Instead of flippant, alcoholic responses, she could hold her own in an intelligent conversation. They started to see plays together, followed by tea and long discussions and debates similar to the ones of their courting days. Ann's opinions were insightful and often unexpected. Mike's pride in Ann's accomplishment is touching. I ask him to tell me about the book, and he hardly takes a breath before responding. *"She works in a field where there is practically no recognition, art therapy. I work in a field where there is a good deal of recognition. I get my name in print all the time! Well, she struggled with her ego or whatever, and eventually she wrote this book. She just stopped worrying about the lack of recognition or what people would think of it. She stopped worrying about whether it was going to be rejected. I think she had always thought of me as the verbal person, while she was the visual person. I was rather surprised when she decided to write a book. And, she wrote it! She sent it to a lot of publishers. It was rejected over and over and finally accepted by one, and now it has become a standard in the field."*

Ann believes that the book has changed their relationship. *"Partly, it seems like you* [Mike] *started to respond to me more as someone who had something to say. You started really talking about my accomplishment with other people. He tells people what I did, because I started doing something."*

Mike adds, *"I think it is in it's third printing, and she has a regular income from that book. That was quite a feather in her cap. That took overcoming her ideas of what her limitations were to do it. A number of things like that have happened."*

Doing significant things and being a more interesting person are partly the result of simply getting sober. The parts that do not necessarily come with sobriety are being able to assert one's own needs, knowing who one is, and knowing what one's ground is. These constitute a process of self-delineation. Although Mike feels that Ann had "*really come to grips with the whole problem,*" for Ann it was and is an ongoing process. In fact, Ann underwent intensive therapy for years.[3] Clearly, however, Mike could see that he benefited from Ann's hard work, from her no longer being an appendage.

For the first time in years, Mike and Ann felt the spark that had long been dampened by alcohol. As Ann recalls, *"We started communicating in a way we had not communicated in many years. It was fun. I started putting together workshops for art therapists, which took place outside of Philadelphia. Plus, my self-confidence and excitement about being a sober person came with a thrilling feeling that I was no longer sabotaging myself. I could build my career and my contacts. I took chances and I followed things through."*

For Ann, part of seeing herself more clearly is seeing that she is a separate, delineated individual. *"I remember Mike got these big cowboy hats on a trip, and I got real upset. Isn't that ridiculous, he's got these big cowboy hats. I'm thinking, I'm going to be so mortified walking down the street with him. My therapist said, 'What do you care if he has this big hat on—you're not wearing the big hat?' So it was that kind of thing."*

BUILDING TRUST: NO MORE PLEASING

In fact, it was much bigger than cowboy hats. *"Additionally, I stopped trying to please, to be somebody I wasn't. I had always had a hard time keeping up with the kind of life I thought Mike wanted, that I thought I was supposed to lead. I just couldn't do it. I just could not be the person I thought I was supposed to be."* Ann felt that her job was to be entertaining, to host the best and most elaborate parties to advance Mike's career. Recalling the way Mike's parents entertained, Ann felt that this was what would make Mike's career a success. With her ever-growing self-confidence and awareness of what she needed and wanted, this feeling of "keeping up" has largely disappeared. Like Cara Gunderson, who changed her political affiliation at Ken's whim, so too did Ann shift from trying to be what she imagined Mike wanted to being what she wanted to be. What Ann is describing is her own process of learning to be true to herself. She stopped offering to entertain Mike's clients and business associates on a regular basis and, instead, started to focus on her own work.

A MOMENT OF CHOICE: GIVING UP ANGER

What about the bad feelings, the anger that all of this happened? Ann stares out the window, momentarily lost in her own thoughts. *"I remember the anger. I don't remember exactly what the anger was for. Maybe everything, I don't know. But I do remember that at some point I realized I either had to give it up or we weren't going to go on. We couldn't go on like that."*

I ask her if this was a purely intellectual decision. Ann hesitates before responding. *"I just gave it up. I just don't have any. I just don't think anger is something that helps much."* This seems to be a test of will, or a turning toward what will ultimately heal. The options are limited. One can become a prisoner of rage and disappointment, or choose an alternative. I recall one alcoholic who described the near-diabolical force of rage: *"I was full of anger and rage and everything else. I was caught up in it. It's a whirlwind. I realized I had to work to get distance from it. It's a cancerous growth. It feeds on you—it's your being—and you're possessed by it."*

A cancerous growth seems an appropriate term for the kind of anger and rage many of these couples described. Rage is a common feeling of alcoholics as well as spouses. Its origins are many: withholding one's voice, habit, unaddressed childhood pain, and anger at time lost and time wasted because of alcoholism. The list could go on and on. The ability to make a conscious decision to "get a distance from it" or "give it up" is one of the more mysterious aspects of recovery, and one that was noted many times by the participants in the interviews. Perhaps it is related to being emotionally "up against a brick wall"—there simply is no place else to go. The only other possibility is to remain stuck in the "whirlwind" and be blown about by the violent forces of rage.

Similar to the exoneration that Cara Gunderson extended to Ken, this letting go of rage is a kind of self-pardon or self-exoneration. It seems to be necessary for many alcoholics, in particular, to move forward. The shame and remorse, the rage and the despair, will consume them if given the opportunity. Thus, once more, we find the moment of choice—the choice to release oneself from the shackles of the past. Ann's accepting this choice stands out in stark contrast to Dave Royer's continued anger at Peg for, among other things, not responding in the way he wished while he was in the rehabilitation hospital. Dave still speaks with great vehemence about what happened fifteen years ago during his hospitalization. His ongoing anger is a cancerous growth that envelops him and all but guarantees his and Peg's relational stagnation.

BUILDING TRUST: NO MORE PLEASING

Rather than simply trying to please Mike, Ann is able to identify what she needs to do for herself as well. Ann is now willing to entertain Mike's colleagues when she has the time, and in a manner in which she is comfortable. If Mike plans the meal and the get-together, then he is free to make the arrangements he likes. Ann attempts to be thoughtful of Mike's needs, while still considering her own needs. She no longer simply tries to please. According to Martin Buber, the sphere of relationships is made more problematic when people are compelled to please others and, in the process, deny their own needs. "Pleasing" is a form of "seeming." Buber claimed that living from "seeming" is false, a deceitful "foreground" that prevents us from being who we are and, thus, from ever being truly known to another person. If people are never known to one another, real relationship eludes them. They may live a life void of disagreement, but the risk is emptiness—a failure to really know how they themselves think, feel, and know, as well as the failure to really know another. Buber refers to this choice of "seeming" as the "essential problem" in human relationships. Furthermore, he suggests that giving in to pleasing or seeming is the coward's way, and resisting it is courageous.[4] Pleasing is a "dependency on, even an addiction to, external referents as the basis of one's internal terms. It is an abandonment of oneself as an equivalent referent in relating. Pleasing becomes seeming when it leaves out my claim to be and my willingness to disclose it."[5]

Ann's early life was a series of traumatic and irrevocable losses that left her untethered or, as she said, without a center. It requires a great deal to move beyond the apparent ease of pleasing to the difficult task of making a claim in one's own behalf. Returning to school, going after a career, planning for her own well-being, and getting and staying sober are all ways in which Ann grounds herself so that she can make claims for herself. Ann struggled and still struggles with her sense of not having a center. The ultimate loss of center for Ann would be for her to try to be what she thinks Mike needs in a wife rather than finding out who she is. Recall that Peg Royer was schooled to please as well. Feeling that her life is unfair, Peg comments that she is trying to do it all the way "*he wants it done.*" Her alternative, or at least the one she has been able to find, is to "*completely withdraw.*" Peg can identify no happy medium. Instead, she bounces between the two extremes: withdrawal and giving up her own terms. Neither end of the continuum makes room for her needs or for relationship-enhancing behavior. Also, recall Ken Gunderson silencing himself to "keep the peace," another form of pleasing. In all cases, these are, in Ann's words, behaviors aimed at being "the person I thought I was supposed to be." Each person attempts to be something for someone else and, in this process, diminishes his or her own life.

BUILDING TRUST: SEEING THE OTHER

Not only did Ann overcome her ideas about what her limitations were, in the process, Mike shifted his view of Ann. Rather than seeing her as a bit pathetic, out of control, and predictable as she had been, he started to see her as a talented, exciting person once again, the woman he thought he had married years before. *"I don't see her as an alcoholic. We talk about it to the extent that she goes to A.A. and then wants to talk about it. Like most people in A.A. she thinks of herself as a lifetime alcoholic, and I understand why, but it doesn't make me think about her as being an alcoholic in any sense except that sense. I think seeing her succeed has contributed to my not thinking of her as an alcoholic."*

Mike's simple but powerful comment may be at the crux of their relational change: to see the other person as a full human being, as who they are capable of becoming, rather than defining them by their limitations. For some couples, this vision of their spouse (usually the alcoholic) is the result of a dwindling but persistent knowledge of what a good person he/she was before alcohol took over his/her life. One spouse echoes this quite eloquently with these words: *"I'll tell you what's different. I see Hank much differently. No, I don't see him so much different—I knew he was a good, kind, gentle person—but when you are angry at someone, you lose sight of that."* Another said, *"We saw more of the real person. Not that the real person had all of the virtues we wanted them to have* [laugh], *but at least it was bearable."*

For some spouses, this change comes about almost serendipitously and not only through changes in behavior. One wife explained, *"I would see people from his meetings talking about how wonderful and sweet he is. I would think, God, he's this wonderful thing to all these people, and he really is."* One spouse spoke of his alcoholic wife this way: *"I think I see her as a much stronger person than I did before* [she got sober]. *But I also see the pressures that she has and her vulnerabilities—which either I just didn't see before or I didn't care about."* As she becomes more a partner to him, she is seen as more complex. Another alcoholic wife said that she was helped to see her husband in a different light through a psychological test. *"One thing that helped me, the Meyers-Briggs test. Really truly realizing Fred is a thinking type and I am a feeling type. Just knowing how difficult the clash of opposites can be in a relationship has helped."*

According to Nel Noddings, who has written extensively about the nature of caring in relationships, seeing other persons as they are and as they might be is a way of confirming those others. When confirmation is not forthcoming, the result is isolation. "To be talked at by people for whom we do not exist . . . throws us back upon ourselves. To be treated as "types" [alcoholic personalities] instead of individuals, to have strategies exercised on us, objectifies us. We become "cases" instead of persons" (text within brackets added).[6] Recall Dave Royer's comment about Peg being his maid and his own inability, and perhaps refusal, to see Peg as anything more.

In order to move toward relational growth, it is not enough to state who and what we are (self-delineation). There must also be an equal and opposite effort to see who the other person is. This movement is due consideration,[7] the other pole of self-delineation. Recall that the Gundersons spoke eloquently about finding their own voices, taking a stand, and knowing who they were within their relationship. The Bertolinos are speaking of seeking to know themselves and their spouse. They acknowledge, credit, and speak of seeing beyond the labels of alcoholic or alcoholic personality.

Self-delineation and due consideration form an "interhuman dialogue."[8] Rather than being psychological notions about individuals, self-delineation and due consideration are, by definition, relational. These terms describe the need to be a self separate from another (self-delineation) and to consider the viewpoint of the other (due consideration). Self-delineation and due consideration refer to entering into relationships while holding one's ground. If the other person's point of view is not seen and acknowledged, there is no real relationship—only individuals who fail to truly meet and know one another.

BUILDING TRUST: TAKING DELIBERATE ACTION

Mike's ability to see Ann differently has now reached the point that he doesn't even think of her as an alcoholic, except insofar as she attends A.A. meetings. When I ask Mike about the ways he changed, he is direct and self-assured. During the first three years of Ann's sobriety, he adopted the following approach: *"Among other things, part of it was the undoing of this pattern of retreat I built up while she was drinking. That was gradual of course. It was clear that if I wanted the marriage to continue, I'd have to make sure I spent time with her. So the first thing I did was get away from certain habits I picked up. Like reading the newspaper at the dining room table. I just didn't do that anymore. I realized if we wanted to be together at meals, I would just have to put the paper away."*

It is here that it becomes clear that Mike is not simply a passive bystander in the resurrection of his and Ann's marriage. He puts the marriage at center stage. Mike's self-evaluation led him to believe that change had to take place on both sides. In addition to not reading at the table, *"I make sure we have free time every evening. That's when, if we want to go do something, we go and do it. Because of that pattern* [his retreating], *she tended to spend a good deal of time doing her own work, and I was working seven days a week. The point is, that lasted all day, every day, till bedtime. Now, when we feel like taking a day off to do something, we do it."*

It is pertinent that Mike, early on in Ann's sobriety, took it upon himself to change some of his habits and patterns of behavior. When we reflect on this and the other couples in this study, what emerges from the stories of most of these couples is the willingness (as demonstrated by Mike Bertolino and Cara Gunderson), of both the alcoholic and the spouse, to take some "reading" of how each might need to change or how each might have contributed to the problems in the relationship.[9]

In addition to Mike's encouraging Ann's newfound abilities, she did something for Mike early in her sobriety that made him particularly grateful. A beloved friend of Mike's died unexpectedly and Mike was devastated. This friend had been a mentor, almost like a brother to Mike. He was the one person Mike could always depend on. Mike recalls of that time, *"We were at this point both caring for each other. Maybe that hadn't happened for a long time. It had been like one person caring and the other person joined in. I guess one of the things that is reciprocal is my wife respected my grief—and I felt that strongly. She was very present there. Both of us were at the same time doing for each other. It* [the relationship] *was never as bad after that."*

After so many years of Mike's caring for Ann and Michael, supporting the house, making certain that Ann was safe and that she could not harm Michael, Ann was finally able to offer care to Mike in the way and at the time that he needed it most. Slowly, their relationship was coming into balance. But some of these shifts came in some surprising ways.

BUILDING TRUST: ENTERING THERAPY

Unexpectedly, Mike decided to go into therapy himself when Ann was in her fourth year of sobriety. Interestingly, it is Ann who brings up this topic. Her voice is almost childlike, as she can hardly contain her enthusiasm. *"To me, what shifted was Mike admitting to himself that he needed help. Instead of acting the way he had for a couple of years, like he was just fine. I thought . . . there was an arrogance to him. I don't know what was going on, but I felt a kind of chip on his shoulder. So what shifted was that I felt that he had admitted that he needed help, and that was OK."*

Much as Mike had spoken with pride about Ann a few minutes earlier, Ann now spoke with pride about Mike. Ann looks to him, obviously awaiting his approval to go on talking about his own need for help. Mike raises his eyebrows to give her the go-ahead. *"About five years ago, Mike decided to see a therapist. He came home and he said he was going because he knew he needed help. I had always sort of hoped he would go to Al-Anon or something, but he didn't do that. Going to the therapist is the next best thing! It was the thing that helped us pull ourselves together."*

Ann admits that Mike's going to therapy helps her to feel that the entire burden of their past is not squarely on her shoulders. Rather than allowing Ann to feel that she is the only "flawed" or "inept" spouse in need of help, Mike is actively taking responsibility to improve their relationship. Mike, although reluctant to discuss this, admits that the therapy has been helpful. He sees it as a practical step. *"I guess we had just been through so much, I decided I needed help looking at my own life. It was very beneficial to me personally and also to our marriage. With the therapist, I was talking about the problems I had. So it wasn't the case of Ann and me, it was me talking. I had never talked about my problems. That was a very positive issue and I benefited from it, and subsequently, our marriage benefited from it."* When I ask him in what ways the marriage benefited, Mike smiles as if the answer is obvious. *"We stayed together. That in itself is an answer. I had never even looked at myself. I had never addressed any problems that I had, relative to my family, to growing up, to work. I am a better person to be around."* He looks at Ann, *"That's something that Ann told me."*

Ann smiles approvingly. When I again press Mike for details on the therapy, for the first time all evening he seems almost at a loss for words. *"There really were long-standing problems. They had to do with her role and how I push and dominate and things like that. We both wanted to make it work, so I really had to look at the whole thing and renegotiate and make considerable changes in my attitudes. We were both living on my income, and I think I felt for a number of reasons that had to do with assumptions about me, about being male, that I accepted. I always felt that meant that I should make most of the decisions. I was the one who pushed in that direction, and it took me a long time to learn that that isn't the way to maintain a good relationship with somebody."* Ann adds, *"He stopped trying to live up to this idea of what he should be, too—Mr. Hardy Person or something like that. He wasn't so defensive. Before, he would very easily take offense."*

One of the most important areas for Mike has been addressing his own tendency to *"take care of everything."* As the eldest child, he has always felt the need to make everything right. Ann recalls an incident a few years ago in Hawaii. They were at a resort hotel and Mike's brother and sister-in-law came to visit them. Ann recalls Mike getting very agitated, wanting everything to be perfect. *"I looked at him and said, 'It's not all your responsibility.' He looked at me and without a moment's hesitation yelled at me, 'Yes it is. It is all my responsibility!' Whenever something has to be done, he'll say 'I'll take care of it.' A lot of times when he says that, it is totally unnecessary. He jumps in to take care of things that don't need taken care of, and I wish he would stop. I often wondered, gee, if he does this at work, no wonder he's so overworked. If he's always volunteering to take care of things he doesn't need to be doing . . . so if there is a problem, the fastest thing that jumps into his mind is, 'I'll take care of it.'"*

Mike glares at Ann. She sheepishly admits that she too held unrealistic expectations of him. Unable to envision herself as a person with the capacity to create a life of her own, she made Mike responsible for everything. *"Well, I expected him to fix everything. He couldn't possibly do that, but I managed to think that it was all Mike's fault. Nothing was my fault. It was like being a kid and expecting your parents to take care of it—whatever it was. I feel like an adult now instead of a victim. I hardly ever feel like a victim."*

Mike's therapy, although brief in duration, led Mike and Ann to attend several sessions together for the specific purpose of learning negotiating skills. An example that they both laugh at is the number of open rolls of toilet paper in the bathroom. Mike wants only one open in the bathroom at a time; Ann prefers several open. Their compromise is to open two at a time. Mike says this is an *"acceptable compromise, not a happy compromise."* It is, however, a better alternative than years past when they would end up in what they describe as a "standoff," with neither one willing to compromise at all. Mike, in a serious tone of voice, adds, *"I would only accept one roll of tissue and she would only accept four or more. It was really asinine. We would deal with it by turning our heads and ignoring it. The difference is that now we've got this commitment to try and negotiate."*

In fact, they negotiate on many issues. The volatility of their relationship makes this an important skill for them, as the alternatives are prolonged conflict or silence. Both Mike and Ann seem embarrassed that they must work at a basic skill such as negotiation, yet both agree that learning to consider the other's point of view is essential.

Mike adds in a suddenly tense voice, *"If you* [Ann] *made up your mind about something, you were never going to change your mind. That I have learned. You never change your mind about anything. You're judgmental and absolutely unwavering. You can't deal with change unless you want to have some sort of irreconcilable difference. It would take something like brain surgery or something. If you have your mind made up about something, you've never given an inch, as far as I know."* The tension in the room is once again palpable.

Mike's diatribe is lengthy, but I let it go on, because I want to see what happens. As soon as he is done speaking, he says that he may have made Ann sound very *"difficult and intractable and judgmental, but she has had no easy life."* Ann concurs that she is not easy to live with, but she interjects with barely contained anger, *"I have always said that I work with brain-injured people and Mike has a social disability. Now we have the tools to work with. It has taken us where we are today and that's good."*

Mike looks exasperated but only sits back in his chair, quiet. As has happened throughout the interview, their caring and love are interspersed with sarcasm and anger.

NOTES

1. Newcomers to A.A. are encouraged to attend ninety meetings in ninety days.
2. Again, Mike praises Ann extensively, just as she praises him.
3. This was unusual among the people I interviewed, although therapy was not unusual.

4. M. Buber, *The Knowledge of Man: A Philosophy of the Interhuman* (New York: Harper and Row, 1965a), 77–78.

5. B. R. Krasner and A. J. Joyce, *Truth, Trust, and Relationship: Healing Interventions in Contextual Therapy* (New York: Brunner/Mazel, 1995), 49.

6. N. Noddings, *Caring: A Feminine Approach to Ethics and Moral Education* (Berkeley: University of California Press, 1984), 66–67.

7. I. Boszormenyi-Nagy and B. R. Krasner, *Between Give and Take: A Clinical Guide to Contextual Therapy* (New York: Brunner/Mazel, 1986).

8. J. Buhl, *Intergenerational Inter-Gender Voice: Shared Narratives between Adult Sons and Their Mothers: An Ethical Perspective* (Unpublished doctoral dissertation, University of Pennsylvania, Philadelphia, 1992).

9. The literature that is critical of the notion of codependency suggests that it inappropriately places blame on spouses. Although this is presented in the appendixes, it is important to note that regardless of how one feels about the notion of codependency, it appears that marriages in which there is relational growth are marriages in which there is some belief by both spouses that there is a need to change.

Chapter 9

Blessed in the Midst of Love and Regret

Sweet are the uses of adversity.

—William Shakespeare, *As You Like It,* Act II

As the interview neared its end, both Mike and Ann got more playful—their personal attacks an odd mixture of sharp daggers tinged with humor. Their years of struggle, their passion, and their dedication to one another, as well as their volatility, were always right on the surface. In thinking back on the thirteen years of her sobriety, Ann recalls her very first year. *"It was the beginning of a long road. We started to get close and enjoy a period of being comfortable—which I would say we are today. But we still struggle—it really is a very difficult relationship."* Mike nods his head in agreement. *"Marriage is . . . at least as far as I've experienced it, an extremely difficult struggle. I think it's very demanding. The problems and challenges change all the time. Our problems are so manifest and interesting."*

Mike still struggles to avoid taking responsibility for everything, and Ann has to remind herself that she does not have to be what she thinks Mike wants her to be. She can also walk beside him when he wears his cowboy hat, knowing that it is not a reflection on her. *"And you, Mike?"* I ask. Mike shakes his head and explains that it was Ann who was hurt by alcoholism. He bears no grudges. Mostly, he expresses his admiration for Ann's efforts to change and build a satisfying life. He feels that, for the two of them, the biggest challenge was getting reacquainted. *"It was more like dating. It took a lot for us to get to know each other. Getting to know each other, that is the hardest part."* Ann chimes in with a grin: *"What's your name?"* They both laugh. When I ask them what they wish could be different between them, Mike begins to explain, *"We go into long periods and not speak to each other."* Ann rebuts him. *"Miiike! It does not last for months—a couple of days."* Again, the volatility rises to the surface. Mike pushes his point: *"You know Ann. She goes on a long boil, and there is no getting her off it. That's what we learned the first night of our honeymoon, what I learned, anyway."* Ann, looking annoyed at Mike once again, responds, *"I take a long time to get over it, partly because there has been no sufficient expression of—no expression of sufficient remorse—an understanding of what happened."*

I ask Ann if she can give me an example of "insufficient remorse." She and Mike both break into a big grin. I feel like I am in the middle of a private joke and hope that they can allow me to understand its meaning. Ann tells me about Mike's doing yard work and ripping out a tree that he mistook for a weed. *"I wasn't angry about that. I understand he thought it was a weed, so I wasn't angry about that. I was angry about his attitude. You know, he said, 'It looked like a weed.' There was no expression of remorse, and that's what got me real angry."* I ask Mike if he has done this yet, and Ann jumps in to respond. *"No, but I'm alright with that. So there is a concrete example of my being better, and there hasn't been any expression of remorse at all. I knew that would happen. I really should have told him that that was a tree. So that's good, it's a concrete example of having come a long way. That I was able to live without getting any kind of apology."* And the tree is? I joke. Mike and Ann respond in unison: *"Gone."* We all smile even though the story is more poignant than humorous; more painful than redemptive. But it is also a clear window into their world—a world that is a series of contradictions, of herculean efforts, of passion and volatility.

What, I ask them, is good about their marriage? Mike responds: *"We're getting better about that. We know what is crucial. I think we are more aware of where the problems are going to arise. When I am ready to travel, I get very difficult and sort of hyper and fussy, not fit to be with. I think we work around those kinds of things. We recognize stressful periods more or less involuntarily—we're a little more conscious, a little more on good behavior. Over the last ten years, the good periods have been increasing in frequency and longevity. I realize some things we've been trying to solve are not going to be solved. We put them into their proper perspective."* He hesitates for a moment and then reiterates his earlier comment. *"I do think relationships are very difficult. We are both very intense people. What has made the difference for me is I am learning about myself."* He hesitates again and then adds, *"We're getting closer by inches."*

Ann nods in agreement. It is easy to understand that Mike's and Ann's backgrounds left them with limited "knowledge" or examples of how to be in a carefree relationship. Their comments about the difficulties and challenges of relationships highlight the tremendous effort and strength it takes for them to be a couple, to make it work.

Ann: *"One thing, Mike has always been enormously supportive of me in any endeavor. The least little thing I do well, he is so full of praise. He is so nurturing and supportive."* Mike smiles. He appreciates and responds to Ann's praise of him. Mike adds, *"We've had a very interesting life—the things we've done and places we've been. Ann's own peculiar situation and my own peculiar situation—my career, job, family."*

Ann adds, *"There is always a slight residue. You can't do away with that. I think living with that remorse is probably part of getting sober too. It's just there. Remorse is probably a good word, sorrow, regret for time lost and damage done. There is just loss and regret all around, and maybe that is part of the human condition too. I think alcohol sort of crystallizes the human condition. We all, alcoholic or not, do or say things we regret. Alcohol sort of throws a very harsh light on all of it."* Ann looks down at her hands folded on the table. She recalls a story, which to this day makes her wonder what it has all really meant for her son. *"We were driving to the mall or someplace. Michael was in about ninth grade, and he was in a health class on drugs and sex, or something like that. I knew that the class was very detailed. They brought in speakers and really did a good job of educating these kids about alcohol and other drugs. I was wondering what it was like for him knowing his mother was in A.A. and listening to all of the antidrug talk. We were talking, and it was nice. I asked him if, in all of these discussions he or any other kids whose parents were in the program, and I knew there were a few others with parents in A.A., if they ever spoke up and said anything about that. Michael looked at me as if I was crazy. And I'll never forget what he said. He said, 'Are you nuts? They think that anyone who is an alcoholic is a bum or something.'"*

Ann looked at her hands for several more seconds. In the car that day with Michael she was unable to say anything more. Michael's words had silenced and pained her. This was a part of the remorse and shame that she carries. Today, she and Michael talk about A.A. and her years of drinking, but only in a limited way. Michael claims not to remember it, not to feel resentful about Ann being absent from his life in his early years. A quiet young man now, he calls Ann and Mike regularly from his work in Nevada and spends holidays with them. They talk on the phone once every week or two. Ann adds, *"I told him you were coming here tonight. He thought that was neat. I feel that the topic is as open as he wants it to be. I can't imagine not telling him things. Mike was remarking today that the past few months, Michael has been calling more and sounds happier."*

Ann smiles with a satisfied look. *"He wrote me a note on a mother's day card that he feels our relationship is so much better now, that he feels better coming home. He thinks we have more fun together—which is true."* She bites her lip as if she is not certain she should keep speaking. And then, again in a very soft voice, she says, *"I am sometimes overwhelmed with this sense of fatigue. There's no way to make up for what went on fifteen years ago. I don't know what to do with that."*

Mike, looking calmer and responding to Ann's expression of her own remorse, responds, *"What a tragedy it would be if she got sober and we couldn't handle that. It would be awful, because that would be the thing that would be the tragedy. To go through something like this is kind of a—death. And to be resurrected, as it were, and then not to have your marriage survive. That is just a horrible irony. What a great—irony is not enough of a word—it's a travesty. I mean that is the thing, you know. God, to go through all that and then not have Ann would be awful. I think we have been very lucky in our lives, really."*

Ann speaks for the last time before I turn the tape recorder off. *"Now, we have a very simple life together . . . we're very happy just sort of sitting and enjoying our house, walking, meeting for coffee, talking about stuff. . . . We've been very blessed. I truly think our marriage has become something wonderful, with plenty of conflict. Now, we accept our relationship—problems and all. I think we're very committed and we always loved each other, no matter what. We encourage each other, 'Go ahead, you can do it!'"* And then she adds once again, *"We're survivors."*

I drive the city streets feeling an odd combination of high and low. High because I feel that I have just heard a very loving exchange, because they are resolute in their commitment to one another. Yet I feel low because their childhood difficulties seem to persist in their lives today. Unlike many of the couples I interviewed, Mike and Ann engaged in frequent flashes of anger and accusation, but were equally passionate with their praise for one another.

Their verbal dueling cut each of them to the quick, and, at times, seemed particularly cruel. Gottman, in his study of marriage types, states that volatile couples tend to be open with their feelings—both positive and negative. It is this openness and volatility that fuels both the romance and the battles.[1] Yet, for all of the difficulty, it is also an invigorating and wonderful relationship. As Mike says, they are very lucky.

Mike and Ann have a stable but volatile marriage that has endured the ravages of alcoholism. Yet, they provide us with so much more to think about. They are also survivors. In fact, it is their difficult pasts that function as a resource for them. They are determined not to repeat the pain of their own childhoods and to build a more balanced and rewarding marriage than those of their parents. This determination to survive was strengthened by their religious faith, Catholicism, which makes divorce an unwanted outcome. Their commitment and love are also supported by the fact that during Ann's drinking, Mike accepted this as a fact of the relationship. Although some may call this codependency, for Mike and Ann it functioned as a relational resource to keep them together. This should not be interpreted as support of such a position but only as acknowledgment that, in their case, it held them together through thick and thin.

Mike and Ann were also helped by Mike's ability to identify with Ann's struggle by relating it to his own struggles with tobacco and chocolates. This served to make Ann's situation more understandable to him. Rather than see Ann as something or someone altogether "other," or as a "volcano," as Peg Royer sees Dave, Mike was able to see her in a more compassionate and humane light. Mike's comparing Ann's alcoholism with his own struggles makes her seem more like him, instead of less like him.

The overall result of this ability is that each can see the other person in his and her complexity—the strengths, the weaknesses, and the possibilities. Despite all of these resources, Mike and Ann grew more distant as the drinking continued and the years marched on. Although Mike never expressed the loss of trust or despair that many spouses talked about, there was clearly a reduced connection between them. What has helped then to reconnect and bridge this distance to fortify the trust between them?

Certainly, Ann's sobriety is a major factor. Beyond that, trust was strengthened by therapy, from which each claims to have benefited. One positive effect for Mike was the opportunity to look at himself in a way he had never done before, to address his tendency to always feel responsible for everything. Therapy along with A.A. enabled Ann to stop trying to please Mike at her own expense, to carry out her decision not to be simply an appendage, and to give up her rage.

Similar to Cara Gunderson, who looked to her own behavior for clues as to how to improve her marriage, Mike identified some simple ways that he could improve the marriage. His decision to no longer read the paper at the dinner table is one such example of a spouse's ability to evaluate his or her own behavior and make changes that embrace the relationship.

Like Cara Gunderson, who is a realist, Ann notes that she and Mike accept their relationship, problems and all. Ann would like Mike to express remorse over the tree, but she accepts that he will not. Mike and Ann continue to struggle with their difficult and volatile relationship. Yet, rather than harp on the problems, they whittle away at them. They believe they have a very rewarding and cherished "good enough marriage."[2] Mike and Ann work diligently on their marriage. This work is not so much a search for perfection or for dramatic breakthroughs as it is an attempt to move "closer by inches"—volatility and all.

NOTES

1. J. Gottman also states that volatile couples tend to see themselves as equals, both consider themselves analytical, and they "leave no hurt unstated." Their marriages are passionate and exciting. Yet they are also at risk for overstepping boundaries to the point that quarrels consume the marriage. J. Gottman (with N. Silver), *Why Marriages Succeed or Fail* (New York: Simon & Schuster, 1994), 43.

2. According to M. Karpel, a "good enough" marriage is a couple relationship in which both partners find relative contentment. They are able to define their relationship in a way that is comfortable for them until the time comes when that definition must be changed. A good enough couple has a healthy balance between togetherness ("we") and autonomy ("I").

M. A. Karpel, ed., *Family Resources: The Hidden Partner in Family Therapy.*

Part IV

The Abbotts: Victim, Victimizer, Victory

On entering into family life he saw at every step that it was not at all what he had imagined. At every step he felt as a man might feel who, after admiring the smooth, cheerful motion of a boat on the water, actually gets into the boat himself. He saw that apart from having to sit steadily in the boat without rocking, he also had to keep in mind, without forgetting for a moment where he was going, that there was water beneath his feet, that he had to row, that his unaccustomed hands hurt, and that it was easy only when you looked at it, but that doing it, though it made you very happy, was very hard.

—Leo Tolstoy, *Anna Karenina*

Chapter 10

Exquisitely in Love and Balanced on the Knife's Edge

Luke and Jan Abbott
Married thirty-one years; three children
Luke: fifty-two years old, history department head, St. Stephen's Academy, a private religious high school; sober twenty years
Jan: fifty years old, retired school librarian
Children: Elyse, twenty-nine (teacher); Katherine, twenty-eight (artist); Daniel, twenty-six (graduate student).

It is July. The drive to Baltimore takes longer than the usual hour and a half; everyone, it seems, is headed to or from a vacation. I met the Abbotts in an unlikely way. In my attempt to recruit couples, I made cold calls to organizations listed in the Philadelphia yellow pages under "alcoholism treatment." One such attempt put me in touch with a volunteer who suggested I interview her good friends in Baltimore, Jan and Luke Abbott. After the exchange of telephone numbers and phone calls, I spoke with Jan and Luke. We chose to get together on what turned out to be one of the hottest days of the summer.

Jan and Luke's neighborhood is a development of middle-class, two-story homes, which appear to be about forty years old. The trees are stately and the lawns manicured. Jan and Luke's home is a traditional Cape Cod backed up against a ravine. Jan greets me in the driveway with a handshake, her left hand full of weeds from the flower garden, which lines the driveway.

Her voice is soft with a slight accent I cannot place. She is my height, about five feet six inches, but thinner and somewhat muscular looking. Her hair is short, exposing a pair of beaded earrings reminiscent of the 1970s. Her blue jeans and pink cotton T-shirt seem to hang on her sinewy frame. I know from my initial telephone contact with them that Jan is an avid tennis player. Her movements are smooth, coordinated, and controlled.

After Jan tosses the weeds into a cardboard box by the front door, we enter the air-conditioned comfort of their home. While Jan gets Luke, I note that the meticulous exterior of the house contrasts with what appears to be "organized disorder" on the inside. Both the living room and the dining room are piled high with stacks of magazines, newspapers, catalogues, and mail. There are multiple pairs of shoes on the tile floor of the entryway as well as unopened mail and a box delivered by UPS that also appears to be unopened. The dining room table is stacked with dishes, more books, and some clothes. Much of the furniture is antique, a mix of styles, materials, and time periods. Later, when we take a coffee break, Jan refers to their furniture style as "early American poverty." I guess that the pieces are from different relatives, as there is no apparent logic or order to the variety. A set of French doors leads from the dining and living rooms to an enclosed porch. There is light coming from that room, although for the moment my eyes rest in the darkness of the entryway and the hard, cool look of the tile floor, which offers a welcome reprieve from the blistering heat outside.

Luke appears after a few moments. Like Jan, he has a slight accent, but his is clearly southern. Of medium height and build, he does not share Jan's erect posture. His shoulders curve in a bit, and his shirt is pulled tight at the buttons. His wire rim glasses are bent the slightest bit up on the left side; his hair is a mass of gray curls jutting out in all directions. He doesn't shake hands, but makes eye contact, says "Hello," and then indicates that we should move to the porch.

The porch, a recent addition, runs along the side of the house. The walls are a soft lavender, and the furniture, white wicker. A blue and white Chinese vase on a corner table overflows with flowers. Unlike the living room and dining room, the porch is very neat. In one corner is a four-foot ficus tree and in another, a cushion holding their black cat, Tamerlane. Tamerlane takes a look around the room when we enter, but other than that, never moves a muscle.

Both ends of the room have floor-to-ceiling built-in bookshelves. Yet what is most striking is the view from the picture windows, which face into the ravine and overlook the garden. It is when I comment on the garden that Luke becomes livelier and a bit friendlier. He describes how the garden had always been Jan's hobby. In recent years, as he watched her transform it from a perfectly attractive backyard to a wonderland of fragrance, color, and texture, he became increasingly intrigued. In particular, he loves the hydrangeas. Lining the yard are twenty-seven different types of hydrangea, each chosen for its particular characteristics. Luke pulls several books off of the shelves—all books about hydrangeas—and he explains that, as a history teacher, he has developed a side interest in the history of gardens and garden design. In fact, he and Jan will travel to Europe with a group of students next spring to visit famous historical sights, including some gardens.

As Jan enters the room, she smiles when she realizes that Luke is talking about gardens. She shakes her head and suggests that I should have come for the entire day because Luke can go on about hydrangeas for hours. She then explains with a laugh that she does all of the dirty work—the weeding and planting—while

Luke sits inside in the comfort of the air-conditioning and reads so that he can tell her how to do what she's been doing on her own for years. They smile at one another, seemingly to acknowledge the truth of Jan's comment. Their interaction is easygoing. After a few more moments of chatting, we get started. Each of us is comfortably seated in one of the wicker chairs cushioned by overstuffed purple pillows.

THE INTERVIEW

Luke's Childhood: Middle-Class Privilege

Luke grew up in Charleston, South Carolina. His parents had come from poor but stable families. His father's family were poor but loving "dirt farmers." With twelve brothers and sisters, Luke's father, Frank, joined the Navy to escape the poverty of rural Georgia. His mother, Leeta, was the middle of three children. Like Luke's father, she was also born and raised in the South. When Leeta was about three her father abandoned the family and was never heard from again. Leeta's mother reared the children alone by taking in sewing, laundry, and lodgers. A strict woman, Leeta's mother stressed education and making a better life for yourself. As soon as Leeta graduated from a local teacher's college, she left the rural poverty so familiar to her for the "big" city of Charleston. It was there that she met and married Luke's father, who had recently returned from his stint in the Navy.

Through hard work (and aided by a booming economy), Luke's parents built a solidly upper-middle-class life for Luke and his older brother, Jed. Leeta taught in public school, while Frank went into business for himself. An unassuming man with the soft drawl of the South, Frank was successful and built up a thriving home contracting business. Relying on a small pension from the Navy, Leeta's salary, tight budgeting, and Frank's eventually successful business, they prospered.

Just as Leeta was, Luke and Jed were encouraged to "better their lot in life" through education, saving, and planning for the future. Unlike many of their friends, they traveled during the summer months—mostly to visit relatives. Luke recalls that his mother used these trips to remind him and Jed of their privileged life and of the need to get a good education so that they would never end up taking in lodgers like her mother had done.

Leeta and Frank were and are devoted to one another and to Jed and Luke. It was clear that Leeta ran the house. She was always convinced that she knew best. Jan and Luke recall with both humor and a touch of incredulity a recent visit with Luke's parents in which Leeta stated emphatically that she simply could not understand why anyone would want to live a life any different from her own! In fact, Luke and Jed learned at an early age to toe the line and not question their mother's opinion. They did it Leeta's way or not at all.

Luke acquiesced; Jed, his brother, rebelled. An artist and free spirit at heart, Jed found Leeta's dictates too constrictive. Jed dropped out of college and married a woman ten years older than he. He was nineteen at the time. Luke took a completely different path, one that guaranteed Leeta's approval: academics. Leeta and Frank's belief in education meant that Luke received constant praise and encouragement for his academic success. Unlike his brother, who seemed to hear the beat of a different drummer, Luke did what his mother expected and more. An honors student throughout school, Luke's educational achievements were always center stage. In the early days of Luke's sobriety he confided to Jan that his secret fear as a child was of waking up one morning having lost his ability to think, to do well at school. He would then be an empty shell. Totally tied to his identity of being smart, Luke defined his worth by how well he performed academically.

As his brother was dropping out of college, Luke was accepted at a prestigious college that would take him hundreds of miles away from home and into Jan's life. He recalls that he wanted to get as far away from his parents and family as possible. Why? Jan tells of recently unpacking boxes they stored in their basement for many years. One box was full of the letters Luke sent his parents from college. All of the letters were apologies—for why Luke hadn't written, why he wasn't going home for holidays, why he hadn't called. Luke's explanation: It was easier to apologize than to discuss, so he apologized over and over again.

More than a thousand miles north, in a small town in Maine, Jan grew up surrounded by cousins, aunts and uncles, and the beauty of nature. Today, she and Luke maintain a cottage that they hope to winterize for their retirement on the family property. She recalls her early childhood as being nearly idyllic: family picnics, long hours of ice-skating, sledding, and reading by her favorite pond. As she approached adolescence, however, she started to understand another side of her home life.

The youngest of four children, Jan now believes that she was practically destined to marry an alcoholic. Jan's parents, Stella and Earl, were married young. She has little memory of her father. Earl was an alcoholic who abandoned the family when Jan was a toddler. Fortunately, they lived among relatives and in a close community where people cared for one another, so the effects on her at that time were minimal.

Because Stella was a housewife, she had no means of supporting Jan and her siblings. *"My mother took my siblings and me home to her family. Her father was a full-blown alcoholic, and my grandmother was very ill from the effects of alcoholism. My mother was the typical daughter of an alcoholic. All of this stuff got passed on to me. She was a very passive person—she would not make waves, she would do anything to avoid an argument. Basically, she would never defend herself or what she thought. We more or less adopted this behavior."* Stella's father, Jan's grandfather, was financially comfortable and willing to care for his eldest daughter and her children, but he was also domineering. He told Jan's mother what to do and when to do it. As Jan got older she realized that there was a tradeoff: Accept the financial support in exchange for going along with her grandfather's rules and regulations.

On the surface, Jan's life was much as it had been before her father left. There were still family outings, the comfort of money and food, and lovely sylvan surroundings. But behind it all was an unspoken mandate to keep silent. *"We looked like we were perfect, but there was a lot of imperfection there, and that's more or less what I grew up with."* Although Jan felt the tension acutely, it was never directly addressed. She never heard the word *alcoholism* and never concluded that that was a primary cause of her uneasiness. In fact, as the youngest grandchild, she was spoiled by her grandfather and loved him dearly. Rather than see the alcohol or her grandfather as problems, she eventually identified her mother's behavior as the problem. This is not uncommon in families where alcoholism is present. Children often blame the nonalcoholic parent (in this case, Jan's mother). Like Peg Royer, who has mostly fond feelings about her alcoholic parents, Jan was quite fond of her doting grandfather. Just as the alcoholic can be the source of trauma and pain, he or she can also be the person remembered for his or her laughter and sense of fun and excitement.

Jan, her siblings, and her cousins provided a support network for one another, and today they still maintain close relationships. Although she sees the harm her mother caused her, she understands it in the light of her knowledge about alcoholism. It is a deep sadness for her. At the same time, she is grateful that she had a stable childhood. Her grandfather sent her and each of her siblings to college—a gift for which Jan feels immensely grateful. Stella never really escaped her father's dominance until she remarried while Jan was in college.

Jan's relationship with her siblings is primarily one of friendship and support. They stay in touch and visit often. Jan feels that her brother suffered most by the disappearance of her father and her grandfather's subsequent heavy-handed control, but even he benefited from the loving community and extended family within which they grew up. Each summer, they all return to Maine to spend the first two weeks of August together.

Unlike Jan's grandfather, Luke's parents drink only socially, and in limited, appropriate amounts. Luke grew up without being exposed to alcoholism. His parents kept liquor in the house for company, but Luke has no memory of ever drinking it. His early drinking was mostly social and not very dissimilar from the drinking of his friends, none of whom from that time in his life, were alcoholics.

Jan and Luke met while at college. Although Luke was two years ahead of Jan, they were soul mates, best friends. Life was pretty much ideal. Both were supported by their parents at a prestigious liberal arts college on the East Coast. Both were academically successful, outgoing, popular but down to earth, and believed by friends and family to be "made for each other."

Like their classmates, they drank at parties and occasionally at a local bar. As did many of the other couples interviewed, they did what was socially acceptable, and never gave it a second thought. Yet Jan, like Cara Gunderson, admits that she should have realized something wasn't quite right. In Luke's last semester, as they sat in a local college bar and contemplated living apart, Luke asked Jan to buy him a drink. She agreed and when she returned to their booth, Luke gulped the drink and then proposed to her.

Marriage: Drawn Together

That spring, Luke graduated with a degree in history and accepted a position teaching middle school in a nearby town. He and Jan married in August at Jan's family's home in Maine. It was a hot and humid day, not dissimilar from the day of the interview. Luke's parents were pleased. They felt that Jan was steady, a calming influence on Luke. Jan's mother and new stepfather, on the other hand, seemed concerned about the relationship. Although they liked Luke because he was articulate and bright, they didn't quite trust his excitability and what they saw as his efforts to control Jan. They thought Jan was too young for marriage, but Jan recalls feeling very grown up and not understanding her parent's concerns. Now she feels that their wariness was right on target. *"I think Luke was looking for something and I was looking for something. Maybe I was looking for the father figure I never had. I think there are certain personality traits that draw people together."*

Their life consisted of get-togethers with friends, Friday night spaghetti dinners, late-night movies on television, sharing opinions on books they had read, and, when they could afford it, a movie out followed by a cheeseburger and French fries at the local diner. Often they shared a bottle of wine, but nothing in excess. Luke describes their early relationship in this way: *"I just had this very comfortable person I was married to. We enjoyed each other, but there was a certain sick attraction. Jan was an over giver. I was an over taker. We fit together like a lock and a key."*

Jan continued in her undergraduate studies—a decision that pleased her family. As a junior, she decided to major in library science so that she would have a job when she finished college. She loved books so her choice of career was fitting. Her grandfather continued to help out with her tuition, although she and Luke managed to pay most of it. Jan took a part-time job in the college library to cover their day-to-day expenses. Luke's paycheck covered the big items such as rent and tuition. Jan describes these early years of marriage with enthusiasm. Of Luke, she says, *"He was fun to be with, and he was affectionate and attractive."* They talked books and big ideas. Jan's life was largely content and unremarkable.

Luke taught middle school and hated it. He recalls that it made him feel completely inept. He can smile at it today, but at the time, it was a painful experience. His sense of ineffectuality undermined his self-confidence. He recalls that his unhappiness led to an increase in his drinking. It was mostly controlled—a glass of wine or beer at night, a half bottle perhaps, often after Jan had gone to bed. No longer limited to social situations, Luke's drinking became a private matter. The more inept he felt about his work, the more he drank. The more he drank, the harder it became to keep up with the never-ending flow of homework to be graded, lesson plans to be written, and tests to design and score. But keep up he did, hating every minute of it.

Luke's teaching had the benefit of prompting him to apply to graduate school in history the following year. He knew that he would succeed *as* a student, not *teaching* them. Luke also knew that he could not survive another year like that first one. He fondly recalls that in those days, graduate students had paid teaching fellowships. Besides, he and Jan were already poor, so Luke's return to school had little impact on their financial security—or lack thereof.[1]

The Black Cloud above Us

The following fall, the start of Jan's final undergraduate year, Luke began graduate school at a nearby university. For the most part, life looked remarkably unchanged from the year before, except for the fact that Luke was much happier. In fact, he was downright enthusiastic and driven. The university gave them ample financial aid, including all of Luke's tuition.

Jan was busy with her own classes and a part-time job in the library. She recalls that at about this time, she started to feel some distance from Luke. She dismissed it as his anxiety about doing well in graduate school and her oversensitivity. Still a student herself, she couldn't fault him for feeling pressured.

What made her feel uneasy? Although Luke was happy to be out of the middle school "prison," the pressure to perform as a graduate student was extreme. He devoted all of his time to his schoolwork. It seemed excessive to Jan, but she had no way to judge. She had noticed that his late nights of study usually included wine or beer. Socially, they continued to see friends, and overall she felt good about the relationship. By the end of this second year, Jan believes she saw a change in Luke's behavior. There was a tension in his usual good nature, which concerned Jan.

Throughout this phase of their marriage, and then later as Luke's alcohol consumption escalated, Jan and Luke, like Ken and Cara Gunderson, developed healthy sides of their relationship. If this development did not transpire, more marriages affected by alcoholism would probably end in divorce. In fact, most alcoholics continue to live in intact family situations. The alcoholism is not enough to lead to automatic expulsion from the family.[2]

Jan had the beginnings of a career, a nearly complete college degree, and a husband who loved her. Luke was pursuing his dream of studying history, and they hoped to have a family. They had not yet attained the white picket fence, but that was just a matter of time. Yet the black cloud was a foreshadowing of a brewing storm, which was increasingly difficult for Jan to ignore.

Behavioral Directives and Practicing to Deceive

The year following Jan's graduation, she was employed by the local public library. Luke continued in his pursuit of his master's degree. In addition, they awaited the birth of their first child. Everything they had hoped for was coming to pass. But more so than in the previous year, Jan felt Luke's distance very keenly. She became acutely aware of the tension between them. She recalls one very disturbing incident in about the fourth month of her pregnancy. Headed to a party to celebrate the publication of a book by a good friend and the friend's coauthor, Jan felt the need to warn Luke to be careful not to drink too much. Luke recalls, *"Jan would launch into this long list of behavioral directives, of what to do. That got to be real common."*

Jan knew from experience that parties were occasions when Luke would drink excessively, and, more and more, he would make a fool of himself. As it turned out, this party was no different—except that things escalated to a more embarrassing point than usual. The coauthor was a prominent young physician and researcher. Jan recalls that his very stature seemed to incite Luke to belligerence. Luke, eloquent when drunk, proceeded to insult this poor physician without mercy: Luke suggested that the physician wrote books to make up for his failure as a doctor. Unlike get-togethers with college friends, who enjoyed and encouraged Luke's verbal agility, the physician was insulted. The young doctor turned to his coauthor, the friend who had invited Jan and Luke to the party, and asked sarcastically, *"Where did you dig this guy up, anyway?"*

Luke cringes as Jan recounts this. He has only vague recollections of the specifics of what he said at that party. He recalls only that he knew he had done exactly what he set out to do—to insult this physician—in no uncertain terms. Jan, on the other hand, recalls most vividly her anger and embarrassment. Even today if she thinks about it, those feelings can be tapped.

Incidents such as insulting the physician, a wild drunken ride home from another party, as well as other misadventures, began to force a wedge between Luke and Jan. From Jan's point of view, Luke was becoming a different person. From Luke's point of view, he was so stressed, so pressured, that he just needed Jan's understanding, not her criticisms or directives. With no let up in the pressure he felt, Luke began to further isolate himself from Jan. *"I was very cool and very aloof. I just kept everything bottled up inside—pressure, anxiety, how to support a family, how to get through school—all of it. I would practice to deceive, and I stayed very self-contained. Jan is an incredibly able person. She was always so able to deal with life."*

Jan moves her head slightly, her beaded earrings shimmering as they catch the light through the window. The signs of alcoholism were amply clear for many of the couples, and yet they themselves could not comprehend what was happening. Why? The usual description of alcoholism is that it is a "disease of denial." Ramona Asher notes that wives of alcoholics go through a predictable process of change in their self-definitions.[3] She identified four phases through which wives of alcoholics pass. The first phase, the early problem phase, involves sporadic questioning by the spouse and the normalizing of deviant behaviors. Luke's behavior at the party serves as an example. Jan "chose" to see the incident as a result of pressures and stress and typical of the more exaggerated behavior she often saw when Luke drank around friends. Asher notes that there is not a sudden early-stage "ah-ha" experience for spouses in which they note, acknowledge, and address the alcoholism, but rather a protracted period of interpretation, reinterpretation, and small awarenesses that build to the eventual acceptance that this person is an alcoholic. "A key struggle and challenge in the moral career of becoming the wife of an alcoholic is to sort out, sift through, and arrive at views of selves and situations among competing and changing definitions."[4]

It is easy to hear such competing definitions: Luke was interesting and fun to be with, yet he was becoming more tense. They had a full life with friends and soon, children, yet Luke started to withdraw and cut Jan off. As Luke's drinking escalated, Jan had to continually adjust her view of reality. She now says, as she and the other spouses did, that she/he *should* have seen it, *should* have known what was going on, *should* have been quicker to put two and two together. As Cara Gunderson said, *"I wasn't dumb."* With Luke, his early drinking was not "alcoholic" per se: He drank socially, as did Jan. As circumstances changed, he consumed more and more alcohol, especially late at night, and the normally delightful parts of his personality moved steadily to the background, replaced by more problematic behaviors. Jan remembers, with a slight sign of embarrassment, *"Near the end of his drinking, he wet his side of the bed; I got up in the morning and I remember looking at the bed. My side was dry, but his side was all wet and I said* [to myself], *'gee, he must have wet the bed.' And he's convincing me he didn't wet the bed. I remember scratching my head and walking away and saying, 'gee, I must have wet the bed because it wasn't him.' . . . It really struck me because I knew in reality I didn't wet that bed. But I was so mushy—just mushy!"*

RESIDUAL RESOURCE: BUILDING A LIFE IN THE MIDST OF DESTRUCTION

Adjusting to alcoholism is a complex process. Most people go into a marriage with a certain trust in their spouses, with the expectation that good things will happen, that they will give their partners the benefit of the doubt, and with the idea that marriage means commitment. Doing anything other than attempting to normalize inappropriate behaviors would, at least initially, be surprising. Besides, Jan and Luke were building a life together as surely as it was being simultaneously dismantled.

The birth of their daughter Elyse was a joyous occasion. Healthy and content, her first year was, nonetheless, a time of adjustment for Jan and Luke. Jan again noticed that Luke's drinking was increasing. She continued to rationalize—it was the pressure of school, of having a family. Jan became pregnant again. By the time Elyse turned one, Jan was ready to deliver their second child, Katherine.

Jan took a great deal of pleasure in being a mother. She worked only one day per week to stay current in her field. In Jan's view, she had the best of all worlds: She could spend time with Elyse, and she had contact with the outside world. Luke took care of Elyse on the day Jan worked, using the other six days a week to complete his master's degree and teach several undergraduate college courses.

But finances were tight, and he had made the decision to seek a full-time job in the fall. Unlike his middle school teaching experience, teaching undergraduates was an experience Luke enjoyed. Based on that and the financial realities of their life, he accepted a teaching position at Kingston Prep, a competitive private high school not far from the university.[5] This would provide enough to support the family and leave enough time for him to pursue his Ph.D., if he so chose. It also put him in the desirable position of working with highly motivated high school students.

Katherine was born at the university hospital in the early hours of the morning. As Jan describes that morning, her posture remains erect, as it does throughout the interview, but her voice shows the first hint of tightly held emotion. *"Everything seemed fine, but after she was born and I was taken to my room, Luke came to visit. I was exhausted and elated but I sensed, no, I knew that Luke just wanted to leave. He just wanted to get out of there. I told myself it was his exhaustion too. He had had no sleep at all. I just had this sense that he couldn't wait to get out of there. Over the next few days, while I was in the hospital, he hardly made it to see me. Luke was a ten-minute walk across campus to my room. He actually called up on the second day, an hour into visiting hours, to tell me he couldn't make it. He was in the middle of a bridge game with the other graduate students!"*

Hurt by Luke's behavior, Jan once again rationalized: Her hurt feelings were a result of hormonal changes related to Katherine's birth. As Jan speaks, Luke stares at the floor. *"On the day we left the hospital, we picked up our older daughter, Elyse, and went home. Within ten, maybe thirty minutes, Luke was out the door. He spent all of his time at the university anyway, but this was painful. He went to an out-of-town meeting, a conference. I woke up in the middle of the night shaking. I wasn't sick—I think all of this was just beginning to register. But still, it didn't register as alcoholism. Not yet. I just felt hurt and alone."*

Asher describes the second phase through which wives pass as the problem-amplification phase. During this time, questioning of the situation becomes more intensified, there tends to be self-doubt, confrontations, and an acknowledgment of a problem—but still, not alcoholism. Asher found that the questions raised by the wives of alcoholics in her study could be reduced to, "What has happened to the man I married or used to know?" "Why is he like this?" "What does he want from me?" "What do I want from him?"[6] I observe that Luke had Jan and two beautiful children, a job, and a good education. What then, pushed him to drink? Luke's face contorts into an odd half-smile. *"I got to the point I tried to convince myself that the reason I drank was because of my family.* [My thinking was], *if I've got to write I can't sit up without a gallon of wine. I was stressed because of my family. A lot of things were really difficult because I was becoming really miserable. I was becoming paranoid. I didn't think, 'Oh, I want something different between us.' That seems like a very logical connection. But it was not there for me at the time. At the time, all I really wanted to do was finish graduate school, and I wanted everybody to be happy and not to be under such pressure."*

Luke was successful to some extent as far as the family's happiness was concerned. He prepared to return to full-time teaching while continuing on in the doctoral program. Jan continued to work part-time, but at a better job at the university. This enabled them to enroll Elyse and Katherine in a university-run day care center. Jan thought about working full time so that Luke could remain in school, but she felt that she could not trust him with the girls. Besides, full-time day care for young children was not her idea of how to raise a family. She enjoyed Elyse and Katherine and didn't want to turn their care over to a stranger. She also knew that she could not depend on Luke for much emotional or child care support. However, both Jan and Luke took great delight in their daughters' growth. Jan took primary responsibility for their care. In part, this included protecting them from Luke's outbursts of anger—a new development, which was becoming a greater concern. In fact, Jan was in a slow process of coming to see the connection between alcohol and the distance between her and Luke.

She recalls that, on the morning when she got word from her doctor that she was pregnant with their third child, she had just gone through the garbage cans to count the empty beer bottles, now a morning ritual. Did she see this as unusual or aberrant behavior on her part? Not really. She saw it as a way to gauge his mood: Fewer bottles, better mood; more bottles, more volatility. To her, it seemed practical, rather than irrational. *"It wasn't like he became an ogre over night,"* she reminds me, *"I didn't recognize it as a problem 'til our relationship was in fairly deep trouble."*

WORKING TO CREATE A FAMILY

Jan had little understanding of what she was up against, and Luke was almost completely unaware as well. But his lack of awareness transcended alcoholism and included relationships in general. He explains: *"There were distances, also there was an awareness thing—I was not aware. The idea that anybody had to do work to create a family was pretty alien to me. I would say in the real problem times, I did a lot of covering up more than anything else. Trying to cover up that I was drinking as much as I was. I was hiding the fact of the amount I was drinking.* (Luke pauses at this point, smiles at Jan, and then corrects his statement) *"Well, I thought I was. I was trying to hide the effects of it and trying to appear like a legitimate sober person. I was thinking I was doing a pretty good job of it. But the longer my drinking went on, I think I struggled to stay sane and worrying about other people and relationships kind of dropped. I was stressed, and I became increasingly stressed."*

Stress seems to summarize Luke's overall relationship to the world at this point. In fact, everything did become more stressful as his abilities to cope and to compensate for his deficient behavior could no longer protect him from the hard reality of alcoholism. To compound the almost overwhelming sense of pressure, Jan gave birth to their first son and last child, Daniel. They now had a newborn, a two-year-old, and a three-year-old. Jan continued to work part time, and Luke carried on with his teaching and graduate school.

Luke was well liked at Kingston Prep. He worked hard, as was expected of all of the teachers, and he was recognized for his ability to bring history to life. This was not the case at the university. Luke tells the story of the day that he arrived late, as usual, for a research seminar. But this time, rather than blithely continuing on with not so much as a pause in his rhythm as he usually did, the professor stopped, scowled at Luke, and announced with barely contained anger and a strong dose of sarcasm that he and the class had agreed to take up a collection to buy Luke an alarm clock.

At about this time, Jan recalls that other people were also beginning to notice Luke's behavior. She remembers one such incident. At a dinner party at the home of an acquaintance, Luke drank too much. When he left the room to go to the bathroom, the host looked at Jan, who was then the mother of three, and said, *"Whatever you do, don't let him ruin your life."* Jan was taken back by this unexpected and pointed warning by a near stranger. But she says that incidents like this enabled her to finally comprehend what was happening with Luke.

Even as she describes the incident today, some twenty years after the fact, Luke's embarrassment is apparent. Everything Luke was attempting to hide was eventually cruelly exposed for the world to see. The night of the dinner party, Luke told Jan of his decision to drop out of school so that he would be able to concentrate on his job and the family. After two part-time semesters while teaching at Kingston Prep, Luke formally dropped out of his Ph.D. program. Although Jan knew what a Ph.D. meant to Luke, she was angry at never seeing him and felt this might be a solution. No longer could he use "research in the library" as an excuse to ignore her and the children. Besides, his behavior had continued to deteriorate everywhere except at Kingston Prep.

Even though less responsibility should have reduced Luke's level of stress, the buildup of pressure gained momentum; he felt that he always had to work, always had to prove himself. Jan experienced a growing sense of disappointment, even despair. Her response was to further distance herself from Luke. Maintaining this distance was a less painful option for her than being told in so many words that spending time with her was no longer a priority in Luke's life. She recalls bitterly how she approached Luke in June of that year to plan their modest summer vacation. His response: *"All vacation means to me is more time to do work!"* Luke remembers it as a period of being *"emotionally split up."*

A MOMENT OF CHOICE: SEEKING HELP

Jan sulked. Two nights after the discussion about their vacation came the "ah-ha" experience that would catapult her to action. She and her son, Daniel, both had bad colds, so Luke had agreed to attend to Daniel if he awoke during the night. Jan remembers hearing Daniel cry in the wee hours of the morning for what seemed like an hour. Finally, she forced herself out of bed and out into the hallway to go to him. She was angry at Luke. Once again, he was leaving her to take care of the children even though he was awake and working. When she stepped into the hallway, she saw Luke fumbling with Daniel at the top of the steps. Luke was drunk, and Daniel was screaming. Fear shot through Jan, and it was at this moment that she understood the extent of Luke's drinking. She remembers that everything seemed to move in slow motion as she watched Daniel squirm in Luke's arms. Paralyzed with fear for several seconds, Jan suddenly saw the harsh reality of Luke's drinking. According to Asher this would be the third phase, the proximal treatment phase. It includes facing the fact that competing definitions are no longer realistic.[7] For Jan, it meant facing the fact that she needed help.

With three small children and a husband who was in serious trouble, Jan was panicky. She contacted a city drug abuse agency and made an appointment with a counselor. The counselor gave Jan reading material and assured her that she was in the right place. Even at that time Jan recalls having trouble accepting that Luke was an alcoholic. She remembers asking the counselor, "Was he really an alcoholic?" "Did beer count as alcohol?" "Did a few quarts a night make a person an alcoholic?"

Jan never considered divorce until after she met her alcoholism counselor. At the first meeting, the counselor, a recovering alcoholic, suggested that Jan set a time limit she was comfortable with. If Luke wasn't sober by the end of that time limit, Jan should consider divorce. Jan set the limit of five years. She smiles at the memory of how "generous" she was. But the time limit gave Jan a sense of freedom and control—something she had not felt for quite awhile.

She left that counseling session buoyed by the sense that help was available and that she had some control over her life. Her feeling of impending doom was temporarily reduced. She had been exposed to alcoholism as a child, although it was never labeled as such, and the problems it incurred had never been addressed. Jan arranged biweekly meetings with her counselor and agreed to attend two Al-Anon meetings. In addition, she bought a book on her way home from that first appointment. To this day, Jan remembers the book and its author: Ruth Maxwell's *The Booze Battle*. Jan read it cover-to-cover that evening, and in the next few months she read all the literature that was available. The shock of seeing Daniel dangling from Luke's arms at the top of the steps was clearly a turning point for Jan—a moment of choice. It marked her acknowledgment of a significant problem, alcoholism, and her decision to seek help. Another spouse recalls a similar time in her life and how her own changed behavior quickly led to changes in her marriage. *"I started making some changes around the house. One of the changes was I started to smile again, and my husband actually says he came into A.A. because he was really jealous. I was doing things like not getting into the car if he was drinking all night. I would have two sets of plans if he came home and had really been drinking and we were supposed to go out. I would have a second set of plans for myself. This was dramatic."*

COMING UNRAVELED

Luke's first turning point occurred the week following Jan's visit to the alcoholism center. More agitated than usual, he asked Jan if she would go for a walk with him to the local park. Luke recalls, *"I had the sense of our relationship being very fragile, like fine china. But I thought of it in a positive and negative way. The fragility was part of what was beautiful, exquisite perhaps. I remember there was a lot of silence. And I remember sitting there by the lake thinking we're exquisitely in love even though we're kind of balanced on the knife's edge. Are we going to stay in the frozen silence or lash out at each other? This thought of this relationship where you actually get along with your kids and you love them and you actually enjoy each other, this was kind of like taking someone homeless and saying, 'You can live in a house like this;'* (Luke makes a sweeping movement with his arms to indicate their house) *there was that much of a gap emotionally for me."*

Jan remembers the conversation on their walk around the lake as well. *"Luke talked about his mother. I mostly listened. He said that he understood for the first time that everything he did was really to please her, his mother, in some way. But the conversation was disjointed—it didn't all make sense. He talked about his stomach pains and a lot of, well, kind of crazy sounding things. Although it seemed meaningful to him, I actually felt kind of afraid. It was like he was having a breakdown. It was eerie. I actually felt afraid of him."*

A MOMENT OF CHOICE: MORE HELP

Although Jan felt afraid, she also felt that Luke's pain might make him open to getting help. She took a chance and asked Luke if he trusted her. To her relief, Luke agreed and only a few days later, Luke made a visit to the social worker, a middle-aged man known for his work with alcoholics. Upon his return from that one visit, Luke announced to Jan that the social worker told him he was not an alcoholic, but he had a 98 percent chance of becoming one. In addition to this single visit, Luke attended a series of DUI classes at the suggestion of the social worker.[8]

Jan recalls feeling disappointed that Luke had been told that he wasn't *quite* an alcoholic. But she kept her silence and allowed the drama to unfold. Over the next three weeks, Luke's moods rose and fell in rapid succession, like waves on the high seas. The deterioration of their relationship was underscored for Jan by one particular outburst. While sitting in the living room chatting with neighbors who had stopped by to finalize nursery school transportation plans, Luke became agitated by a comment Jan had made. He picked up a pillow from the couch and threw it across the room at Jan. It hit her on the shoulder. Jan recalls this as not only humiliating but a real warning. *"I didn't grow up with people hitting one another, and this felt like a qualitatively different kind of behavior. Although it was a pillow, it might as well have been a rock. To me, it felt like Luke was on the edge of becoming physically violent. I didn't do or say anything. I felt, well, so embarrassed. I looked down at the floor for what seemed like a long, long time."*

In addition to incidents like the pillow, Jan felt that she could no longer trust Luke to keep an eye on the children. He was simply too preoccupied with himself and too agitated. His temper was wildly unpredictable. Although it was under control most of the time, incidents like the thrown pillow were becoming more common. Jan remembers that this was the first time she explicitly acknowledged his mood swings. The mood swings were widening the gap between them. Equally disturbing was the fact that she could no longer confide in Luke. When Luke drank, he would pull comments out of context and repeat anything to anyone. Their most personal conversations were suddenly open to anyone who would listen. Their relationship was rapidly coming unraveled.

Luke did attend the DUI classes the social worker had suggested. Following the third week of DUI classes, he came home and unemotionally told Jan that he believed he was an alcoholic. Jan remembers her surprise at his calm and rational tone of voice. Within a few days, he was attending A.A. meetings. Meanwhile, Jan had seen her counselor several more times, and she had begun attending Al-Anon meetings on a regular basis.

RESIDUAL RESOURCE: DOUBLE VISION

On the surface, it sounds like a time to rejoice. In fact, this could be the end of Jan and Luke's story—if life were that simple. However, the distance, pain, distrust, and disappointment that had accumulated over the years persisted. As Jan recalls, their ability to talk to one another about anything of importance had all but ceased. In addition, she could no longer recall what it was about Luke that had once been so attractive to her. Even so, she remembers, *"I held on to the knowledge that the parts of Luke that I had loved, although no longer within my memory's grasp, were still there. I couldn't see them, but I just knew that they had once been there. I held on to that."*

Echoing the residual resources shared by the Gundersons and the Bertolinos—"chemistry," love, commitment, and friendship—Jan called on those same dormant resources that form the foundation of relationships. Although Jan's memory failed her in terms of what specifically she had loved about Luke, she had faith in their past existence and hope that she might once again *feel* those good feelings.

Judith Wallerstein and Sandra Blakeslee note the presence of a "double vision" as essential to maintaining a satisfying and rewarding marriage. "The powerful memories provide a reservoir of past indulgences on which people can draw when things look dark. Beloved recollections of a better past soften the blows of the present."[9] Asher described the transformation of the wives of alcoholics as seeing that "he's this *and* he's that."[10] In other words, they must bring back into their awareness that there is more than one side to their spouse. One wife of an alcoholic described the moment that this double vision came into play for her. She had gotten into an altercation with a construction foreman whom her husband had treated badly. In utter frustration, she found herself pleading with the foreman. *"The man that he is, is not the man you see."* She recalls further: *"I began to cry on the way home in the car, and I thought, 'How true. That is not Larry* [her husband]. *That is some other man.' And that was the beginning of me realizing he was sick."*[11] Another spouse described the presence of a double vision in their relationship today, many years after the start of sobriety. *"I can look at my husband's eyes and see the dark side of him and know it and accept it. And I can look at his eyes and see a lot of love too. And he can do the same thing with me."*

For couples like Jan and Luke, the softening of the present by the past, like the feelings of love described by Cara Gunderson, is a powerful buffer in the face of alcoholism. A double vision is a residual resource. Its presence and persistence are necessary to hold people together in the midst of despair.[12]

This double vision is a paradox of sorts, for what is healing is also problematic. The double vision that prevents divorce can also function in some cases to keep people in hopeless, even dangerous, situations. As some of the codependency literature suggests, seeing what is good can be indicative of a dependent and weak person. Yet, it is this very same double vision that may help to maintain the relationship during some of its most trying times. For these couples, a double vision of the good along with the bad is dependent on residual resources. For couples like Jan and Luke, the question becomes, how do you bring the good to the forefront?

NOTES

1. Their parents/grandparents helped out with tuition but not living expenses.
2. P. Steinglass, L. A. Bennett, S. J. Wolin, and D. Reiss, *The Alcoholic Family (*New York: Basic Books, 1987).
3. R. M. Asher, *Women with Alcoholic Husbands: Ambivalence and the Trap of Codependency (*Chapel Hill: University of North Carolina Press, 1992), 28.
4. R. M. Asher, *Women with Alcoholic Husbands,* 5.
5. Kingston Prep is a pseudonym.
6. R. M. Asher, *Women with Alcoholic Husbands*, 10.
7. This phase also includes introspection, resocialization, self-assertion, revitalization, seeking outside help, and becoming proactive rather than feeling like one is the recipient of other people's actions and has no choices to make on one's behalf.
8. DUI is the acronym for driving under the influence. These classes were mandated by the justice system for drivers who were found to abuse alcohol. Another term is *driving while intoxicated,* or DWI.
9. J. S. Wallerstein and S. Blakeslee, *The Good Marriage: How and Why Love Lasts* (New York: Houghton Mifflin, 1995), 324.
10. R. M. Asher, *Women with Alcoholic Husbands*, 169.

11. This also relates to the disease concept raised by Cara Gunderson. "Sick" people deserve some understanding, some compassion. They are also capable of change and recovery because, rather than being a permanent aspect of their personality, the "sickness" may be a temporary state.

12. To underscore the level of despair felt by many spouses and the tenacity of the double vision, it is worth noting that many spouses at their most desperate and despairing times imagine the deaths of their alcoholic partner. As one spouse explained, looking surprised at her own words: *"I couldn't tolerate him. I used to wish he wouldn't come home. I used to wish he would wrap himself around a telephone pole before he would kill someone. I felt complete disgust more than anything else. I remember thinking that we had life insurance and maybe the easiest would be if he was killed and I just got the life insurance.* (Pause.) *Is this on tape?"* Another spouse recalls expressing her sentiments directly to her husband: *"I remember one time saying to Alan, 'You know, it would be much kinder if you say you love me like you do, it would be much kinder if you just take a gun and shoot yourself.'"*

Chapter 11

Insight Is Not Enough: Therapy and Beyond

"A soul is never sick alone, but always a between-ness also, a situation between it and another existing being."

—Martin Buber, *Pointing the Way*

Luke became committed to his A.A. meetings early in sobriety. Jan's memory of Luke's first year of sobriety is vivid. *"Sobriety was hard. I had also built an identity for myself. I was this ignored person. The victim. And suddenly I wasn't the victim any more. Luke was sober so I couldn't as easily explain my bad feelings."* Jan's identity was shattered, leaving her adrift at least initially. What had once anchored her, her victim status, although in a negative way, was no longer available, and she had nothing new to replace it with. In addition, Luke had little energy and was distracted. Asher describes the fourth, the posttreatment phase, as a period of reflections and harmonization when the wife must establish a new identity as "wife of an alcoholic." Just as there is a gradual awareness or acceptance that one's spouse is an alcoholic, there is an equally slow-moving period of acceptance of oneself as the wife of an alcoholic. This identity can be disturbing because of all it does and does not imply. Being the spouse of an alcoholic is a permanent label, full of stigma and unknown meanings. At the same time, it may be quite freeing because at last the pieces of the puzzle make some sense. Simply having a label helps some people to contain the disorder and understand it. "Alcoholism" is a framework that provides a semblance of meaning and structure for determining how to proceed. For many, it is a beginning.

BUILDING TRUST: THE NEED FOR SELF-CARE

For Luke, the experience of early sobriety provided time to focus on himself even more. *"To me, the first two years was about myself and making connection with other people in A.A. The focus was on myself in a different way. I was aware, if anything, of even less stress. It was important to me not to worry so much about making money, not worry so much about work, not worry about keeping everybody happy. I felt that I had this permission to not be as responsible for things. To me, that included my job, my family—that was all secondary to getting sober. There was this awareness: 'You will never get sober for somebody else; you have to get sober for yourself.' Yes, it is not a question of whether my marriage goes on, whether our marriage goes on—all that stuff is secondary. I'm here for myself to be sober. I needed space, I really did. And I just didn't have the energy. I probably became less concerned sober, than when I was drinking."*

The ability of the alcoholic to say, in essence, "All I can do is take care of myself," is a self-affirming statement. It reflects the recognition that one's own needs are crucial and must take precedence over their responsibility to other people. Unfortunately, this self-focus often comes at a time when the spouse's need to receive attention is at an all-time high. As in the case of Peg Royer, who chafed at the thought that Dave needed five more years before he could pay attention to her, early sobriety can be yet another very trying time for couples. For some couples, one spouse's involvement in Al-Anon can provide a needed counterweight to the focus on the alcoholic. As one spouse said of Al-Anon, *"I liked that the focus was on me."*

A year or more passed in which the intentional acts of destruction between Jan and Luke came to a halt and there was relative quiet: no more pillow throwing, no more volatile outbursts. But as Luke points out, *"Holding things in stasis may have been stopping destruction but almost in the same way as you might say we stopped fighting. Almost like you might say, 'I grabbed a rampaging child and held him firmly.' The child may see that hold as a very aggressive act. My focus on myself stopped the destruction on the obvious level. But that sort of insistence of, 'It's not my problem,' may have been its own negativity."*

STILL A SECOND FIDDLE

Luke is quite right. This focus by the alcoholic on himself, the position that he or she cannot be responsible for other peoples' needs, is often experienced by his or her spouse as one more rejection or one more insult.[1] Luke acknowledges the tension that such a stance generates. Just as "holding the child firmly" can be experienced as aggression by the child, so too can the spouse interpret this self-focus as aggression. The spouse who hears, "It's not my problem," or "Sobriety comes first" also feels a stinging rejection. It is in fact a case of equally opposing and valid needs: the need of the alcoholic to focus on him or herself, and the need of the spouse to feel that he or she is finally no longer a second fiddle.

When marriages are functioning well, both spouses feel that they are treated fairly over all. This enables them to adjust to periods of time in which one is required to give more than 50 percent and the other receives more than 50 percent. With couples such as Jan and Luke, for whom there is a history of imbalance, both spouses need to receive more than they are able to give at the moment. Both are depleted, leaving little if any energy to offer each other comfort. Sometimes, as in Mike and Ann Bertolino's case, there are circumstances that facilitate a rebalancing. In their case, the unfortunate death of Mike's friend and mentor became an opening for Ann to offer Mike support and unwittingly help to rebalance the relational scales.

Luke's lethargy and her ongoing feeling that she was a second fiddle were difficult for Jan to ignore. What does being a second fiddle feel like, and why is it so harmful? Two wives of alcoholics provide some sense of what it is like: *"I was at the hospital with our daughter* [who had almost drowned during the time my husband was in rehab] *and his* [the alcoholic's] *mother was screaming at me: 'Don't call him—he's in such a delicate state, you know!"*

"As things got worse, I needed some assurance that I was central to my husband's life. . . . It became less clear to me that I was significant to him and I guess what I wanted was to know that I was significant."

Why do these feelings prove problematic for marriages? Research on long-term marriage suggests that feeling respected and feeling central to one's spouse are essential ingredients to satisfying relationships. As long as a spouse does not feel central, or like number one, there tends to be discontent. In the early periods of marriage this centrality must be established. For the couples in this book the alcohol either prevented establishment of centrality altogether or reversed it after it had been established. One spouse being second for extended periods of time often depletes the trust between the spouses.

For Jan and Luke, there was gradual improvement during the latter part of the first year of sobriety. Luke began to take more interest in the children, a responsibility that had fallen almost entirely to Jan. She recalls that he also became more interested in how bills were paid and how the house was run. But it was in the spring of that first year of sobriety that their lives underwent a second major change: Luke was offered a job as department head at a private secondary school in Baltimore. To make the offer more attractive, the school offered Jan a part-time position as librarian and agreed to cover most of his expenses if Luke decided to return to school to complete his Ph.D.

After much soul searching, Jan and Luke accepted the positions and moved their family to Baltimore. For Luke, it felt like the opportunity to begin again. Jan was less sanguine. In fact, she confides that she considered staying behind on a permanent basis. Although the move was logical and only an hour and a half away, Jan knew that she would lose her daily support system. Nonetheless, she felt that overall the move made sense. Like Luke, she also saw it as an opportunity to begin again.

The move was a dream come true for Luke. He loved his new school and the responsibility of being chairperson. Within the first year, he was admitted to a graduate program, made numerous A.A. friends, and, much to Jan's dismay, spent most nights at A.A. meetings. Jan, on the other hand, was less enthusiastic about her job. She and the head librarian did not get along well. After six months, Jan left the school in search of a more satisfying position. Although the tumultuous emotions of the first year of sobriety were behind them, their relationship seemed to level off. Luke became increasingly consumed by A.A., teaching, and graduate school, and once again, Jan found herself taking responsibility for most things around the house. Although the children were in preschool and elementary school so that she had a reprieve from their constant demands, she still felt alone and abandoned. Jan came to resent Luke's A.A. commitments and his failure to pay attention to her. To Jan, it seemed that everything and everyone else came before her and the children. As far as she was concerned, Luke had exchanged alcohol for A.A.

Jan's sense of abandonment was keen. She recalls making plans for her birthday during their second year in Baltimore. It was the beginning of Luke's fourth year of sobriety. They had always celebrated family birthdays together, but this year, Luke announced to Jan that he could not be home for her birthday because he had to take a total stranger to an A.A. meeting. Jan's voice falters for a moment. *"He told me his number one priority was being sober. I could intellectually hear that—but emotionally, how do you stake a claim in the face of 'Well, if I don't have this* [A.A.] *I'll die.' I struggled with that although I did make claims, but at the cost of insisting you stay home for my birthday. After you insist that someone celebrates your birthday with you, there is kind of a feeling of not much real joy and spontaneity."*

Neither Jan nor Luke could recall exactly what happened with the birthday celebration, but Jan remembers that it made her realize one more time that she was not satisfied with their relationship. She was still second fiddle. Not only had alcohol been replaced by A.A., but now family was being replaced by strangers. Also, Luke's work never seemed to end. Summers were filled with graduate school and research. Winters comprised a dizzying number of school commitments, papers to grade, parents to meet, faculty meetings, and an array of social obligations. More and more, Jan found herself refusing to be involved as the supportive wife. One day, after reading her Al-Anon book, she threw the book across the bedroom. She remembers feeling nothing but anger at that moment.

Jan and Luke both realized that tensions were once again brewing between them. Frustrated and hurt, not knowing where else to turn, Jan made an appointment with a family therapist. Luke grudgingly went along, certain that Jan's problems were hers and hers alone. What else could be expected of him? He was sober, working, in graduate school, and he spent time with his children. Jan, on the other hand, felt that the problems boiled down to just one: Luke. Yes, he had his good points, and he wasn't an evil person, but he simply wasn't giving Jan what she needed. They entered therapy almost five years after Luke got sober, both filled with trepidation.

BUILDING TRUST: ACKNOWLEDGING THE PAIN OF "GOOD" DESTRUCTION

When I ask what therapy was like, Luke smiles and says, *"This is the really good destruction."* Luke says they had picked up this phrase during a family trip to see the ravages of the eruption of Mount Saint Helens. When they entered the park visitor center, the ranger on duty had smiled and directed them to where they could see *"some really good destruction."* The incongruity of a ranger, a protector of the environment, directing them to "good destruction," had been incorporated into the family's story telling. It had also become a metaphor for one aspect of their relationship. Jan and Luke smile at one another once again. I think back to Jan's early excitement while talking about being engaged to Luke. At this moment, even as we talk of "good" destruction, I see the sparkle in her eyes that I imagine was there early in their relationship.

Surviving five years of sobriety was noted by many couples as being the beginning of a new phase, a new era in their relationship. The hopefulness had by then been tempered by the ongoing needs of family and the realization that sobriety alone is not the answer to everything. The excitement of newly won sobriety for the alcoholic has become a more routine part of life. No longer having to concentrate totally on staying sober, the alcoholic realizes there are relationships to be built or mended.

BUILDING TRUST: THERAPY

Of the forty-nine people interviewed, twenty-five noted that they attend or have received some kind of psychological counseling. Twenty-three have had individual counseling, seventeen couples have had couple counseling, and eight couples have participated in family counseling. Some have been in and out of counseling, trying different types. Others made use of counseling only once. One couple had entered counseling prompted by what they termed *"crisis situations,"* and now, after many years of being sober, they are again seeking counseling to help them "fine-tune" their relationship. Overall, people felt that their counseling was helpful. One alcoholic said that the therapy *"made me feel that I could reach out and talk to people—one of the things I lost was the ability to speak seriously or intimately other than in the context of the A.A. meetings. How do you speak seriously? That's something people often do over a drink or that people get comfortable doing in A.A. with A.A. friends. You know, it's hard to know how to talk unless you've got people who are certain kinds of friends to really talk to. You can't do that in an ordinary environment. So I think really talking was prompted by therapy."*[2] Another alcoholic described the benefits of therapy: *"As nebulous as this sounds, it has been a matter of finding out who I am . . . trying to make the world into something I felt safe in. Therapy created that ground for me that I never had. It's like kind of relaxing and realizing I'm safe."* One spouse, who was a great believer in the A.A. and Al-Anon programs, suggested that therapy was an essential component of relationship healing. *"The program* (A.A./Al-Anon) *doesn't help you much with your relationship. It helps you with yourself, and it helps you find a way of life for yourself, and then it kind of leaves you there. It leaves you there, and you're not hooked into your spousal relationship. You're healthier, but I feel you are kind of left with that."* A few people found therapy unhelpful or neither helpful nor unhelpful. Yet by and large, a majority felt that counseling had been valuable for them.

For some couples, the goals of counseling were very specific, while for others the goal was a general attempt to make their relationship work and to ease some of their pain. Very concrete goals included learning to negotiate or argue, and learning how to dispense with guilt. As one alcoholic recalled about a visit to his counselor, *"I wanted to get rid of everything* [guilt, rage, etc.]*—the very last thing that I never told anybody else . . .* [the result of counseling was] *I lost that guilt, I lost that guilt of the past, and I don't even walk around thinking about it any more."*

Jan and Luke entered therapy together at Jan's insistence.[3] For Jan, the exterior of her life was in order. The children were relatively happy and healthy. She and Luke had been able to afford a comfortable if not extravagant home. Luke was experiencing professional success. They had friends. Yet, she still felt empty. *"I was just depleted. One thing I felt was that I was taking care of people and not getting anything back. I was so low I really felt that I was crossing a very fine line between sanity and insanity. I was scared for myself."* Just as Luke determined that he had to focus on his own needs in early sobriety, Jan now found it necessary to focus on herself. As she describes it, *"It really had nothing to do with Luke at a certain point—it really had to do with me."*

So here they were a full five years into sobriety, and desperately needing help. Both recall being nervous when they met the therapist. The initial sessions consisted primarily of the therapist asking them questions about their childhoods, their children, their lives together. Jan recalls the therapist asking her if she wanted the marriage to survive or if she imagined it coming to an end.

Given that they wanted to work on the marriage, what exactly had brought them to therapy? For Jan, it was now an overwhelming sense of sadness and feeling that she had been abandoned by Luke. Luke was in therapy because he wanted Jan to be happy; he couldn't figure out why she wasn't. What neither Jan nor Luke articulated in those first therapy sessions, but which they both agree was their expectation, was their hope that the therapist would assess the situation and assign blame appropriately. To Jan, this meant blaming Luke for all of his poor behavior, for his overwork, and for ignoring her. Luke hoped that the therapist would straighten Jan out. After all, Luke made money, held a job, went to school, and he was sober. What more could Jan expect of him? Why couldn't she be content?

From the beginning, their therapist elicited disappointment and anger from both of them. For Jan, it came rushing out like air from an overinflated balloon. The slights, her feelings of abandonment, her birthday party that didn't happen, the births of their children, which Luke had barely attended, the insults, the volatility. Luke held steadfastly to the fact that everything was really fine, if only Jan would see that, if only Jan could enjoy life, if only Jan. If Luke was in pain, it was only because of Jan's failure to acknowledge that everything was really fine.

BUILDING TRUST: REEVALUATION

Although initially Luke took the position that all was fine, their therapist, Dr. Madison, acknowledged Jan's pain. Jan repeated Dr. Madison's words in a particularly firm voice: "*'Of course you are angry—you have every right to be angry.' That was such an acknowledgment. It was such a relief to feel that it's OK, the anger's appropriate. And at that point I was able to let go.*" Dr. Madison suggested to Luke that his simply wanting Jan to be happy was a form of scapegoating her, of failing to take responsibility for past transgressions. Luke's stance that she should "just be happy" suggested that he believed Jan had no reason for her dissatisfaction. Furthermore, it implied that Jan was solely at fault. It effectively removed Luke from the equation of all that had brought them into therapy.

At the same time, Dr. Madison proposed that Luke also had suffered—he too had been abandoned. Jan recalls that it was almost impossible for her to sit and hear their therapist speak of Luke's suffering. After all, he was the alcoholic, not Jan; he had not gone along with the original marriage plan; he was the one who was volatile, who lost his temper with no provocation—and now he was the one who was still too busy to be at home. How could *he* be hurting? Wasn't *he* the perpetrator? How could anyone think that *Luke* was in pain? He was the one who caused the pain, thought Jan. Another interviewee recalled a similar point in her therapy when the therapist suggested that she have compassion for her alcoholic husband. Calmly she recalls, *"It really struck me as odd—to think about it in a whole different way."*

The therapist's insistence that Luke had suffered as well eventually paid off by starting a process of humanization and reevaluation. Part of this reevaluation took the form of helping Jan and Luke each see the ways they had contributed to their own unhappiness. Dr. Madison suggested to Jan that she had become the "doormat" in the relationship.[4] Dr. Madison insisted that Luke respond to questions directly rather than deflect them and suggest that it was Jan's responsibility to change.

How was Jan a "doormat," and how did she respond to being called one? She was a doormat in that she simply responded to Luke's schedule and busy life rather than having demands of her own. Jan seemed resigned to Luke's ways—somewhat like her own mother had remained silent in the face of her grandfather, all the time seething inside. Jan recognized her failure to focus on her own life, to give it as much attention as she gave to Luke. Another spouse described her initial therapy visit and how it led to the realization of being "addicted" to her husband because she had no life in her own right.[5] With incredulity she recounted, *"I talked with my counselor for an hour and a half. I talked for quite awhile and I realized that the whole time I talked about my husband. It was like I was totally addicted to my husband. It was all I could think about. I kept putting myself in his head. I had not one idea about myself. And at the end of the session, the counselor said, 'But what about you?' And I had absolutely nothing to say about me."*

Jan remembers feeling strangely relieved by the therapist's pronouncement of her being a doormat. *"I knew she was right. It helped to hear someone else say it. I think I could hear that because Dr. Madison had also told me that my disappointment and discouragement were real and they were warranted; what wasn't OK was my own staying that way."*

BUILDING TRUST: JUST LISTENING

How did their therapist interrupt Luke's pattern of deflection? Dr. Madison would steer Luke's responses and discussion to his own behavior, feelings, and past. She repeatedly asked him to talk to Jan about his own pain, his own loss, without reference to Jan's behavior. Jan recalls, near the end of one very long and frustrating session, four or five months into therapy, *"Dr. Madison said, 'Now, tell Jan what was happening with you.' Luke looked over at me to say, 'Are you sure you want to hear what I have to say?' And I said, 'Yeah, I do. I want to hear the pain more than the anger because the anger scares me.' It was really a big moment because he was able, for the first time, to share what was in his heart. Without sharing the pain, he couldn't let my love in either. You know, you can't have one without the other."*

Although Luke does not recall this moment, and Jan does not remember exactly what Luke said about the pain, it was part of an important process for Jan and, she believes, for Luke. Why was it significant? Jan continues, *"We went over the hurts and pains of those last three to five years and talked on each side without attacking each other. It was important for me just to sit and listen. For Luke to see that it was OK to share his pain, for him to think he has permission. I'm living with a man I know more than I know any other person, and, for all those years, he could never share what was going on within himself. So you know, that has made a tremendous difference in our relationship. . . . That was the key for me."*

The idea that there is pain and loss on both sides is part of the humanizing that can take place. In addition to the recognition that alcoholism is a disease, there must be acknowledgment of the humanity of the alcoholic; only then does compassion filter through. In this way the alcoholic can move beyond the single role of victimizer. At the same time, the spouse's suffering must also be acknowledged so that the reality of his or her experience is not diminished. The spouse must be held accountable so that he or she can begin to form an identity other than that of victim.

Along with identifying the pain, Dr. Madison encouraged each of them to say what it was they wanted from each other. Rather than allow them to simply unleash blame, she also steered them into talking about the disappointments they had felt and about what they needed and hoped for from the other. The simple question of what they each wanted from the other initially left Jan and Luke speechless. Then they both responded with what they needed the other *not* to do: Don't go to so many A.A. meetings, don't make all of the decisions in the house, don't, don't, don't. So, Dr. Madison prodded them to think of what they wanted in a positive vein. Perhaps a walk together on Sunday afternoons, a night out together or separately. Thinking in terms of what they wanted was almost beyond Jan and Luke's grasp. So accustomed were they to thinking of how they wanted the other to change and of their disappointment when they failed to do so, the simple question, "What do you need from this person?" had long ago ceased to be part of their awareness. With Dr. Madison's help, Jan and Luke slowly started to think in terms of wants and needs rather than blame.

Throughout the sessions, Dr. Madison also facilitated Jan's and Luke's exploration of their childhoods. Through these recollections they gained insight into the dynamics that had shaped some of their behaviors and expectations. The shared exploration of family loyalties helped them see themselves and each other in the full context of their lives. Rather than each seeing the other in isolation and acting out of ill will or goodwill based on how they felt about their relationship, they discovered that the exploration of dynamics in their own families placed their expectations and behaviors in a larger context: that of family loyalties.

Family loyalty refers to the tendency of patterns of parenting to be repeated generation after generation. Examples of loyalty include the fact that most parents raise their children similarly to the way they themselves were raised. They also tend to hold attitudes toward money, education, religion, work, and lifestyle preferences that are similar to those of their parents. Loyalty can be manifested in negative as well as positive ways. The son whose mother cannot let go of him, and thereby prevents him from forming other close relationships, and the woman who was abused by her parents, and so now abuses her own children, are examples of negative loyalty. Thus, loyalty represents the potential for both health and pathology.[6]

Luke recalls his struggle to differentiate his own opinions from those of his parents: *"It made me split in the sense of having to be responsible for Jan. My mother's image of what Jan ought to be and what I wanted—how do you know what you want out of your relationship versus what you are taking over from what your mother and father taught you a relationship ought to be?"*

For Jan, the effects of having grown up with her grandfather's alcoholism were compounded by her mother's passivity. Jan was reluctant, nearly incapable, of making demands on Luke. On the other hand, both Jan and Luke had been loved and cared for as children. Luke had seen his parents' commitment—and in fact still sees it today. Although Jan harbors resentment for her mother, she was adored by her grandfather and thus thrived in her childhood.

In addition to helping Luke and Jan untangle their pasts to help them in the present, the therapeutic emphasis on their families of origin deflected some of their intense scrutinizing and blaming of each other. Most importantly, it helped them to see that some of their disappointment and pain was really a result of their pasts not their present. Instead of seeing the other as controlling or as behaving just as one would expect an alcoholic to behave, Luke and Jan entertained the possibility that each, in part, behaved according to what they had received from their parents and what their parents had withheld from them—intentionally or not.

Jan recalls that Dr. Madison never demonized their parents; instead, she helped them to put their relationship into a different perspective. "*Because of the intergenerational pieces,* [I came to understand that] *some of Luke's responses didn't have to do with me but maybe his mother or stress at work. My responsibility was to* [stop being a doormat and] *stand up to him.*"

BUILDING TRUST: SEEING THE OTHER WITH NEW EYES

What was the outcome of learning to see the other person in a larger context? Jan put it this way: "*Our therapist sided with both of us—Luke as a person had a side. So I started to think that this was a turning point for me—if he wasn't just a victimizer, who was he? It may sound corny, but I could see the man that he really was, or the man I had fallen in love with. That person was still there, and that other monster was all gone.*"

Jan describes a crucial shift. For the first time since Luke's early sobriety, she realizes that the designation of victimizer is not clear-cut. This realization occurred as a result of her fair assessment of both sides of the past. Forced to see beyond her own perspective, Jan was able to entertain the notion that Luke was not simply a victimizer. This does not mean that she had to forget what had happened in the past, but it did mean that she had to shift her thinking. In so doing, she made room once again for Luke's human aspect to be taken into consideration. This harks back to the interview I had with Dave Royer, in which he stated emphatically that he certainly could not imagine Peg's experience. With this failure of imagination, Dave was trapped and Peg held hostage as his maid.

Once Jan no longer maintains the identity of victim, as she noted earlier, and once she sees Luke as more than a victimizer, presumably there is room for some shifting of labels. In fact, Jan has come to see that as the doormat in the relationship, she shares the victimizer role with Luke. If this is true, then perhaps he shared the victim role with her.

The process of being able to see the other is made possible in the first place by the same residual resources that helped Jan and Luke maintain their relationship. It comes to fruition only through the willingness of both partners to enter into the difficult process of due consideration. Like the Bertolinos, Jan and Luke can each once again see a glimmer of who the other person is. This means acknowledging the good and the bad and refusing to hold the other captive by any label so restrictive as victim or victimizer. This shift is difficult because it requires the people involved to give up the benefits of a clear stance of blame, which makes life neat but disregards the many complexities that in fact exist.

The type of understanding Jan experiences "leads the victim to a position where he or she need not condemn the victimizer as a monster . . . understanding of the victimizing family member allows the victim without condemnation to resolve the questions of how a trusted loved one could cause such unjustified pain."[7] As long as we see another person as a monster (or a maid), we force them to remain outside the reach of our reason.[8] Our own anger separates us from the real person, and we see only the monster or the maid. Jan slowly came to recall Luke's kinder and more human qualities, the qualities she had temporarily lost sight of. Such changes have been referred to as a softening of attitudes, the willingness to be open to taking a risk, to trust the victimizer once again.[9]

As Jan struggled to rediscover Luke's personal qualities and see who he really was, Luke, like Ken Gunderson, struggled to escape the shackles of his own vision of himself. *"I didn't want to be a beast. I think that one of the things that changed for me was that ability to see that, with love, it would be possible to go through something and actually, yeah, recognize damage and make some retribution and then go on."*

BUILDING TRUST: TAKING RESPONSIBILITY

About six months into therapy, Luke left town to go to a conference. He extended the trip to include short visits with his parents as well as his longtime friend Seth. These visits provided pivotal moments that built trust between Jan and Luke. *"I went out to visit my parents. I wanted support . . . and didn't get it. I went out with a friend, Seth, and he accused me of being very insensitive. I felt really emotionally and personally beat up. But it forced me to rethink what my role was, what both of them had said was, or what I heard was, 'You're really insensitive—you take no responsibility for any of this stuff.' And it really hurt."*

What was it that hurt Luke about his visits with Seth and his parents? They forced him to face facts. *"It's related to the image I've always used. Thinking that one has maybe dented the fender of the car, in terms of our relationship and then trying to own up to the fact that there has been this real smash-up."* Although Jan had begun to forgive Luke, he had yet to acknowledge his part in their difficulties. Luke returned home with a new sense of his own responsibility in the near-demise of his and Jan's relationship. No matter how much he struggled to avoid this admission and continued to convince himself that he had really contributed more than he had taken, he finally faced the realization that his behavior during his active alcoholism, and even now in sobriety, had cost him and Jan dearly. Once he acknowledged what his parents and Seth had said, he returned home and began to apply this new insight and became more willingly engaged with therapy. A similar trust-building experience was described by an alcoholic wife at the moment she realized her husband's dedication and sacrifice. *"Once we watched a movie,* The Promise *with James Woods. Well, James Woods has a schizophrenic brother, and he promises his mother he'll take care of his bother when she dies. The whole picture is about that. At the end, he takes the brother to a beautiful hospital where he belonged. James Woods is fulfilling his promise. He gave up his money and his everything to put his brother in that hospital, and I realized how much my husband suffered. We both cried. . . . I knew then what he suffered, but I didn't know it before. He stuck by me the whole time, no matter what I did. No matter how crazy, he stuck by me, and I am very grateful for that."*

While Luke was out of town, Jan had gone to a physician seeking medication for depression. *"I felt like I was crossing the line between sanity and insanity. I had always been this together person, and here I was, feeling like I just couldn't do it any more. I was so depleted."* Although Jan and Luke were making some progress in therapy, the overwhelming feelings and emotions, pent up all those years, were almost more than Jan could take. She started taking antidepressants, and did so for six months. The medication provided the strength she required to keep trying.

Luke's realization of the harsh truth that he was insensitive and irresponsible, combined with his love for Jan and his desire to have the relationship continue, effectively shifted the direction of their therapy sessions. Because Dr. Madison had credited Luke for his contributions, elicited descriptions of his losses, and had refused to be diverted by his attempts to place blame in inappropriate places, Luke began to see that he had a safe haven in which his feelings and needs could be explored.

Jan's own changing self-assessment and new, stronger sense of self were gradually emerging. It helped her to identify what she needed from Luke and also what she wanted for herself. Relinquishing her role as the doormat in the marriage, Jan knew she must take a stand in her own behalf. Dr. Madison admonished her that it would not be in anyone else's apparent best interest for Jan to put herself first. With Dr. Madison's support, she made strides in this direction. Both Jan and Luke had to face their own complicity in the destruction of the relationship. Regardless of who was at fault and in what ways, the relationship had been harmed, and it clearly would not be mended by the efforts of one person alone. In reality, the many years of instability and built up resentment had left their marriage imbalanced. It would require the efforts of both to right it.

BUILDING TRUST: DELIBERATE ACTIONS, NOT JUST INSIGHT

Meanwhile, Luke's forthrightness about his personal responsibility for damage to the marriage signaled an important turn. The A.A. program encourages making amends by undertaking deliberate actions to right wrongs. Among couples who had the most satisfying relationships, this notion was manifest through their actions not just through words and insights. One spouse said, *"It was the action that counted, of being involved together, doing something, but first of all really recognizing that our relationship needed working on, and then practicing, and making a commitment, too."* Luke's actions included small acts of thoughtfulness: *"I was driving home one night and there were flowers along the road, and I stopped and picked them for Jan. It seems like for a long time I would bring a flower home for her every night and put it next to her bed. No words. You don't have to be nice to me; you don't have to say anything."* Another alcoholic explained, *"I tried to keep Friday and Saturday free so I wasn't consumed with A.A. seven days a week—I kept that open for anything we could do together. I made a point of that and I did it intentionally. A lot of guys I know never got any balance in their life. I think that might have been the unknown factor"* [in our remaining together and finding happiness].

Movingly, another alcoholic recounts a similar kind of effort. *"I made a conscientious effort. I became aware that I wasn't paying much attention to Catherine and hadn't for a long time. There's been a progression. I used to ask Catherine how did her day go, and then I wouldn't listen to anything she said. And then it got to where I really made myself concentrate and listen, and all she would talk about was work, paperwork, and projects. It kind of progressed to the point I didn't really have to make that concerted effort to say, 'How was your day?' I really want to know, 'How was your day?' And progressively, she explained how her day went in a much more people-oriented way, instead of stuff-oriented."*[10] The wife of an alcoholic notes that every night they read a passage from a self-help book together. *"We talk about it. Just a couple of minutes. We also always cuddle for a couple of minutes before we get up in the morning, too."* Another spouse, in describing the ways they pay attention to each other and how this differs from their past, said on the evening of our interview, *"My husband left this morning and said he is going to try and coordinate his night at A.A. with my night out just so we're not out without each other. It is just thinking like that."*

Intriguingly, Jan hardly recalls the flowers Luke left at her bedside. What she remembers is *"being so angry at Luke. Then being in therapy and seeing Luke struggle through these therapy sessions which were not fun, which were exhausting and brutal. I don't know, it was like seeing him do something for the relationship. Seeing him subject himself to it and so forth. But seeing him there and being there in this therapy he didn't want to be in . . . I mean, I was subjecting myself to the therapy but I wanted to be there. It was like this tangible contribution that was clearly atypical for him. I felt like I could see him shifting."* The idea that one's spouse is *trying* came up repeatedly during the interviews. In her interview Cara Gunderson describes that she felt commitment to the relationship because she could see that Ken was making an effort.[11]

Luke's earlier comment that he was surprised when he learned that making a family required work is very revealing and pertinent at this point. Our understanding of what is really required to live with another person and to create a satisfying life is often limited to happy endings and quick solutions. But as Luke and others discover, this simply isn't so. It takes ongoing effort, even when the returns on that effort are not apparent. It is somewhat like raising a child: The time you invest in the child's early years to create feelings of security and to instill manners, to teach them problem solving skills, and facilitate their ability to test themselves in the world, only pay off years later. For most of us, the simple fact is that all relationships require nurturing care. For marriages that survive alcoholism and other crises characterized by the development of mistrust, there is perhaps a greater than usual need to direct attention to the relationship. Luke had to repair not only his relationship with Jan but also that with his three children. Doing so strengthened his marital relationship and increased his sense of belonging in the family.

BUILDING TRUST: REENTRY INTO THE FAMILY

Luke admitted to Dr. Madison that he felt distanced emotionally from his three children, especially their eldest, Elyse. Elyse had been old enough to remember much of the tension between him and Jan, caused by his drinking. She was young at the time but nonetheless, she had seemed to ally herself with Jan and now remained a staunch defender of Jan. Although Jan felt close to all three of the children, she worried about the effects of marital strife and alcoholism on their lives.

Dr. Madison saw all five family members on several occasions. As a result of these meetings, and based on her earlier sessions with Jan and Luke alone, she encouraged Luke to actively work to restore his relationship with Elyse. For Jan, this was another unexpected but all-important shift in their relationship. *"What I saw him doing was going after our children, and I think I saw that as more his contribution. I was totally depleted by that time. So the thought of Luke being more involved in their lives was wonderful. I didn't have any struggle: I wanted it. . . . I gave over much of the parenting to Luke."*

What Jan describes is a process in which Luke gave Jan time to recharge her energy by taking over some of the care of the children. His presence in the therapy, his assumption of his increasing child-care and involvement with other family members—all combined to make Jan more forgiving and more open to Luke's efforts. But if it was not a struggle for Jan, Luke's story was quite different. Jan recalls Luke's efforts with the children: *"He worked to get some of it* [the relationship] *back. I would say that Elyse in particular didn't make it easy for him."*

Jan points out that Luke had always been so busy with work and graduate school that he hadn't had a lot of time for the children. He loved them dearly, she believed, but his job responsibilities pressed upon him. The pressures from the outside world were always imposing on Luke. He always seemed to be under pressure for one reason or another. As the head of the history department he not only had his teaching and administrative duties, but he was also responsible for what other faculty members in his department were teaching and intradepartmental staff relations. Even summer breaks did not free him of his responsibilities completely. Summer provided time for him to take extra classes, prepare for comprehensive exams, and plan for the upcoming year of teaching. The demands seemed to be never ending.

Elyse met Luke's overtures with rejection and anger. Her loyalty to her mother was unequivocal. Luke recounts a short vacation he took with Elyse while Katherine and Daniel were away at summer camp. *"I went away with Elyse on a vacation, and Elyse was more like the dog defending Jan! I think me creating my own relationship with Elyse—it took persistence. She was determined to be true to her mother. I guess she was angry at what she saw as Jan getting the short end of the stick. Not that she consciously saw it that way, but that was about the size of it. She would hardly talk to me. She just seemed angry all the time. It made it very hard to stay with it."* But Luke persevered with painstaking effort, and Elyse eventually responded affirmatively. Luke recalls that it took several years—years of going to school events with her, taking her out for ice cream, withstanding her silences, doing things with Elyse and her friends—doing whatever he could to be involved in her life, he did. Just as when he began leaving the flowers by Jan's bedside with no expectation of being thanked, Luke accepted Elyse's initial rejections. Ever so slowly, the anger and distance between them began to dissipate.

Jan describes what this meant to her: *"I guess I ran the show for so many years. Finally, he would suggest we do something for fun and 'Oh my gosh!' I'd think, 'I don't have to suggest we do this or that.' I felt like all of a sudden I wasn't this witch!"* Not only could Jan stop seeing Luke as a monster but, because of his increasing involvement with the children, she was freed from seeing herself as a witch.[12]

Reentering the family constellation was usually accomplished with great difficulty and a fair amount of uncertainty, if it was accomplished at all. One alcoholic, sober for many years, recalled a defining moment of action. *"My daughter was giving me a whole raft of blarney. She got finished, and she went back upstairs, and my wife looked at me and she said, 'When are you going to take over?' I got up out of that chair, and I went upstairs, and I said to that kid, 'If you ever talk to me like that again, I'm gonna knock your head off. This is no way to treat someone who is trying like the devil to be a good person.' At that point, my wife had been playing both roles for fifteen years—I'm sure it was pretty wearing!"*

Often approaching a child who is loyal to the other parent is difficult. One father, sober only five years and on the cusp of creating a relationship with his college-aged daughter, described his efforts with a combination of despair and hope: *"I'm almost glad when she's away at school. I think part of it is the normal father–daughter thing. I remember making a feeble attempt to apologize to her, but it came out guilty. We were riding in the car, and I said, 'I don't know if you ever think about it, Kim, but I really am sorry for a lot of the crap that happened.' Kim said, 'I really don't think about it a whole lot, I'm just trying to get on with my life.' I immediately got irritated: God damn it! I wanted her to say, 'Dad, it's okay—you're wonderful today and the past is the past.' But she wouldn't say that. I think I would like to spend the rest of my life or a big part of it saying, 'I'm sorry Kim. I'm sorry for the summers that I didn't have the guts to be a father. And when you wanted to play, I wasn't capable of playing with you 'cause that was too scary—we'd just go over to the toy store, and I'd buy you a lot of toys with Mommy's money and the credit card and just send you off somewhere so I could go hide in the basement.' I really feel that inside—I spent so much energy hiding from Kim. I still don't feel like much of a father. I think she'll be twenty-one, and I don't have to be a father any more 'cause she's grown up. Ellen and Kim had this alliance for years: I wasn't there, and they hung together."*

One couple agreed that what they had not been able to do for their children because of alcoholism they were now doing for their grandchildren. An alcoholic father described how surprised he was at the moment he realized the hard, even unpleasant, work required daily to build and maintain a relationship with his toddler daughter. *"And I was astounded that here is this thing* [child] *that really means a lot to me, but you know,* [I realized] *I thought, you've got to change diapers!"*

Jan and Luke were fortunate that their children were relatively young when Luke began to rebuild his relationships with them. In addition, Jan's decision or need to step back and let Luke be a parent, also worked to their advantage—and to the children's advantage.

Although Jan and Luke say that therapy did not, in itself, cure everything, and they admit that it was hard work, they do acknowledge that it provided some tools to make progress in rebuilding their marriage and their family. Now, years later, they make use of therapy only occasionally. Jan returned to graduate school after about a year of therapy. With their therapist's encouragement, she became a part-time rather than full-time student, even though this was less than ideal for her program. She simply felt that the children were too young to have both parents working or going to school full time. Luke eventually completed his Ph.D. and, after some soul searching, decided to remain in his position as a department head and prep school teacher so that he could devote summers to being with his children. Although he admits the lure of a college position was very tempting, he made a choice in favor of a comfortable lifestyle and time to be with his children while they were still at home. Besides, he occasionally teaches a course at the university and often gives guest lectures. He has recently been contacted by the landscape design department of a nearby university to give a slide show about the gardens he has visited. Luke is thrilled.

NOTES

1. This feeling of being ignored by the spouse seemed to be relevant for couples in which the husband is the alcoholic.

2. Belenky et al. (1986) present a brief but informative discussion on "real talk." They distinguish real talk from didactic talk. Real talk requires "careful listening; it implies mutually shared agreement that together you are creating the optimum setting so that the half-baked or emergent ideas can grow. Real talk reaches deep into the experience of each participant; it also draws on the analytical abilities of each." True conversation, or real talk, includes discourse, exploration, talking and listening, questions, argument, speculation, and sharing. Didactic talk, on the other hand, exists when the speaker intends to hold forth rather than share.

M. F. Belenky, B. M. Clinchy, N. R. Goldberger, and J. M. Tarule, *Women's Ways of Knowing: The Development of Self, Voice, and Mind* (New York: Basic Books, 1986), 144.

3. Wives were more likely to be interested in therapy than were husbands, especially couples therapy.

4. Spouses saying that they were "doormats," "mushy," or had no identity, was common. K. J. Shirley, *Journey into Contextual Therapy: A Primer on Building Trust.* (Malvern, Pa.: Contextual Media, mimeo., 1987).

5. The phrase, "being addicted" to her husband, probably comes out of the codependency movement, which tends to use quasi-medical terms.

6. M. S. Friedman, "Martin Buber and Ivan Boszormenyi-Nagy: The Role of Dialogue in Contextual Therapy," *Psychotherapy* 26 (1989): 402–409.

7. T. Hargrave, *Families and Forgiveness: Healing Wounds in the Intergenerational Family* (New York: Brunner/Mazel, 1994), 46.

8. The spiritual guide and writer Deepak Chopra has suggested that addicts are seekers, albeit misguided seekers. He brings them squarely into the realm of humanity. D. Chopra, *Overcoming Addictions* (Pittsburgh: Three Rivers Press, 1998).

9. T. Hargrave, *Families and Forgiveness*, 66.

10. It is striking how this quote captures the sheer effort involved in investing in a relationship. As one wife of an alcoholic said, *"I had to work very hard at this. The thing that helps me is my continually going to Al-Anon meetings, and I read my literature every day."* The idea that effort is required to make a relationship work is understood.

11. Research suggests that women married to men who invest more tangible resources, emotional resources, time, energy, and effort in the relationship, experience more satisfaction in their marriages.

R. S. Sternberg and M. Hojjat, eds., *Satisfaction in Close Relationships* (New York: Guilford Press, 1997).

12. It should be underscored that this book was not intended to explore the views of children. There is tremendous literature exploring the lives of children of alcoholics. What Jan and Luke describe is the slow process of shifting the balance in their lives to giving and taking in more equal ways.

Chapter 12

Renewal and Healing: The Mysterious Nature of Marriage

Feelings are a mere accompaniment to the metaphysical fact of the relation which is fulfilled, not in the soul, but between the I and Thou.

—Martin Buber, *I and Thou*

As we end, I ask Jan and Luke how they would describe their relationship today. Both sit for a moment, pensive. Jan speaks first. *"I keep a journal, and every once in a while I go back and read it because I don't want to get into a sticky place again. . . . I have a friend who says you can never take a 'nap.'"* The pain has been so great, that even today, Jan must remain vigilant. "*What I mean by 'not taking a nap' is that I have to be aware of what's going on.*"

Jan pauses as if waiting for Luke to comment. When he doesn't, she continues, *"I mean, he is very good. I think our relationship has really gotten good. I get what I need, I think he gets what he needs. We know what each other's needs are."* Jan begins to shift the flowers around in the vase on the table beside her. Luke is pensive, as he has been throughout the interview. He looks confused for the first time, or tentative, as if his mouth won't quite form the words he needs. "*We are complementary. I am a great global strategist. I have creative ideas and am very good at kind of creative global plans, but when it comes to details, the focus is her department. I am more emotional, and Jan will have the tendency to kind of slow down and look at things more objectively.*"

Once he seems satisfied that he is addressing the right question, he continues: *"I don't think I trusted relationships as much; the thought of real renewal, healing, or whatever you want to call it was not present for me. I started off thinking, 'well, you try to hold on to as much of the relationship as you can—you arrest the decline.' And now I have this sense of being in love. I feel incredibly happy about where we are, and it was not possible to imagine that before."* He pauses again and then adds, *"It's mysterious—I know that it's not enough for one person to say 'I love you': the other person has got to be ready to hear that."*

As the interview comes to an end, Luke turns on the spotlights and we wander out into their yard to see the hydrangeas. Jan points out a lace-cap in the process of changing from pink to lavender. The color change is subtle but nonetheless dramatic. Yet as I drive away, it is not the hydrangeas or the heat of the summer that I think of. It is Luke's analogy of building loving relationships being like saying to someone who is homeless, *"You can live in a house like this."* It is possible; it can be done.

The rebalancing and strengthening of Jan and Luke's marriage took many years, and the process was sporadic. They initiated and built trust, like most couples, in a variety of ways. First, Luke used A.A., while Jan used Al-Anon. They also made use of therapy after five years of sobriety. Although they were at an apparent dead end in their relationship, the therapy provided a level playing field on which each of them could not only face the depth of their responsibility but also surface the possibilities for healing. These possibilities were revealed through the painstaking efforts of each to hear the other's side; to listen to each other; to explore some of the repercussions, both good and bad, of their childhood loyalties; and to identify what it was they wanted from each other rather than remain stuck in a vicious cycle of blame.

Although the therapist acknowledged the victimization Jan experienced as a result of Luke's drinking, both Jan and Luke took responsibility for having harmed the relationship. This had several effects. First, it became less clear that either was just victim or victimizer. This left room for each of them to think about themselves in a new way as well as to discover the other. This was an opening for Luke to see himself not simply as a beast but as a person. For Jan, it was the opportunity to stop identifying herself as the victim and to be able to see the ways she had inadvertently contributed to their problems.

Luke's acknowledgment that he had indeed done much more than "dent the fender" went beyond this important insight and set him on a path of attempting to give to Jan in some very concrete ways. He gave her flowers, but from Jan's viewpoint, his real contribution was in sitting through the very difficult therapy sessions. For the first time in a long time, she was able to see his effort, to acknowledge his commitment to the marriage.

Luke also sought out better relationships with his children—a task that exposed him to their rebukes. In addition to his building these relationships, Luke's increasing involvement with the children freed Jan from feeling overburdened by the children's needs and enabled her to see herself in a better light. Luke's reentry into the family constellation presumably served all of the family members by strengthening ties and, thus, contributed to the rebalancing of the family.

Their story highlights Luke's slow realization that good relationships don't simply happen—they require effort and attention to create and maintain. Effort is also required to fortify trust between spouses. Rather than simply "arresting the decline," as Luke said, he discovered the possibility of building something better than he had imagined. The existence of a positive early relationship and Jan's faith in what was good in Luke helped her to maintain a double vision of the relationship during the worst of times. Unlike some spouses who could recall the good times in earlier years, or who noted that some aspects of their lives remained good throughout the drinking years, Jan's memory was dim and she had to rely on faith that whatever those good qualities had been, they still existed. Her faith helped her conjure up a double vision of better times that served as a residual resource at a particularly crucial juncture of their marriage.

Part V

Lessons on Resiliency

It does not begin in the upper story of humanity. It begins no higher than where humanity begins. There are no gifted and ungifted here, only those who give themselves and those who withhold themselves.

—Martin Buber, *Between Man and Man*

Conclusion

In order to save their marriages, the Gundersons, the Royers, the Bertolinos, and the Abbotts all had to navigate the treacherous and shifting waters of relational crises. Rather than simply focusing on the dangers and pitfalls, they also have provided a panoramic view of the terrain of resilience. The development of resilience was not a smooth continuum but sometimes was characterized by an awkward, timid, and wavering path with stretches of self-assured and directed behavior. These accounts highlight the facts that the couples are endowed with both assets and weaknesses and that their relationships are a combination of fragility and immeasurable strength. They have spoken openly about their struggles, both failures and successes. In doing so, they have offered us parables about the possibilities for relational renewal. They speak as well about what happens when these possibilities are obscured. The couples have provided extensive views of the mechanisms that came into play in their ongoing struggles and shared a glimpse of the slow yet deliberate regeneration and growth of their relationships. In their essence, they offer us hope that even in the darkest times and places, there exist the possibilities of redemption and growth.

Ken and Cara Gunderson have been married twice—to each other. Ken's alcoholism and eventual involvement with illicit drugs took them down a path so bleak it is amazing that Ken is alive and that they are still married; it is even more amazing that they are living together in harmony. Ken and Cara's story is dramatic. Today, they are happily married. Yet, as explained in chapter three, this is no storybook marriage. Cara wishes for a bit more, but, as she says, she is a realist. She takes the best and tries diligently to make small but significant changes. Also, she sees Ken's very genuine efforts. With courage, stamina, and determination, Ken and Cara weave a true love story.

Married nearly thirty years, and their relationship steeped in volatility from its inception, Mike and Ann Bertolino provide an inside view on the surprising strength of absolute commitment. Mike's and Ann's abilities to look past the labels and the stigma to see each other's potential are as moving as they are pivotal. Their commitment to each other in conjunction with their flashes of anger underscores the fact that good marriages and resiliency take many different forms. There is not just one kind of alcoholic marriage, just as there is not only one kind of nonalcoholic marriage; and there is not only one way for resiliency to take form.[1] Mike and Ann's marriage will stand out for both its strength and its struggle.

Years of emotional turmoil and exploitation had nearly eradicated the limited trust between Jan and Luke Abbott. After a period of five or more years of Luke's sobriety, they found that sobriety and individual support groups simply were not enough. Their story takes us on a journey through the therapeutic process of rebuilding their marriage and investing in each other. Jan and Luke show us that insight alone is not enough. To move solidly out of the abyss of crisis requires deliberate action. Their story is about the hard work of finding one's footing, of reassessing blame, and of building trust. Today they both report a mutually satisfying relationship. Their ability to address their past leaves them both content and on solid ground, although Jan admits she remains vigilant to this day.

In sharp contrast to these couples is the Royers. Peg and Dave maintain a strictly enforced distance. They inhabit parallel worlds, or, as Peg expressed it, they are on *"two different tracks."* For all intents and purposes, Peg and Dave Royer are relationally bankrupt. Peg timidly longs for more, and Dave gave up expecting anything from Peg many years ago. Dave finds reward and meaning in his volunteer work and expresses satisfaction in having his life parallel to Peg. Peg, on the other hand, is sad and in despair that nothing better will come to pass. Yet the distance between Peg and Dave may be no greater than the distance that once existed between the Gundersons, Abbotts, or Bertolinos. What is different is the Royer's failure to imagine a way to traverse the abyss that separates them or, in Dave's case, to even want that to happen. The cost of alcoholism has simply been too high, the pain, too acute. Neither one is willing to address still-festering wounds or long-term disappointment or to take the risk of exploring what might be possible.

What Peg and Dave do have is a truce of sorts. But this truce is no victory: Dave's anger is palpable, and Peg's disappointment, profound. They are victims, and not only in the ways they think they are. Rather than simply being victims of each other, they are also victims of their own inability to grasp the resources in front of them. Although they are caught in a web of anger, blame, and despair, their predicament helps us to discover some of the points at which they might have chosen other options. They remind us of the fragility of relationships and of the human suffering that results from the diminishment of trust.

Clearly, all four couples experienced something quite different from what they imagined on their wedding days. But that is not uncommon. When couples stand at the altar and recite their marriage vows, they promise to love, to honor, and to cherish. In fact, this is what most couples celebrate. But they also pledge to remain together during bad times, indeed until death. In other words, the idea that rough times and treacherous terrain are as much a part of marriage as are love and adoration is a given. Unfortunately, much of the marriage literature over the past fifty years has focused primarily on the pathology of relationships, with a relatively scant focus on ideal relationships. But this dichotomy has left us stranded. In fact, most relationships are neither pathological nor ideal. Instead, the majority fall into a middle ground of good-enough marriages.

The Gundersons, Bertolinos, and Abbotts achieved this middle ground after a long descent into the abyss of mistrust and despair. The question is, how did they reach this middle ground? How did they reconnect to rebuild their relationships? What was required of them as individuals, and what was required of them as couples to do this? Fortunately, they have provided us with a road map that reveals their journey—the residual resources they brought with them for the journey, the moments of choice that moved them, and, finally, the ways they built trust that ultimately made their relationships strong.

THE JOURNEY: WHAT THEY BROUGHT

Research that has explored what constitutes satisfying marriages and the ingredients that may contribute to divorce has identified important elements of each. What has been largely missing has been a more nuanced and comprehensive understanding of a relationship that is grounded in the context of individual couples. By being grounded in a context, we have the possibility of moving beyond discrete variables and the narrow spheres of pathological and ideal relationships. Instead, we can look squarely at those more elusive aspects of relationship—the residual resources. For these are what each couple brought along on their journey. These resources are what held them together in the worst of times, what enabled them to maintain hope in the midst of despair, and what provided some ground under their feet. This ground was not solid, but soft and shifting. Like the sand beneath a person's feet as the ocean waves wash over them, these resources were often hard to hold on to. What were the resources?

In these interviews, we have heard of many resources, such as love, liking each other, a sense of hopefulness, devotion to family, feelings of friendship, shared commitment, shared religion and values, and basic trust in the other. Couples also reported that having good experiences and positive images to remember to buoy the relationship in the worst of times, sharing a common identity, the acceptance of alcoholism in their marriage, and the ability to exercise personal insight, provided residual resources for keeping their marriages together and for serving as a foundation on which to rebuild. That some couples described their experience of finding goodness and pleasure in the midst of the destructive forces of alcoholism was unexpected. Even while the relationship between spouses was in the active process of being nearly destroyed, they still shared in the construction of a life together. Thus, they were in a building process even as the process of destruction shook the very foundations of their relationships. Finally, their sheer determination held them together. These residual resources are often overlooked or taken for granted.

THE JOURNEY: WHAT MOVED THEM

Although the journey for many of these couples is and has been slow and circuitous, it has at times moved forward by great leaps rather than by inches. These leaps were the "moments of choice," described by the couples. Moments of choice often require people to make dramatic changes in their assumptions about themselves and their marriages as well as changes in their behaviors. Often these moments of choice proved to be life altering. With the exception of the Royers, the moments of choice moved each partner *into* the relationship rather than *away from it*. For some, like Ken Gunderson, it was the moment in sobriety while living in a distant city when he first asked himself, *"What the hell am I doing here?"* It was this question, along with the choice to quit drinking, that moved him to return to his family and begin again. Cara's moment of choice was her decision to exonerate Ken, to offer him unconditional love. Given her options, this may have been the least painful choice for her and the most expedient for their relationship. Ann Bertolino's moment of choice was when she decided to relinquish her anger and her rage. In fact, these couples often felt that they could be destroyed by the whirlwind of rage—a rage they often could not explain. The power of the rage was so great they had little choice for their own survival, let alone the relationship's survival, but to turn away from ire and embrace love. The alternative was an all-consuming rage. The couples were also moved toward one another by the decision of some spouses to seek help, most often through self-help groups, in order to learn about alcoholism and its effects. What these moments have in common for the Gundersons, Bertolinos, and Abbotts is that their force catapulted the spouses toward insight, action, and change.

THE JOURNEY: WHAT MADE THEM STRONG?

What made them strong? Quite simply, trust. But like resources, trust can be elusive. Few people would argue that trust is not an essential ingredient of most healthy and satisfying relationships. The crises in which these couples found themselves were primarily crises of trust. Having diminished respect, reciprocity, and reliability, the very existence of their marriages was threatened by an avalanche of mistrust. In relationships largely characterized by mistrust, the challenge to find trust was daunting. How did this happen? What shifted? And what have we learned from it?

Three primary changes occurred within these relationships that served to nurture trust. These couples were willing to make an assessment of their need to change and to accept some personal responsibility for the near demise of the relationship, to find the delicate balance between caring for oneself while offering care to one's partner, and to take deliberate action to invest in the relationship.

The Gundersons, Bertolinos, and Abbotts had to look at themselves with a critical eye and say, "In what ways are my expectations out of line, and what can I do to change them? How have I contributed to the destruction of the relationship?" Ann Bertolino said that, early in their marriage, she expected Mike to take care of everything, but she has come to realize that this was not helpful to her or to their relationship. Cara Gunderson had to take a hard look at her own shortcomings. For Jan Abbott, it meant no longer being the doormat of the relationship. Mike Bertolino went to therapy, and Ann stopped acting as and viewing herself as merely an appendage. These changes required a careful examination of how these individuals intentionally or unintentionally contributed to the devolution of their marriages. For those situations in which both partners were aware that they needed to make some adjustments in the relationship, balance and fairness eventually prevailed. When both shared the burden to change the relationship, the couple felt a greater sense of balance in their relationship. Once more we note, that the nonalcoholic spouses did not take responsibility for the alcoholism. These spouses did, however, take responsibility for their own behaviors that were not useful, that were at times destructive, and that made their own development, if not the development of their spouse, more problematic. There have been criticisms of nonalcoholic spouses taking some responsibility when it is the alcoholic's behavior that directly led to the marital crisis. However, if one spouse becomes ill or unemployed, the other spouse would usually make some adjustments in their behaviors to accommodate the illness or the unemployment. For example, a wife who has cancer might be "responsible" for the marital crisis, but presumably her husband would make some alterations in his behavior while she is undergoing treatment. Part of being in a balanced relationship is the ability to distribute the burdens and share in the pain. Furthermore, it is the *relationship* that has suffered, not simply the individuals. Thus, it is the relationship, not simply the individuals, that needs to be repaired. To suggest that repair and balance could come about from the efforts of one spouse only is, perhaps, unrealistic.

Seeking that balance between caring for one's own needs and the needs of one's spouse was another central task. To focus exclusively on one's own needs is as destructive as it is to focus exclusively on the needs of others. In order to feel fairly treated, care must be both given and received. Recall Peg Royer's comment that, *"It's very easy to get lost in this shuffle of people who all they do is make their needs known to you. Why am I angry? Unfairness or what I perceive as being unfair in our relationship makes me have a lot of rage."* If there is not a relative balance, the relationship becomes one-sided and each of the partners is likely to feel that he or she is being treated unfairly by the other.

What did caring for one's own needs look like in these marriages? Early in recovery, couples often made the choice to attend A.A. or Al-Anon, which provided them with support and knowledge about alcoholism. In addition to gaining knowledge and immediate support, they also learned a common language that made it easier to "hear" the other's voice. For most couples, the schism between them, which was caused or at least exacerbated by alcoholism, was so great that they had lost the ability to communicate. By attending self-help groups and learning a unique vocabulary, they could finally talk to each other in terms both could understand. Thus these couples found a language that enabled them to reestablish trust. Given the often vituperative nature of some of these relationships prior to the group meetings, it is no small accomplishment that they were able to discover and use this "common language."

Letting go of responsibility for the behavior of others was a critical form of self-care for both partners, but particularly for the alcoholic. Even if problematic, it was necessary. Just when the partner expected the alcoholic to be more involved in direct and positive ways in the relationship, the alcoholic needed to do the opposite: to take care of his or her own needs. Even though the initial stages of recovery are difficult for the alcoholic's partner, a period of almost total self-focus appeared to be a necessary mechanism of self-nurturing for most of the alcoholics. Many spouses and couples invested in their own hobbies and careers. Ann Bertolino wrote a book, and Ken Gunderson became an accomplished woodworker. In both cases, they were caring for themselves by investing in meaningful enterprises.

An important mechanism for caring for one's own needs was finding one's "voice." The couples spoke quite passionately about this.[2] This was true for males as well as females, alcoholics as well as nonalcoholics. As noted previously, these couples did not support the notion that women "lose their voices" while men do not. Part of voice was the expression of feelings and emotions. Partners commented that talking about their emotions made them feel better, and it also made their spouses feel better. No longer left in the dark, the partner found grist for discussion. Recall that Cara Gunderson referred to her response upon hearing Ken's feelings as *"like striking gold."*

Finding oneself, finding a voice, and expressing feelings are aspects of self-delineation. Self-delineation also includes the decision to stop pleasing others at the expense of oneself. Cara Gunderson politely gave her daughter, Mara, a second choice of dates when she could visit, because Cara refused to disrupt her own plans to accommodate Mara. Ann Bertolino spoke of feeling like she was "supposed to be" a certain kind of wife even though she was drowning in all of those expectations. The men experienced these aspects also. In order to keep the peace, they not only withheld their voices but also "went-along-to-get-along." Many of those interviewed were experts at pleasing—at saying and seeming to be what they believed others wanted them to be. As noted, this sacrificial pleasing prohibits others from knowing who we really are. The more we try to appear to be what or who we think others expect us to be, the more impossible it becomes to have an intimate relationship because our partners will only know the side of us that pleases (or we think pleases) them. Persisting in this pleasing behavior means failing to self-delineate. This deprives other people of knowing who we truly are, as we deprive ourselves of experiencing emotional intimacy.

If caring for oneself is important, it must be balanced by offering care to others. *Due consideration* is the term applied to the offer of care to others. One spouse said simply, *"It's a two-way street."* How did these couples care for each other? Luke Abbott's gift of flowers by the nightstand every night was an example of offering care. Another way of offering care was taking the simple but often elusive step of asking about the other. One of the most notable examples of this was the alcoholic who described the chronology of asking his wife how her day was until he no longer had to force himself to ask about her day; he truly wanted to know. This somewhat benign effort provides one example of how change and trust building occur. Such efforts move couples toward connection, toward relational imagination, toward repair.

Taking deliberate action begins with asking oneself what would improve the relationship. Recall that Mike Bertolino realized that if he wanted a better relationship with Ann, he needed to stop reading the newspaper at the table. This is a simple gesture, but illustrates the kind of behavior that says to the other person: You are central to me; this relationship is central to me; I want connection, not disconnection. These are not incidental ways to invest in the marriage, they are calculated. Similar direct actions led another spouse to say about her marriage, *"We've managed our destiny."*

Another form of deliberate action was therapy. The Abbott's detailed story of their experience shows how therapy can move people out of stasis and into action. According to Ann Bertolino, Mike's therapy *"was the thing that helped us pull ourselves together."* For the Abbotts, one of the most notable outcomes was the slow fading of the sharp dividing line between victim and victimizer. Jan sat and watched Luke struggle in therapy. Having acknowledged her own shortcomings and then observing Luke wrestle with the therapy, she arrived at the inevitable question: "If Luke was more than a victimizer, what and who was he?" Furthermore, if he was capable of being the victim, perhaps Jan was capable of victimizing in her own way. For the first time in Luke's sobriety, Jan had to face the fact that Luke's identity was not solely that of alcoholic. Before he was an alcoholic, he was alive with all the possibilities—negative and positive—that personhood implies: "even the most destructively entitled addict was once a devoted, giving person until he reached the critical point of depletion and despair."[3]

For Luke, one of the important shifts was manifest in his reentry into the lives of his children. This effort was slow to produce results and not always welcomed by Luke's daughter. To Jan, it offered a reprieve from being overburdened. Unlike the romantic vision of family automatically arising by dint of birth and marriage, real families and close relationships that have been through a prolonged crisis require effort and time. Reentry into the family is another self-righting action. The spouse who has heretofore been the active, perhaps overly responsible, parent is freed to pursue other interests and activities. The alcoholic obtains the opportunity to have a relationship from which they previously felt disqualified. Although the purpose of this book was not to address issues between parents and children, it became clear from the interviews that establishing or reestablishing relationships with children was an important component of leading a more balanced life.

Many of the spouses accepted the notion that alcoholism is a disease. By equating alcoholism with a common disease such as diabetes, spouses were better able to understand and sympathize with the alcoholic's struggle. No longer viewed as a monster, alcoholics were seen as having an illness. This shift in thinking contributed to the humanization of the alcoholic.

The Gundersons, Bertolinos, and Abbotts are studies in the rebuilding of trust. In the sphere of family studies, the development of trust has been identified as the family's most important task.[4] Once thought to be developed in a finite amount during a short but critical stage of infant development, trust between parent and child is now believed to be continuously shaped and reshaped through reciprocal care or its lack.[5]

Beyond the discovery of residual resources, the experience of moments of choice, and the initiation of building trust, what made a difference for these couples? For one, many were, like Cara Gunderson, realists. They stopped holding their spouses accountable to unrealistic expectations. By becoming realists, they removed an intense pressure from the relationship. If one partner feels continuously disappointed, there is little chance for trust to thrive. Instead, the partners considered not only what their spouses had to offer but also what they could do for themselves. This generated a recalibration of the relationship, which in turn brought their expectations in line with reality.

In contrast to the crises these couples faced, the dramas of their resilience could seem almost mundane to the uninvolved. When Cara Gunderson said that hearing Ken express his feelings was like striking gold, some people might wonder about the analogy. After all, he had been critical of her choice when he rejected her decision to have their child get braces. However, if what people really want is to be loved, cherished, heard, and acknowledged, something so seemingly simple as hearing a spouse express their feelings can actually be quite profound. In fact, people yearn to be accompanied through life. Ken's involvement was a form of accompaniment for Cara. These couples, having seen some of the worst of what marriage can be about, were more than satisfied with the small but crucial improvements in their relationships.

The notion of what is accepted as satisfying can correlate with changes in expectations. These individuals would not have chosen their life situations. Like anyone else who survives a crisis, they felt they had learned important lessons and even grown stronger in the process. But the encounter with adversity was not what they had bargained for, not at all a part of their marital expectations. These are, for the most part, people who feel that they would have been better off if they had had an easier path in life.

Their experiences underscore the fact that change is relational as well as individual. Both spouses had to take stock, make changes, and find ways to rebalance their own lives as well as their marriages. They had to accept certain aspects of their relationship and attempt to modify others. They had to see that they were different from each other, and as such, would always have differences of opinions, needs, and desires.

Among the findings of this study there are three that stand out as particularly surprising. First, these couples continued to build a relationship even as it was being destroyed. Second, the nonalcoholic spouse sooner or later accepted that alcoholism was a disease. Finally, although each of these couples struggled with alcoholism as the presenting problem, their relationships were quite dissimilar. What do these findings suggest?

The idea that relationships can be simultaneously built and destroyed is intriguing. In the words of one spouse, *"It just wasn't all bad."* The concept of marriage in some ideal or abstract sense served as a life preserver for many couples. Children, a home, friends bound them together. They had built a life and were determined not to relinquish it. This suggests that marriages function along different strands at the same time. Although ultimately interdependent, it is possible that these strands are also capable of functioning autonomously or nearly autonomously, at least for certain periods of time. In order to understand the middle ground of relationships, we must understand relationships as both serving and being based upon multiple purposes. Marriage is an intricate complex of relationships, actions, thoughts, feelings, and experiences. One aspect may overfunction if another underfunctions. For example, if the marital relationship is suffering, perhaps children and home or work take on additional importance. While this may appear to be pathological or a form of displaced concern, it may be a transitory adaptation to cope with difficulty. If building a family is a primary function of marriage, it may be that for some people enduring long periods of unfairness, imbalance, and mistrust is simply worth the pain in order to maintain the integrity of the family unit. Orford suggests that failing to understand such complexity in the weave of the strands could lead to misleading shortcuts in understanding. Instead of seeing a context of various behaviors, we identify 'coping failures' and thereby cast relationships in overly simplistic terms. If we are satisfied to categorize all marriages as either ideal or pathological, such oversimplification is necessary. If, however, we can tolerate the idea that marriages are uniquely complex, we are more likely to succeed at understanding both individual situations and the true nature of relationships. Accepting the idea that a marriage can be both built and destroyed at the same time, acknowledges this complexity.

As noted previously, whether or not alcoholism is a disease is a long-standing debate in the literature. For the couples interviewed, the identification of alcoholism as a disease was a helpful piece of the equation these spouses began to understand in order to rebuild their marriages. Almost all of the nonalcoholic spouses noted that they found some comfort in understanding that the alcoholic was not purposely destroying the marriage but instead was struggling with a disease. This seemed to provide a beginning point for compassion to take hold or to at least enter into the realm of possibility. Although some critics might argue that alcoholism is not a disease, my purpose is to identify what helped these couples. And it was clearly helpful to them to consider alcoholism a disease. Whenever a couple is involved in a process of forgiveness for any breach of trust, there must be some means of accessing compassion and initiating insight.

The third unexpected finding was that the couples did not especially resemble one another, although they each happened to face the crisis of alcoholism. It may be that identical or similar destructive patterns are revealed in many people's lives, but there was nothing to suggest that there was some discrete, identifiable flaw in these couples that was the single cause of their difficulties. Instead, there was evidence of unexpected yet similar capacities to cope and rebalance and to resolve problems in the midst of extreme duress and mistrust.

Resiliency, the self-righting of relationships, is a paradox. These couples are healed but not unharmed. The experience of marital crisis is held close to them. In virtually every interview, the couples' painful emotions were just below the surface—and often rose above the surface. As noted in the introduction, these relationships are not fairy tales, nor did they have Hollywood endings. The couples spoke of living with remorse, regret, occasional depression, and of wishing for more from their spouses. Yet, they had found a relatively comfortable balance. They acknowledged their success at holding their marriages and their families together, of building relationships that provided both spouses with comfort and a sense of being well held, and of sharing past times and cultivating ongoing love and friendship. As Mike Bertolino said, the tragedy would have been allowing the relationship to end, even though they still live with some unmet needs and unresolved issues. Even as they celebrated their successes, most couples spoke of continuing struggles to improve their relationships and to find better ways of relating to one another. They know that they must be more aware of the other's needs while being mindful of their own needs and that they must be vigilant in order to make a satisfactory and rewarding relationship even more so.

Many of the actions these couples described as helpful were quite simple—asking a spouse how her day was, making sure the two of them spent time together regularly, learning to talk openly about likes and dislikes. This raises a question of simplicity vis-à-vis complexity. Simplicity is captured in the common themes of residual resources, moments of choice, and building trust. These are pieces that we can point to and say, yes, these are steps toward resiliency that can be identified. Recall the analogy of the father quoted in Part IV—to have a relationship with his child meant he had to change the diapers. Marriages may be analogous to caring for a child—they take time, they take care, and they take doing the hard work of tending to, of being concerned with, of imagining the other side, and of cleaning up the messes: You have to change the diapers.

And yet it would be dishonest to suggest that there is not something more complex and mysterious about the process. Luke Abbott captured it near the end of his interview with Jan: *"It's mysterious—I know that it's not enough for one person to say 'I love you': the other person has got to be ready to hear that."* Luke is correct: there is a mysteriousness about the entire process.

Is there a way to accept both truths, that relationships are both complex and simple? Mysterious and quite basic? Should the mysterious nature of relationships discourage couples who are now, perhaps, in a crisis? I think not. The ability to be in a relationship is, according to Martin Buber, "no privilege of intellectual activity. . . . It does not begin in the upper story of humanity. It begins no higher than where humanity begins. There are no gifted and ungifted here, only those who give themselves and those who withhold themselves."

Mysterious or not, relationships can grow. The Gundersons, Bertolinos, and Abbotts are not more gifted than others. They have awkwardly but ably activated the relational resources between them; they have been drawn to moments of choice that brought them closer to each other rather than farther apart; and they have found and built trust where least expected. Their stories are real, they are informative, and most important, full of hope.

But they are stories of ordinary courage—this is the day-to-day courage that is required of people to live in relationship rather than outside of it, to struggle to be who and what they want to be even when this is in opposition to what others need and want, to balance this with reasonable concern and care for others, to move forward in faith when this is all there is, and to see and seek hope and opportunity even in the face of despair. Their experiences are valuable testaments to the power of resilience.

NOTES

1. J. Gottman (with N. Silver), *Why Marriages Succeed or Fail* (New York: Simon & Schuster, 1994).

J. S. Wallerstein and S. Blakeslee, *The Good Marriage: How and Why Love Lasts* (New York: Houghton Mifflin, 1995).

P. Steinglass, L. A. Bennett, S. J. Wolin, and D. Reiss, *The Alcoholic Family* (New York: Basic Books, 1987).

2. "Voice" is a good example of the dynamic nature of resources and why it is so difficult to identify these resources as simply caring for the self or for the other. With voice, one is able to express one's own needs, opinions, and concerns. It is most obviously a way to care for oneself. On the other hand, by finding one's voice, a person also "gives" to the other. By letting a person know what your opinions, needs, and thoughts are, you offer the other person a window through which to see who you really are. In essence, this becomes a way of giving to that person. Thus, what looks at first glance like caring for one's own needs may well be a way of caring for the needs of another. Likewise, something like taking deliberate action to help the marriage, such as giving your spouse flowers each night, appears to be only an act of giving to another person. However, this offers the spouse who gives the flowers a way to contribute to the relationship in a meaningful way. By so doing, he or she earns entitlement. This may be especially important in marriages in which there has been a breach of trust, such as in cases of domestic violence, an affair, or alcoholism. The person who has contributed to the diminishment of trust needs to find ways to give to their spouse once again.

3. I. Boszormenyi-Nagy, and B. R. Krasner, *Between Give and Take: A Clinical Guide to Contextual Therapy* (New York: Brunner/Mazel, 1986), 387.

4. S. E. Lutz and J. P. Medway, "Contextual Family Therapy and Victims of Incest," *Journal of Adolescence* (7) (1984): 319–327.

5. J. Kagan, *Three Seductive Ideas* (Cambridge, Mass.: Harvard University Press, 1998). M. Cotroneo, "Families and Abuse: A Contextual Approach," in *Family Resources: The Hidden Partner in Family Therapy*, ed. M. A. Karpel (New York: Guilford Press, 1986).

B. J. Hibbs, "The Context of Growth: Relational Ethics between Parents and Children," in *Children in Family Contexts: Perspectives on Treatment*, ed., L. Combrinick-Graham (New York: Guilford Press, 1989).

Appendix 1

Overview of Alcoholism, Alcoholics Anonymous, and Al-Anon

"Alcoholism is a chronic disease characterized by a tendency to drink more than was intended, unsuccessful attempts at stopping drinking, and continued drinking despite adverse social and occupational consequences."[1] Alcoholism produces both psychological and physical dependence for the more than ten million alcoholics in the United States. Because of the stigma attached to alcoholism, it is assumed that estimates are conservative. J. Krestan and C. Bepko point out that every alcoholic affects the lives of several other people. They estimate that a total of thirty-five to forty-four million people in the United States are directly affected by alcoholism.[2]

The cost of alcoholism and alcohol-related problems in 1995 was estimated to be $166.6 billion dollars.[3] This estimate includes costs related to health care, productivity loss, crime, and automobile accidents. More than half of the $166.6 cost was covered by the alcoholics themselves, with the remainder covered by the government, insurance companies, and the victims of crimes and traffic accidents.

The specific effects of alcoholism can include depression, psychosis, and gastrointestinal problems, which can include inflammation of the esophagus and of the stomach, and ulcers. The liver, pancreas, and heart can also be affected adversely. High blood pressure can result, and in some cases this may lead to stroke. In addition, there can be nerve deterioration in the arms and legs. In recent years, as more attention has been paid to women alcoholics, it has become clear that drinking by pregnant women can lead to birth defects and fetal alcohol syndrome (FAS). FAS is the leading cause of mental retardation, an outcome of alcoholism that is 100 percent preventable. FAS can include growth deficiency, facial malformations, and central nervous system dysfunction. The economic cost of FAS was estimated to be $1.6 billion per year in 1985.[4] The incidence is one in every 1,000 live births.

The economic costs of alcoholism, however, are only part of the equation. The emotional costs are staggering. To help address these costs there are a variety of self-help groups available to the public. Among the most well known are Alcoholics Anonymous (A.A.) and Al-Anon. Both are self-help programs, and both use a twelve-step approach. A.A. is primarily for alcoholics, and Al-Anon for family and friends who are affected by an alcoholic.

A.A. (ALCOHOLICS ANONYMOUS)

A.A. was established in 1935 to help alcoholics achieve and maintain sobriety. The only requirement for membership is the desire to stop drinking. Meetings at any one site are usually held weekly, but most communities have multiple sites with meetings held at a variety of times from early morning to late at night. They are free, although participants are invited to make a minimal donation of their choice. A.A. meetings are held throughout the world so that access to them is relatively easy. There are two kinds of meetings: "open" and "closed." Open meetings are for any interested person (including alcoholics); closed meetings are limited to alcoholics. Meetings typically last one to two hours. They vary in size, from a few people to hundreds of people.

The format of both A.A. and Al-Anon meetings vary somewhat but usually includes a chairperson who begins the meeting, introduces the speaker, and brings the meeting to a close. One person, who may be a group member or a member of another group, is the designated speaker. The designated speaker talks on a topic upon which the group has agreed previously. Most often, the talk includes a personal account by the speaker. This is frequently followed by an open discussion wherein anyone in attendance is free to contribute their thoughts and insights. Topics are often based on readings from A.A. literature, and especially the "Twelve Steps" of A.A. Near the end of the meeting, the group often recites what is known as the serenity prayer:

> God grant me the serenity to accept the things I cannot change,
> The courage to change the things I can,
> And the wisdom to know the difference.

The meeting is then adjourned.

A.A. and Al-Anon are "twelve-step" programs. This means that there are twelve guiding steps, or principles, that members study. These twelve steps have been modified in recent years for use by a variety of other self-help groups. For A.A., the twelve steps are:

1. We admitted we were powerless over alcohol, that our lives had become unmanageable.
2. Came to believe that a Power greater than ourselves could restore us to sanity.
3. Made a decision to turn our will and our lives over to the care of God as we understood Him.
4. Made a searching and fearless moral inventory of ourselves.
5. Admitted to God, to ourselves, and to another human being the exact nature of our wrongs.
6. Were entirely ready to have God remove all these defects of character.
7. Humbly asked Him to remove our shortcomings.
8. Made a list of all persons we had harmed, and became willing to make amends to them all.
9. Made direct amends to such people wherever possible, except when to do so would injure them or others.
10. Continued to take personal inventory and when we were wrong, promptly admitted it.

11. Sought through prayer and meditation to improve our conscious contact with God as we understood Him, praying only for knowledge of His will for us and the power to carry that out.
12. Having had a spiritual awakening as the result of these Steps, we tried to carry this message to alcoholics, and to practice these principles in all our affairs.[5]

The topic of "amends" (steps 8 and 9) came up during the interviews. Amends refers to attempts to make up in some way for harm done. This might mean verbal apology, efforts to provide additional care to those harmed, or simply to remain sober. The interpretation of the twelve steps and how they are followed, is largely an individual decision.

In addition to the Twelve Steps, there are Twelve Traditions that address the organizational structure of A.A., and there is also the main text of A.A., "The Big Book." Members usually read and reflect on all of these as well as on the many publications of brochures, booklets, and books, made available through A.A. meetings and A.A. headquarters.

A.A. slogans are also used to help members be mindful of how to live and how to stay sober. Examples of slogans include: "One day at a time," "Keep it simple," and "Let go and let God." Their purpose is to provide guidelines for recovery and for living that can be accessed quickly and easily.

Members also receive guidance, if they choose, by having a sponsor, who is a recovering alcoholic who is willing to serve as a guide or mentor for those with less sobriety. Having a sponsor early on in sobriety is customary. The sponsor is typically available to listen, to guide, and to be contacted in an emergency. Some A.A. members always have a sponsor, and some have a sponsor early in their sobriety but not in later sobriety. Like most of A.A., this is a personal choice.

Although most people who attend A.A. are sober, they do not refer to themselves as "recovered," but "in recovery." This is an important distinction, as most alcoholics view their recovery as an ongoing process of remaining sober and developing themselves as people. Unlike a disease such as pneumonia, which can be cured, alcoholism is a disease thought by some to be incurable, and A.A. members typically remain vigilant for the rest of their lives. An alcoholic knows that they could, at any time, return to drinking. Thus, the term, *in recovery* is standard. It should be noted that there are some who believe that alcoholics do not need to abstain totally from the use of alcohol but can drink in limited amounts. This stance is very controversial and is not the position of A.A., which encourages total abstinence.

A.A. is considered a spiritual program in that there is acknowledgment of a "higher power," or God. However, how members define higher power, or God, is up to them. To some members, their higher power may be the group itself. There is no prescribed definition. In fact, A.A. is not allied with any other organizations, institutions, sects, denominations, or politics. A.A. attempts to remain clear of any controversy and does not endorse or oppose any cause. Its sole purpose is to help alcoholics stay sober.

AL-ANON

Al-Anon is to families of alcoholics what A.A. is to the alcoholic. Structured in a similar way, these are group meetings for families and friends of alcoholics who are sober or still drinking. Typically, these meetings are attended by spouses who seek guidance in dealing with the alcoholic in their lives and guidance in living their own lives in the best way possible. These meetings are also held throughout the world. Like A.A., they are free except for a voluntary modest donation, which the member determines on his own. The structure also includes a speaker who may or may not be a member of that particular meeting. Like A.A., Al-Anon is a twelve-step program. Al-Anon members have sponsors, use slogans, and consider themselves to be involved in a spiritual program that each member defines in their own way. Also like A.A., Al-Anon depends on guidance from the many brochures and books that present the A.A. and Al-Anon beliefs and teachings.

Both A.A. and Al-Anon are listed in telephone directories worldwide. For children who have an alcoholic parent or family member, help is available from Alateen groups. These are also based on the A.A. philosophy and are widely available.

NOTES

1. R. Berkow, M. H. Beers, and A. J. Fletcher, eds., *The Merck Manual of Medical Information*, Home Edition (Whitehouse Station, N.J.: Merck Research Laboratories, 1997), 442.
2. J. Krestan and C. Bepko, *Too Good for Her Own Good: Breaking Free from the Burden of Female Responsibility (*New York: Harper & Row, 1990).
3. G. Bloss and H. Harwood, "New Study Updates Estimates of the Economic Costs of Alcohol Abuse," *Frontline: Linking Alcohol Services and Practice* (Washington, D.C.: National Institute on Alcohol Abuse and Alcoholism in Conjunction with the Association for Health Services Research, November 1989): 6–7.
4. D. P. S. Kelman, L. S. Miller, and S. Dunmeyer, "The Economic Costs of Alcohol and Drug Abuse and Mental Illness: 1985." (Rockville, Md.: National Institute on Drug Abuse, 1990), cited in *Alcohol Alert*, #11, PH 293, National Institute on Alcohol Abuse and Alcoholism, January 1991.
5. The Twelve Steps of Al-Anon are identical to the A.A. Twelve Steps, except for step twelve, which in Al-Anon reads: "Having had a spiritual awakening as the result of these steps, we tried to carry this message to others, and to practice these principles in all our affairs."

Living with an Alcoholic (Cornwall, N.Y.: Al-Anon Family Group Headquarters, Inc., 1976).

Appendix 2

Alcoholism as a Disease and the Codependency Movement

In 1967 the American Medical Association (AMA) declared alcoholism a disease. Since that time, a multitude of books and articles has appeared on the subject. Still, the conceptualization of alcoholism as a disease has been hotly debated. Conrad and Schneider provide a thorough history of the origins of alcoholism conceptualized as a disease as well as the debates about the appropriateness of this conceptualization.[1] They remind us that in the seventeenth and eighteenth centuries in America, drinking was considered an act of free will. In Europe, there was some suggestion that alcoholism might be rooted to insanity. Toward the end of the eighteenth century, there was a slight giving way to a medical model, put forth by Benjamin Rush. Not only did Rush use the word *disease,* he referred to excessive drinking as an addiction

At the crux of the argument are two competing positions: One holds that alcoholism is a moral failure; the other, that it is a physical disease. Many people take the position that alcoholism has a genetic, or biological, basis, but that only some people with this predisposition actually become alcoholics. This of course begs the question: What makes one person become an alcoholic and allows another to bypass its ravages? Some researchers have suggested that certain "triggers" might explain why one person with the predisposition escapes the condition, while another person succumbs to it. Erickson has noted that among recovering and recovered alcoholics, alcoholism has usually caused them such intense suffering that there is no question but that it be considered a disease.[2] Thus, arguing against alcoholism being considered a disease may not be reasonable. Some claim that this label removes responsibility by suggesting that alcoholism is akin to cancer or cystic fibrosis—conditions we have no control over. As many have noted, you can walk away from a bottle of alcohol, but you cannot walk away from cancer or cystic fibrosis.

Yet, such a distinction is not always so easy to maintain. What about lung cancer for the majority of victims? Often caused by smoking (also an addiction), is it reasonable to think that lung cancer is a not a disease but a moral lapse? Asher, in her 1992 book on wives of alcoholics, claims that the disease concept applied to alcoholism is both restrictive and redemptive. On the redemptive side, it suggests the potential for change. As in the case of Cara Gunderson in this book, it minimizes blame and facilitates compassion. But on the restrictive side, it is a deviant label perhaps applied incorrectly and now, difficult to "lift."

Erickson suggests that the main difficulty with alcoholism, as compared with other diseases such as cancer or diabetes, is that alcoholism creates victims who "dangerously and negatively impact thousands of other people with whom they come in contact."[3] Unlike most diseases, this negative impact results in a highly stigmatized condition and highly stigmatized sufferers. Erickson reminds us that many other diseases, including leprosy, epilepsy, and tuberculosis, also carried great stigmas until cures were found.

Conrad and Schneider suggest that the disease notion has been widely accepted because of the legal endorsement of its assumptions, the establishment of the National Institute of Alcoholism and Addictions, the mandate to treatment rather than punishment, and the AMA's acceptance that alcoholism is a disease. They go on to say that it is likely that the debate may be settled through reform rather than revolution.[4] In other words, rather than viewing alcoholism as a disease, it might be relegated to the ranks of a "health problem." This allows alcoholism to remain medicalized but releases it from the realm of "disease" and thereby ends this long-running debate.

CODEPENDENCY

In a related vein, there has been a debate around the popular notion of "codependency." In recent years the impact of addictions on family and close friends has received increased attention. The term *codependency* first appeared in the 1970s but was popularized by Melanie Beattie in the late 1980s, with publication of her seminal work *Co-Dependent No More*.[5] The initial use of the term was to describe someone, most often a wife, whose life was affected by a chemically dependent person. For all intents and purposes, it seems to have replaced terms such as *co-alcoholic* and *co-addiction.*

The origins of codependency are usually traced to psychoanalytic theory, "disturbed personality theory" of the 1950s, and the theory of decompensation, which suggests that when the husband gets sober, the wife "decomposes" because her health is dependent on his remaining "sick." Such thinking enforced the belief that people remained in dysfunctional relationships because of their own pathological tendencies. Because most alcoholics were thought to be men and little attention was paid to female alcoholics, spouses of alcoholics were envisioned as women. In 1953 T. Whalen suggested that there were four character types of wives of alcoholics: suffering wives who were unnecessary martyrs and sought crucifixion; wavering wives who never followed through with attempts to cope with the problem; controllers with a desperate need of their own outside the pathology of the alcoholic; and the punishing wife, who needed to emasculate her husband.[6] Al-Anon literature in the 1970s reflected such thinking through the introduction of characters such as "Suffering Susan," "Wavering Winnie," "Controlling Catherine," and "Punitive Polly." By the 1980s, talk of alcoholism was no longer so stigmatized and the publishing world erupted in a plethora of self-help books. Among these were numerous additions to the codependency literature. In a relatively short period of time, an entire movement was created.

Beattie provides an overall definition of codependency: "A codependent person is one who has let another person's behavior affect him or her, and who is obsessed with controlling that person's behavior."[7] She expands on this definition to include behaviors and personality traits such as helping, caregiving, low-self esteem or low self-worth bordering on self-hatred, self-repression, abundance of anger and guilt, peculiar dependency on peculiar people, attraction to and tolerance for the bizarre, other-centeredness that results in abandonment of self, communication problems, intimacy problems, and ongoing whirlwind trips through the five-stage grief process. In addition, codependency is considered a progressive disease because, as the addict close to the codependent person gets more trapped in their addiction, the codependent person reacts more intensely. According to Beattie, there are at least eighty million people in the United States who are either addicts or codependents.

A variety of other writers in the addictions and family fields published similar and expanded uses of codependency. The term eventually made its way into public discourse and became a euphemism for anyone who did anything that might not have been in his or her own best interest. The "cure" for codependency was based on a twelve-step program similar to A.A.'s Twelve-Step Program. Overall, it encouraged codependents to put their own needs first. Sales of books on the topic often found quick success. Clearly, the popularity of this term and this literature suggests that it offered the public something they wanted. What did it offer?

Codependency seems to have offered people a label for what ailed them in their interpersonal lives. Its encompassing definition, the basic instructions on how to move beyond codependency, and the neatness with which people could identify with other like-minded people, was welcomed. Like the A.A. and Al-Anon literature that tends to avoid, at least on the surface, complex explanations, so too did codependency literature. However, just as the concept of alcoholism as a disease has been debated, so too has the concept of a codependent person.

Overall, critics condemn codependency because of its wide-ranging definition, which makes it possible for almost anyone to be considered codependent, and conversely, makes it virtually impossible for anyone to claim they are not codependent. In the words of Melanie Beattie, it has a "fuzzy definition because it is a gray, fuzzy condition." Others have observed that it also "blames the victim" rather than acknowledging that these "victims" are participants in a relational drama and can be better understood from a different vantage point altogether. In addition, the term *codependency* is overly simplistic, and it relies on the language of family systems yet it lacks the substance of systems theory.[8]

Critics claim that the notion of codependency is not based on research—in fact, it ignores much of the available research by suggesting that people who are codependent have a disease. Babcock and McKay see it as much worse than that: They point out that codependency "sells the idea that the woman herself is the pathogen."[9] In fact, a great deal of research on the functioning of wives of alcoholics suggests that they are involved in an adaptation process, and, although the circumstances may be pathological, their behaviors often are not. Haaken picks up on this by suggesting that the codependency literature fails to identify the positive aspects and developmental experiences that often coexist with the pathology. Furthermore she points out that words like *codependency,* which connote pathology, have a negative influence on the public because they present a distortion of reality.[10]

Overall, those who critique this literature echo Orford's words that addictions work in general has been oversimplified.[11] Menicucci and Wermuth criticized the addictions field for depicting families as unchanging and having a consistent profile. They write: "Even with drug abuse, adult change and development occurs. It proceeds regardless of the covert desires of the family to hold on to children and maintain 'homeostatic balance.' "[12]

Most notable among the critics has been Wendy Kaminer, author of *I'm Dysfunctional, You're Dysfunctional: The Recovery Movement and Other Self-Help Fashions.*[13] Kaminer points to the grandiosity of codependency: "If society and everyone in it are addicted, self-destructing, infected with left-brain rationality, then people in recovery are the chosen few, an elite minority of enlightened, if irrational, self-actualizers with the wisdom to save the world."[14] Regardless of one's acceptance or rejection of this term, it is unmistakable that it has become part of our everyday speech and that for some, it has value. Like the conceptualization of alcoholism as a disease, which may in some way be technically incorrect, the codependency literature may be misleading but at the same time it offers some people solace.

NOTES

1. P. Conrad and J. W. Schneider, *Deviance and Medicalization: From Badness to Sickness* (Philadelphia: Temple University Press, 1992).
2. C. K. Erickson, "A Pharmacologist's Opinion—Alcoholism: The Disease Debate Needs to Stop," *Alcohol & Alcoholism* 27, no. 4 (1992): 325.
3. C. K. Erickson, "A Pharmacologist's Opinion," 326.
4. P. Conrad and J. W. Schneider, *Deviance and Medicalization*, 109.
5. M. Beattie, *Co-Dependent No More: How to Stop Controlling Others and Start Caring for Yourself* (New York: Harper & Row, 1987).
6. T. Whalen, "Wives of Alcoholics: Four Types Observed in a Family Service Agency," *Quarterly Journal of Studies on Alcohol* 14 (1953): 632–641.
7. M. Beattie, *Co-Dependent No More,* 36.
8. J. Harper and C. Capdevilla, "Codependency: A Critique," *Journal of Psychoactive Drugs* 22 (1990): 285–292.
9. M. Babcock and C. McKay, eds., *Challenging Codependency: Feminist Critiques* (Buffalo, N.Y.: University of Toronto Press, 1995).
10. J. Haaken "A Critical Analysis of the Codependency Construct," in *Challenging Codependency: Feminist Critiques,* ed. M. Babcock and C. McKay (Buffalo, N.Y.: University of Toronto Press, 1995), 53–69.
11. J. Orford, "Control, Confront, or Collude: How Family and Society Respond to Excessive Drinking," *British Journal of Addiction* 87 (1992): 1513–1525.
12. L. D. Menicucci and L. Wermuth, "Expanding Family Systems Approach: Culture, Class, Developmental and Gender Influences in Drug Abuse," *American Journal of Family Therapy* 17 (1989): 135.
13. W. Kaminer, *I'm Dysfunctional, You're Dysfunctional: The Recovery Movement and Other Self-Help Fashions* (New York: Vintage Books, 1992).
14. W. Kaminer, "Chances Are You're Codependent Too," 1992, in *Challenging Codependency: Feminist Critiques.*

Appendix 3

Research

STUDY POPULATION AND INTERVIEWS

Demographic Information

This study is based on in-depth interviews of twenty-one couples (husband and wife) and five individuals whose spouses did not agree to participate. The total number of people interviewed was forty-seven. All had been married to their current spouse during the time of active drinking (range of years married: eleven to fifty-six; average number of years married: thirty-three), and each alcoholic had been sober for at least four years. The average number of years sober was fourteen. There were two exceptions made to the criteria for inclusion in the study. Two couples were included in which both spouses are in long-term recovery.

In addition to the interviews, all participants completed a thirty-two-item measure of marital satisfaction, the Dyadic Adjustment Scale.[1] The scores generally reflected what was said during the interviews. The majority of participants rated their marital satisfaction within the average range. None were in the "very much above average range." Four spouses, all wives of alcoholics, scored in the "clinically significant range." Other than providing a general confirmation of what was discussed during the interviews, the DAS was limited in usefulness. Because of the use of composites, specific scores were not incorporated into the main body of the text.

Gender

Of the participants interviewed, seven alcoholics were women and nineteen were men. The women had been sober from eight to twenty-three years. Of the individuals interviewed, three were male alcoholics whose wives declined to be interviewed, and two were female nonalcoholic spouses.

Ethnicity

All except one couple listed Caucasian as their ethnic identity.

Education

Most participants had at least some college, nine had attended graduate school, and one person had not completed high school. Of the female alcoholics, four were college graduates (two of these with graduate degrees), one was a high school graduate, one had less than twelve years of schooling, and one did not complete that item on the form.

Income and Occupations

Reported income levels were high, mostly over fifty thousand dollars per year. Thirteen couples and individuals reported joint incomes of more than $75,000 per year. Two did not report incomes at all (one couple failed to return their demographic and DAS forms). Overall income levels were lower because of the fact that some participants were retired and living on retirement incomes.

Occupations were predominantly professional. A random selection includes teacher, engineer, nurse, business owner, CPA, doctor, therapist, and interpreter.

Age

The ages of participants averaged fifty-seven, with the range between thirty-eight and seventy-eight.

Addictions

When asked about addictions other than alcohol, four people listed drug addictions, one listed gambling, one tobacco, and one listed sex. Only one of the six women alcoholics listed an additional addiction: drugs.

Counseling

Of the forty-seven participants, twenty-five have had some kind of psychological counseling. The majority indicated individual and couple counseling, with only seven indicating "family" counseling. Of the seven women alcoholics, five have had some kind of psychological counseling.

Adult Children of Alcoholics

Approximately 50 percent of those interviewed are adult children of alcoholics. The number of couples in which both partners are adult children of alcoholics is four, although in one case it was unclear and in one case of adoption, there is uncertainty. Of the female alcoholics, one couple noted that both had come from alcoholic homes.

A.A./Al-Anon

Twenty-nine participants attend A.A. or Al-Anon meetings regularly, and thirteen people virtually never attend support group meetings, although in many cases, they did at an earlier point in time. This tends to be truer of spouses than of alcoholics. Of the couples in which the female is the alcoholic, only one husband currently attends A.A. or Al-Anon.

Children

Two couples had no children, and of the couples with children, the number ranged from one to twelve, with the average being 3.5. Children were, for the most part old enough to have left home. A few couples had teenagers at home.

Study Limitations

The number of people interviewed was relatively small. This was primarily because of the difficulty of locating participants who met the criteria and were willing to be interviewed. Given the stigma attached to alcoholism, personal contacts were necessary in order to meet potential participants. Various attempts were made through the use of flyers, but these were not successful.

I did not ask specifically about the couples' sex lives. Although several raised this point, it was not a planned part of the interviews.

INTERVIEW DEVELOPMENT, FORMAT, AND ANALYSIS

One of my first challenges was how to find people to interview. Because of my husband's involvement in A.A., I went to him first. He put me in contact with several friends and acquaintances who had friends in A.A. Through this network of people, approximately two-thirds of the participants were identified. In addition, I distributed flyers at the local video store and library asking for participants. This was not successful. I also made telephone calls to various alcoholism-related groups. Although these groups could not officially endorse the project, I made some contacts through this approach. Overall, alcoholism has so much stigma attached to it, combined with the emphasis on anonymity in A.A./Al-Anon circles, that the vast majority of contacts were made through friends and friends of friends. It took the better part of a year to contact and schedule interviews with the participants who agreed to take part in this project.

It turned out, of course, that finding the participants was not as difficult as identifying exactly what I was trying to learn from them. I believed initially that I wanted to learn how healing occurred between people. So the initial phase of the project was geared toward answering these general questions: "What has contributed to healing between spouses?" and "What does this healing 'look like'?" Because I was interested in healing, I made the decision to begin the interviews at the point of sobriety. In this way, I thought I could avoid spending too much of the interview time on *drunk-alogues* (the A.A. term for a detailed monologue that describes an alcoholic's drinking history) and stories of the real down-and-out periods. But at each interview, I found that the couples simply couldn't do this or chose not to. They would say something to the effect of, "Well, you have to understand . . ." and then tell their entire history. After this happened several times, I was reminded that the reason for using interviews as my primary form of data collection was to gain insight into their context, not to extricate them from it. From that point on, I started the interviews by asking them to discuss their family of origin, or their initial meeting and the time period when they were first married.

After the first several interviews were conducted, I felt dissatisfied with what I was able to elicit by focusing solely on "healing." It seemed that the couples were in a long-term process of change, but healing did not quite capture what I was hearing. At about this time, one of the participants politely explained that *healing* was probably the wrong word and *growth* was much more appropriate. Why? Because healing suggests a completed process as when a cut finger heals and the infection disappears leaving no trace of what has been. For the majority of these couples, there was significant change for the better, but not complete healing in the sense of no memory of the pain. This was evident from the way the spouses spoke of events from the distant past as if they had occurred the day or week before, as well as their own admissions that although their marriages were good, they were not without issues.

Perhaps more importantly, healing suggests returning to a previous state of health or well-being. For some of these couples, their early years were not especially easy. Many dealt with alcoholism from the very first day of marriage—if not in the engagement and dating period. Only one couple, who experienced the effects of alcoholism late in their marriage, said that the alcoholism never really affected the high quality of their relationship. For many, alcoholism, whether it was recognized as such or not, had a profound effect from relatively early on. Their need was to grow, to change, to improve. There was no absolute, ideal state of health to return to. Thus, my search for "healing" was often leading me in the wrong direction. What I did hear described over and over again, was the ability to change and grow.

Once I made this shift in my own thinking, I was able to identify the resources and mechanisms that contributed to relational growth. No longer in search of absolute healing, I was free to see that growth took a variety of forms and occurred by way of various processes or mechanisms and to differing extents. In addition, often the changes were subtle. The question was, what did this growth "look" like?

All interviews for this book were structured, open-ended interviews. It was structured in the sense that I followed an interview guide that was developed to elicit the relational and individual history of the couples and individuals interviewed as well as their present-day feelings about their relationship. It was open-ended in that I went into the interviews with enough flexibility to allow the participants to determine the path the interviews would take. For example, it became clear very early on that some marriages were more satisfying than others. Had I forced a particular "line" of questioning on the participants that suggested that I expected to hear about a certain "level" of growth, it is less likely that they would have been able to provide such rich insight into their marital history and current marital status. Often when people are being interviewed they want to please the interviewer to help them out. Thus, if an interviewer asks a question like, "Please tell me how your relationship has healed?" the participant is likely to attempt to come up with an answer about healing even if they have experienced little or none. I chose to ask questions that would avoid, to the largest extent possible, "putting words into people's mouths." The interview guide appears at the conclusion of this appendix.

The interview guide was used as just that—a guide. For example, most couples talked about their past history, particularly about early drinking, the crisis period of drinking, and then early sobriety. Often at this point, one or both spouses would purposely steer the interview in a direction very pertinent to their current relational workings. For example, one spouse talked very eloquently about how she became more autonomous and built a life for herself once she realized that her entire focus had been on her alcoholic husband. But as the interview went on, she directed it to their current struggle as she sees it—shifting from so much "independence" and autonomy to a balance between autonomy and sharing.

Another aspect of the interviews had to do with the fact that most of the alcoholics were in A.A. and quite a few of the spouses had been in Al-Anon at one time and a few still were. As such, they were comfortable and familiar with "telling their story." At A.A. and at Al-Anon meetings, this is part of sharing, of being a speaker, of how a person is known. They "tell their story" so that others can learn from it if they so choose. Although the stories were clearly relevant and contained valuable information into some of the individual thought processes and experiences of the participants, they often veered away from a relational perspective. The difficulty was that once a "story" was begun, it often seemed like it had to reach its usual conclusion before I could interject a slightly different question or perspective. On several occasions I asked a question aimed at eliciting information, or insight, about how the relationship was construed at the time, and the response was very individually focused and often ended with words to the effect of, "and that's what I always tell in my story." I sometimes wondered if I was truly "connecting" with the participant, or if I was more of a substitute for an A.A. meeting. Whatever the answer, I learned to accept this as an alternate form of responding. At times it seemed to be what was available to people who often could not remember much of their history; the "story" functioned to make a whole out of disparate pieces.

Early in this study I made the decision to not insist that couples meet together for the interview. My thinking was that participants would know what was acceptable to them. Forcing joint interviews could, and would have, eliminated some excellent interviews. Sixteen couples were interviewed jointly, five spouses met with me separately, and five couples interviewed separately.

There was not a clear pattern about the choice of individual verses joint interviews. Some people just seemed more comfortable talking privately, whereas it didn't seem to make a difference to others. One alcoholic said he and his wife would be happy to meet with me jointly. When he asked his wife, she said she would be glad to do the interview but only if they were done individually.

ANALYSIS AND INTERPRETATION OF INTERVIEWS

Immediately following each interview, the audiotapes were transcribed and my thoughts and insights of the interview were recorded. Once this was done, the transcript was read multiple times. Initially it was read to simply get a "sense" of how this couple or individual talked about their relationship. Did they use "positive" or "negative" words to describe their mate? Did they talk of fairness, satisfaction, and growth, and if so, in what ways? Did they focus on disappointment, struggle, and unfairness, and if so, why? How did they describe their own individual transformation? How did they feel the marriage had been affected and how had it evolved since sobriety? What were and perhaps are, the "trouble" points in their relationship? What made them remain a couple? Did they tell a story indicative of growth or indicative of despair?

The initial readings were followed by reading to identify patterns within the transcript. For example, one pattern was the sense by the spouses of not being considered—of being a "second fiddle"; another pattern was considering the other person—what motivated this, what did it look like, what inhibited it, and so on.

Because I had agreed to write only in composite form to protect the identities and anonymity of the participants, I then moved from the patterns to the formation of the composites. It should be noted that the use of composites is not unusual. For example, well-known sociologist Lillian Rubin made use of composites for *Intimate Strangers: Men and Women Together*, as did Steven and Sybil Wolin for *The Resilient Self: How Survivors of Troubled Families Rise above Adversity*.[2] According to Wolin and Wolin, their composites are "psychologically accurate."[3] Well-known writer Peter Whybrow notes in his book on emotions and their disorders that he makes use of composites. "The stories are real, and frequently include verbatim descriptions of illness and recovery, but the characters are composites of the real life experiences of more than one person, transported in time and place to ensure anonymity."[4]

The use of composites has both benefits and limitations. A primary benefit is the protection of the identities of the individual participants and the coverage of many persons in a compact manner, which facilitates the distillation of the essence of the many interviews. Anonymity is especially important among people who attend A.A. and Al-Anon. Because of the stigma attached to alcoholism, protecting peoples' identities is considered to be of paramount importance. Among the participants interviewed for this book, many attend meetings on a regular basis. At these meetings they speak openly about their lives—past and present. Thus, it was incumbent upon me to be certain that entire life stories were not presented. It should be noted, however, that the processes described accurately reflect the facts and family dynamics of the couples in order to preserve the integrity of the findings and conclusions. All names and identifying information have been changed. Thus, the experiences are fairly represented but are not descriptive of any individual. In addition to the use of composites, standard procedures, such as changes of occupation title, physical descriptions, and so on, were used.

As the composites took form, the template of (1) residual resources, (2) moments of choice, and (3) building trust became clear and moved to the forefront as a useful framework to understand the processes and experiences of the couples. It is important to note that this template, or framework, is not always as discreet as the presentation. For example, a moment of choice is also a step toward building trust. This framework serves to help make sense and to provide a structure for a dense and complex reality. All relationships are complex, and certainly long-term relationships are extremely complex. They have shared many years and experiences together and have known good times and bad. The template serves as a convenient and accurate way to talk about the commonalities and the distinctions between how couples experience relational growth, or struggle to do so.

The richness and complexity of lived life is always more than any outsider can know. What I have done here is attempt to capture the most salient points, which may help other people by providing them with a lens or a perspective that is respectful of people's efforts, honest about their limitations, and productive in terms of attempting to identify relational resources and mechanisms of change and trust building rather than simply cataloging pathological behavior.

INTERVIEW GUIDE

History

1. Tell me about the early years of your marriage.
2. When did alcohol start to become a problem in your marriage?

3. What was happening between you when the period of active drinking was at its worst? What did you each feel about the relationship? Think? How did you interact?
4. At what point did you get sober?
5. Tell what happened to each of you around early sobriety? What happened to the relationship? (What did each person think, feel, how did they act vis-à-vis the other?)
6. What are the major changes in you/your spouse?
7. Tell me about "amends."
8. What were your expectations of the other/of yourself?

Current

1. How would you describe your relationship today? Why? What would you like to shift in the relationship? Why? What would you like to keep the same? Why?
2. How do you handle genuine disagreements?
3. How do you acknowledge each other?
4. Tell me about how you interact with your children (if appropriate).

Family of Origin

1. Tell me about each of your parents.
2. Tell me about their relationship with each other; with you.

(These questions were asked in varying order depending on specific circumstances of the interview.)

NOTES

1. The Dyadic Adjustment Scale (Spanier, 1976) is one of the most widely used tools to measure marital quality. The thirty-two items take approximately ten minutes to complete. Marital quality is based on four subscale measures: consensus, satisfaction, affectional expression, and cohesion. The DAS was chosen because of its reliability and validity and because it is easy to complete.

2. L. B. Rubin, *Intimate Strangers: Men and Women Together* (New York: Harper & Row, 1983).

S. J. Wolin and S. Wolin, *The Resilient Self: How Survivors of Troubled Families Rise above Adversity* (NewYork: Villard, 1993).

3. S. J. Wolin and S. Wolin, *The Resilient Self.*

4. P. C. Whybrow, *The Thinkers' Guide to Emotion and Its Disorders.*

Suggested Resources for Clinicians

There is an enormous body of literature on alcoholism and alcoholism treatment. The references listed below represent a small subset of those available that would be useful to clinicians.

BOOKS: GENERAL

Boszormenyi-Nagy, I., and G. M. Spark. *Invisible Loyalties: Reciprocity in Intergenerational Family Therapy.* New York: Brunner/Mazel, 1984.

Presents both the depth and breadth of Contextual Family Therapy, an intergenerational approach to therapy that addresses issues of family justice and trust. The authors include details of clinical challenges and how the contextual framework can be applied. One family's history is presented along with details of the contextual approach.

Karpel, M. A., ed. *Family Resources: The Hidden Partner in Family Therapy.* New York: Guilford Press, 1986.

Provides an extensive overview of the historical shift from a focus on pathology to individual and family resources. Also includes in-depth discussions on how clinicians can identify and make use of resources in families. Topics include: serious illness, trust building, divorce, abuse, death and dying, and remarriage.

Wolin, S. J., and S. Wolin. *The Resilient Self: How Survivors of Troubled Families Rise above Adversity.* New York: Villard Books, 1993.

Written specifically for survivors of deeply troubled families, this book weaves together research with personal stories of resilience into a self-help book that is also appropriate for therapists and educators. The authors note seven "resiliencies" and include a self-help section for each so that the reader can understand their own relationship to that resiliency from early childhood to adulthood.

BOOKS: ALCOHOLISM

Asher, R. M. *Women with Alcoholic Husbands: Ambivalence and the Trap of Codependency.* Chapel Hill: University of North Carolina Press, 1992.

This book is based on the firsthand experiences of wives of alcoholics who were interviewed by the author. Asher, a sociologist, examines the wives' experiences in terms of a "moral career," or what it is that disrupts, challenges, and ultimately, transforms self-identifications. For clinicians, it provides a detailed account of the lived experience of wives of alcoholics and places these experiences in a societal context.

Beck, A. T., F. D. Wright, and C. F. Newman. *Cognitive Therapy of Substance Abuse.* New York: Guilford Press, 1993.

Based on cognitive therapy and education, this text details treatment and education of clients using cognitive and behavioral strategies and techniques. It includes working with clients who are depressed, anxious, those with a low tolerance for frustration, and so forth. Suggestions are very specific. For example, how to deal with a client who catastrophizes, who is angry, and so on.

Brown, S., and I. D. Yalom, eds. *Treating Alcoholism.* San Francisco: Jossey-Bass, 1995.

Contributors to this volume write from a developmental model perspective to emphasize change over time. Vignettes of individual, couple, and family experiences bring the text to life. Divided into four sections (history of alcoholism; working with clients during drinking and transition stages; abstinence; and family) this book is particularly useful to clinicians but also would be appropriate for clients. It presents tasks for therapy of the different stages of recovery and a thorough and realistic portrayal of family and couple recovery. The discussion of alcoholic couple development is especially helpful as it is compared with normal couple development.

Karpel, M. A. *Evaluating Couples: A Handbook for Practitioners* New York: W. W. Norton, 1994.

Provides a succinct chapter discussion of alcoholism, its impact on couples, therapeutic interventions, and recommended readings for therapists and clients.

O'Farrell, T. J., *Treating Alcohol Problems: Marital and Family Interventions.* New York: Guilford Press, 1993.

Written specifically for the clinician with an interest in research, this is a practical guide to marital and family therapy. Text is divided into four sections: (1) When the alcoholic is unwilling to seek help; (2) How to stabilize the family during treatment; (3) Methods to maintain long-term recovery and prevent relapse; and (4) Future directions. Each chapter describes a different method of treatment and includes an overview of the method, special clinical considerations, guidelines and case studies related to the method, and a summary of the method's effectiveness.

Steinglass, P., L. A. Bennett, S. J. Wolin, and D. Reiss. *The Alcoholic Family.* New York: Basic Books, 1987.

Based on a systems oriented perspective, this book provides a comprehensive view of family systems affected by alcoholism and family-based interventions. By drawing on clinical interviews and an array of research data, the authors provide a thorough portrait of families that are organized around alcoholism. The final section of the book presents family therapy approaches useful to such families.

Vaillant, G. E. *The Natural History of Alcoholism Revisited.* Cambridge, Mass.: Harvard University Press, 1995.

Appropriate for the clinician with an interest in alcoholism research, Vaillant's text is thorough and readable. He addresses seven primary questions in depth: (1) Is alcoholism a symptom or a disease? (2) Does alcoholism usually get progressively worse? (3) Are alcoholics, before they begin to abuse alcohol, different from nonalcoholics? (4) Is abstinence a necessary goal of treatment, or can insisting on abstinence sometimes be counterproductive? (5) Is returning to safe social drinking possible for some alcoholics? (6) Does treatment alter the natural history of alcoholism? (7) How helpful is Alcoholics Anonymous in the treatment of alcoholism?

ARTICLES

Hawley, D. R., and L. DeHaan. "Toward a Definition of Family Resilience: Integrating Life-Span and Family Perspectives." *Family Process* 35, no. 3 (1996): 283–298.

Walsh, P. "The Concept of Family Resilience: Crisis and Challenge." *Family Process* 35, no. 3 (1996): 261–281.

These two articles provide a thorough review of the literature on family/relational resilience and its meaning for clinicians and researchers. Included are definitions of resilience, a review of research on individual resilience that provides a context for understanding the current attempts to expand this notion to families, and theoretical questions remaining to be addressed. The references are helpful for anyone interested in more extensive reading.

Lauer, R. H., J. C. Lauer, and S. T. Kerr. "The Long-Term Marriage: Perceptions of Stability and Satisfaction." *International Journal of Aging and Human Development* 31, no. 3 (1990): 189–195.

Robinson, L. C., and P. W. Blanton. "Marital Strengths in Enduring Marriages." *Family Relations* 42 (1993): 38–45.

These two articles provide valuable overviews of what helps marriages endure. Although not focused on alcoholism per se, these articles highlight the notion of strengths in ongoing relationships.

Steinglass, P. "A Life History Model of the Alcoholic Family." *Family Process* 19, no. 3 (1980): 211–226.

This article takes a developmental life-history view of families and alcoholism. Based on the notion of the family life cycle (premarriage, early marriage, mid-life plateau, mid-life crisis, and late resolution) and the concepts of the alcoholic family, homeostasis, and the family alcohol phase, the author takes a macroscopic view of families, which includes "wet," "dry," and "transitional" phases. Four case histories (stable-wet alcoholic family; stable-dry nonalcoholic family; stable-dry alcoholic family; and stable controlled-drinking nonalcoholic family) are presented, along with ample discussion. This article provides a nuanced depiction of the different ways families are affected by alcoholism over time and places them in a developmental framework.

CONTACTS

A.A. and Al-Anon publish a great deal of literature on the A.A. and Al-Anon philosophy and various aspects of alcoholism. All are based on the twelve-step tradition, which is valuable for any clinician to be familiar with.

FrontLines is published twice yearly by the NIAAA in conjunction with the Association for Health Services Research (AHSR): 202-223-2477.

National Institute on Alcohol Abuse and Alcoholism (NIAAA): Publishes *Alcohol Alert*, a newsletter of the Office for Substance Abuse Prevention's National Clearinghouse for Alcohol and Drug Information: 800-729-6686.

Bibliography

Al-Anon Family Group. *Living with an Alcoholic*. Cornwall, N.Y.: Al-Anon Family Group, Inc., 1976.

Anthony, E. J., and B. J. Cohler. *The Invulnerable Child*. New York: Guilford Press, 1987.

Asher, R. M. *Women with Alcoholic Husbands: Ambivalence and the Trap of Codependency*. Chapel Hill: University of North Carolina Press, 1992.

Atkinson, M. P. "Conceptualizations of the Parent–Child Relationship: Solidarity, Attachment, Crescive Bonds, and Identity." In *Aging Parents and Adult Children*, edited by J. A. Mancini. Lexington, Mass.: Lexington Books, 1989.

Babcock, M., and C. McKay, eds. *Challenging Codependency: Feminist Critiques*. Buffalo, N.Y.: University of Toronto Press, 1995.

Batshaw, J. *Healing the Shame That Binds You*. Deerfield Beach, Fla.: Health Communications, 1988.

Beattie, M. *Co-dependent No More: How to Stop Controlling Others and Start Caring for Yourself*. New York: Harper & Row, 1987.

Beck, A. T., F. D. Wright, and C. F. Newman. *Cognitive Therapy of Substance Abuse*. New York: Guilford Press. 1993.

Belenky, M. F., B. M. Clinchy, N. R. Goldberger, and J. M. Tarule. *Women's Ways of Knowing: The Development of Self, Voice, and Mind*. New York: Basic Books, 1986.

Bepko, C., and J. Krestan. *Too Good for Her Own Good: Breaking Free from the Burden of Female Responsibility*. New York: Harper & Row, 1990.

Berkow, R., M. H. Beers, and A. J. Fletcher, eds. *The Merck Manual of Medical Information*, Home Edition. Whitehouse Station, N.J.: Merck Research Laboratories, 1997.

Bloss, G., and H. Harwood. "New Study Updates Estimates of the Economic Costs of Alcohol Abuse." *Frontline: Linking Alcohol Services and Practice*. (Washington, D.C.: National Institute on Alcohol Abuse and Alcoholism in Conjunction with the Association for Health Services Research (November 1989): 6–7.

Blum, D. "Finding the Strength: How to Overcome Anything." *Psychology Today* (31) 3 (1998 May/June): 32–38.

Boszormenyi-Nagy, I., and B. R. Krasner. *Between Give and Take: A Clinical Guide to Contextual Therapy*. New York: Brunner/Mazel, 1986.

Boszormenyi-Nagy, I., and G. M. Spark. *Invisible Loyalties: Reciprocity in Intergenerational Family Therapy*. New York: Brunner/Mazel, 1984.

Buber, M. *The Knowledge of Man: A Philosophy of the Interhuman.* New York: Harper & Row, 1965a.
———. *Between Man and Man.* New York: Macmillan, 1965a.
———. *I and Thou.* New York: Charles Scribner's Sons, 1970.
Buhl, J. "Intergenerational Inter-Gender Voice: Shared Narratives between Adult Sons and Their Mothers: An Ethical Perspective." Unpublished doctoral dissertation, University of Pennsylvania, Philadelphia, 1992.
Chopra, D. *Overcoming Addictions.* Pittsburgh, Pa.: Three Rivers Press, 1998.
Conrad, P., and J. W. Schneider. *Deviance and Medicalization: From Badness to Sickness.* Philadelphia: Temple University Press, 1992.
Cotroneo, M. "Families and Abuse: A Contextual Approach." In *Family Resources: The Hidden Partner in Family Therapy*, edited by M. A. Karpel. New York: Guilford Press, 1986.
Cotroneo, M., and B. J. Hibbs. "Ethical Discourse in Families." *American Family Therapy Association Newsletter* (46) (1991): 11–13.
Erickson, C. K. "A Pharmacologist's Opinion—Alcoholism: The Disease Debate Needs to Stop." *Alcohol & Alcoholism* (27) 4 (1992): 325–328.
Friedman, M. S. *The Healing Dialogue in Psychotherapy.* New York: Jason Aronson, 1985.
———. "Martin Buber and Ivan Boszormenyi-Nagy: The Role of Dialogue in Contextual Therapy." *Psychotherapy* (26) (1989): 402–409.
Gilligan, C. "Do the Social Sciences Have an Adequate Theory of Moral Development?" In *Social Science as Moral Inquiry,* edited by N. Haan, R. N. Bellah, P. Rabinow, and W. M. Sullivan. New York: Columbia University Press, 1983.
Gottman, J. (with N. Silver). *Why Marriages Succeed or Fail.* New York: Simon & Schuster, 1994.
Haaken, J. "A Critical Analysis of the Codependency Construct." In *Challenging Codependency: Feminist Critiques*, edited by M. Babcock and C. McKay. Buffalo, N.Y.: University of Toronto Press, 1995.
Hargrave, T. *Families and Forgiveness: Healing Wounds in the Intergenerational Family.* New York: Brunner/Mazel, 1994.
Harper, J. "Recovery for the Relationship: A Treatment Model for Couples with a Recovering Chemically Dependent Partner." *Alcoholism Treatment Quarterly* (7) 2 (1990): 1–21.
Harper, J., and C. Capdevilla. "Codependency: A Critique." *Journal of Psychoactive Drugs* (22) (1990): 285–292.
Hawley, D. R., and L. DeHaan. "Toward a Definition of Family Resilience: Integrating Life-Span and Family Perspectives." *Family Process* 35, no. 3 (1996): 283–298.
Hibbs, B. J. "The Context of Growth: Relational Ethics between Parents and Children." In *Children in Family Contexts: Perspectives on Treatment*, edited by L. Combrinick-Graham. New York: Guilford Press, 1989.
Higgins, G. O. *Resilient Adults: Overcoming a Cruel Past.* San Francisco, Calif.: Jossey-Bass, 1994.
Hycner, R. *Between Person and Person: Toward a Dialogical Psychotherapy.* Highland, N.Y.: *The Gestalt Journal* (1991).
Jack, D. C. *Silencing the Self: Women and Depression.* New York: Harper-Collins, 1991.
Kagan, J. *Three Seductive Ideas.* Cambridge, Mass.: Harvard University Press, 1998.

Kaminer, W. *I'm Dysfunctional, You're Dysfunctional: The Recovery Movement and Other Self-Help Fashions*. New York: Vintage Books, 1992.

———. "Chances Are You're Codependent Too." *New York Times* (February 11, 1992). Cited in *Challenging Codependency: Feminist Critiques*, edited by M. Babcock and C. McKay. Buffalo, N.Y.: University of Toronto Press, 1995.

Karpel, M. A. *Evaluating Couples: A Handbook for Practitioners*. New York: W. W. Norton, 1994.

Karpel, M. A., ed. *Family Resources: The Hidden Partner in Family Therapy*. New York: Guilford Press, 1986.

Kaufman, G. *Shame: The Power of Caring*. Rochester, Vt.: Schenkamn Books, 1992.

Kegan, R. *The Evolving Self: Problem and Process in Human Development*. Cambridge, Mass.: Harvard University Press, 1982.

Kelman, D. P. S., L. S. Miller, and S. Dunmeyer. "The Economic Costs of Alcohol and Drug Abuse and Mental Illness: 1985." Rockville, Md.: National Institute on Drug Abuse, 1990.

Krasner, B. R. "Towards a Trustworthy Context in Family and Community." Paper presented at Villanova University, Villanova, Pa., July 1983.

———. "Trustworthiness: The Primal Family Resource." In *Family Resources: The Hidden Partner in Family Therapy*, edited by M. A. Karpel. New York: Guilford Press, 1986.

———. "Adult Children, Adult Parents: Key to Direct Address." Paper presented in San Diego, California, 1991.

Krasner, B. R., and A. J. Joyce. *Truth, Trust, and Relationship: Healing Interventions in Contextual Therapy*. New York: Brunner/Mazel, 1995.

Krebs-McMullen, B. "Depression and Survival." Manuscript, Fairhaven College, Western Washington University, 1989.

Krestan, J., and C. Bepko. "Alcohol Problems and the Family Life Cycle." In *The Changing Family Life Cycle: A Framework for Family Therapy* (2nd ed.), edited by B. Carter and M. McGoldrick. Boston: Allyn & Bacon, 1989.

Krone, L. C. "Justice as a Relational and Theological Cornerstone." *Journal of Psychology & Christianity* (2) (1983): 36–46.

Lauer, R. H., and J. C. Lauer. "Factors in Long-Term Marriages." *Journal of Family Issues* (7) (1987): 382–390.

Lauer, R. H., J. C. Lauer, and S. T. Kerr. "The Long-Term Marriage: Perceptions of Stability and Satisfaction." *International Journal of Aging and Human Development* 31, no. 3 (1990): 189–195.

Ludwig, A. M. *Understanding the Alcoholic's Mind: The Nature of Craving and How to Control It*. New York: Oxford University Press, 1988.

Lutz, S. E., and J. P. Medway. "Contextual Family Therapy and Victims of Incest." *Journal of Adolescence* (7) (1984): 319–327.

Mackey, R. A., and B. A. O'Brien. *Lasting Marriages: Men and Women Growing Together*. Whitehouse, Conn.: Praeger, 1995.

Maxwell, R. *The Booze Battle*. New York: Prager, 1976.

Menicucci, L. D., and L. Wermuth. "Expanding Family Systems Approach: Culture, Class, Developmental and Gender Influences in Drug Abuse." *American Journal of Family Therapy* (17) (1989): 129–142.

Mitchell, S. A. *Relational Concepts in Psychoanalysis: An Integration*. Cambridge, Mass.: Harvard University Press, 1988.

Nathanson, D. L. *Shame and Pride: Affect, Sex, and the Birth of Self.* New York: W. W. Norton, 1992.

National Institute on Alcohol Abuse and Alcoholism. "Children of Alcoholics: Are They Different?" (U.S. Department of Health and Human Services #9, PH288). Rockville, Md.: Public Health Service, 1990.

———. "Estimating the Economic Cost of Alcohol Abuse." (U.S. Department of Health and Human Services. #11, PH293) Rockville, Md.: Public Health Service, 1991.

Noddings, N. *Caring: A Feminine Approach to Ethics and Moral Education*. Berkeley: University of California Press, 1984.

Orford, J. "Alcoholism and Marriage: The Argument against Specialism." *Journal of Studies on Alcoholism* (36) 11 (1975): 1537–1563.

———. "Control, Confront or Collude: How Family and Society Respond to Excessive Drinking." *British Journal of Addiction* (87) (1992): 1513–1525.

Peckham, V. C., A. T. Meadows, N. Bartel, and O. Marrero. "Educational Late Effects in Long-Term Survivors of Childhood Acute Lymphocytic Leukemia." *Pediatrics* (81) (1988): 127–133.

Potter-Efron, R. T., and P. S. Potter-Efron. *Anger, Alcoholism, and Addiction: Treating Individuals, Couples, and Families*. New York: W. W. Norton, 1991.

Rice, D. P., S. Kelman, L. S. Miller, and S. Dunmeyer. "The Economic Costs of Alcohol and Drug Abuse and Mental Illness: 1985." Rockville, Md.: National Institute on Drug Abuse, 1990. Cited in *Alcohol Alert* 11, PH 293, National Institute on Alcohol Abuse and Alcoholism, January 1991.

Robinson, L. C., and P. W. Blanton. "Marital Strengths in Enduring Marriages." *Family Relations* (42) (1993): 38–45.

Rogers, V. *Adult Development through Relationships*. Philadelphia, Pa.: Praeger, 1983.

Rubin, L. B. *Intimate Strangers: Men and Women Together*. New York: Harper & Row, 1983.

Sampson, E. E. "Justice Idealogy and Social Legitimation: A Revised Agenda for Psychological Inquiry." In *Justice in Social Relations*, edited by H. W. Bierhoff, R. L. Cohen, and J. Greenberg. New York: Plenam Press, 1986.

Satir, V. *Conjoint Family Therapy*. Palo Alto, Calif.: Science and Behavior Books, 1967.

Scarf, M. *Intimate Partners: Patterns in Love and Marriage*. New York: Ballantine Books, 1987.

———. *Intimate Worlds: Life inside the Family*. New York: Random House, 1995.

Shapiro, J. P., D. Friedman, M. Meyer, and M. Loftus. "Invincible Kids." *U.S. News & World Report* (November 11, 1996): 62–71.

Shirley, K. J. *Journey into Contextual Therapy: A Primer on Building Trust* (Malvern, Pa.: Contextual Media, mimeo., 1987).

———. "Adults with Spina Bifida: Relational Reciprocity within the Family." Unpublished doctoral dissertation, Temple University, Philadelphia, 1992.

Smith, R., and E. Werner. *Vulnerable but Invincible: A Longitudinal Study of Resilient Children and Youth*. New York: McGraw-Hill, 1982.

Spanier, G. B. "Measuring Dyadic Adjustment: New Scales for Assessing the Quality of Marriage and Similar Dyads." *Journal of Marriage and the Family* 38 (1976):15–28.

———. *Dyadic Adjustment Scale Manual*. North Tonawanda, N.Y.: Multi-Health Systems, Inc., 1989.

Steinglass, P. "A Life History Model of the Alcoholic Family." *Family Process* 19, no. 3 (1980): 211–226.

Steinglass, P., L. A. Bennett, S. J. Wolin, and D. Reiss. *The Alcoholic Family*. New York: Basic Books, 1987.

Sternberg, R. S., and M. Hojjat, eds. *Satisfaction in Close Relationships*. New York: Guilford Press, 1997.

Strauss, E. S. "The Therapist's Personal Impact on Family Resources." *In Family Resources: The Hidden Partner in Family Therapy*, edited by M. A. Karpel, New York: Guilford Press, 1986.

Strauss, M., R. Gelles, and S. Steinmetz. *Behind Closed Doors: Violence in the American Family*, New York: Doubleday, 1980.

Thompson, L. "Contextual and Relational Morality: Intergenerational Responsibility in Later Life." In *Aging Parents and Adult Children*, edited by J. A. Mancini. Lexington, Mass.: Lexington Books, 1989.

Tronto, J. C. "Beyond Gender Difference to a Theory of Care." *Journal of Women in Culture and Society* (12) (1987): 644–663.

van Heusdan, A., and E. van den Eerenbeemt. *Balance in Motion: Ivan Boszormenyi-Nagy and His Vision of Individual and Family Therapy*. New York: Brunner/Mazel, 1987.

Wallerstein, J. S., and S. Blakeslee. *The Good Marriage: How and Why Love Lasts*. New York: Houghton Mifflin, 1995.

Walsh, P. "The Concept of Family Resilience: Crisis and Challenge." *Family Process* 35, no. 3 (1996): 261–281.

Whalen, T. "Wives of Alcoholics: Four Types Observed in a Family Service Agency." *Quarterly Journal of Studies on Alcohol* (14) (1953): 632–641.

Whybrow, P. C. *The Thinkers' Guide to Emotion and Its Disorders*. New York: Harper Perennial, 1997.

Wiseman, J. P. *Wives of Alcoholics and Their Social Psychology*. New York: Aldine De Gruyer, 1975.

Wolin, S. J., and S. Wolin. *The Resilient Self: How Survivors of Troubled Families Rise above Adversity*. New York: Villard, 1993.

Index

About the Author

Karen J. Shirley received her bachelor's degree from the University of Washington and her Ph.D. from Temple University. For the past decade she has conducted narrative social science and health services research on spina bifida, the cognitive effects of pediatric radiation treatment, and the long-run consequences of alcoholism. She teaches college writing and adult literacy in Philadelphia, where she lives with her husband and children.